Restorative Justice in Education

Restorative Justice in Education

Transforming Teaching and
Learning Through the Disciplines

EDITED BY

Maisha T. Winn and Lawrence T. Winn

HARVARD EDUCATION PRESS
Cambridge, Massachusetts

Copyright © 2021 by the President and Fellows of Harvard College

All rights reserved. No part of this publication may be reproduced or transmitted in any form or by any means, electronic or mechanical, including photocopy, recording, or any information storage and retrieval systems, without permission in writing from the publisher.

Paperback ISBN 978-1-68253-616-2
Library Edition ISBN 978-1-68253-617-9

Library of Congress Cataloging-in-Publication Data is on file.

Published by Harvard Education Press,
an imprint of the Harvard Education Publishing Group

Harvard Education Press
8 Story Street
Cambridge, MA 02138

Cover Design: Endpaper Studio
Cover Photo: iStock.com/pixelliebe

The typefaces used in this book are Arno Pro, D Sari and Helvetica Neue.

*For Breonna Taylor,
Elijah McClain,
Ahmaud Arbery,
and George Floyd*

Contents

Series Foreword — xi
by H. Richard Milner IV

Restorative Justice in Education: An Introduction — 1
Maisha T. Winn and Lawrence T. Winn

SECTION I   Why History Matters
Vanessa Siddle Walker

1 Reimagining Restorative Justice in an Ethnic Studies High School Classroom — 13
Eduardo López, Roxana Dueñas, and Jorge López

2 DisCrit History Matters: An Intersectional Exploration of Injustice and Resistance — 25
Subini Ancy Annamma

3 The Whole Story Matters: Building Historical Capital with Youth — 41
Lawrence T. Winn

SECTION II Why Race Matters
Tyrone C. Howard

4 Race Matters in Early Childhood Education   61
Mariana Souto-Manning, Avanti Chajed, Abby Emerson, Hyeyoung Ghim, and Maureen Nicol

5 Abolition in and Through Mathematics: Three Radical Reimaginings   73
Erika C. Bullock and Erica R. Meiners

6 When Race Matters in Mathematics: Practicing Three Commitments for Children Learning Mathematics While Black   87
Darrius D. Robinson, Maisie L. Gholson, and Deborah Loewenberg Ball

SECTION III Why Justice Matters
Danfeng Soto-Vigil Koon

7 Promoting Equity and Justice in Science Classrooms via (W)holistic Science Pedagogy   105
Alexis Patterson Williams and Salina Gray

8 Building Queens and Kings: The Restructuring of Identity Through Transformative Restorative Justice   119
Bryan A. Brown and Karega Bailey

9 "They Were Just Living Their Lives": Reconceptualizing Civic Identity, Membership, and Agency in Second-Grade Social Studies   137
Noreen Naseem Rodríguez

SECTION IV Why Language Matters
Carla Shalaby

10 Restoring What Matters: Reflections on Classroom Language Practices and Ideologies 153
Hannah Graham and Adam Musser

11 Transforming Social Studies Education: Lessons from Youth on Why Language Matters 165
Elizabeth Montaño

12 When the Game Is Rigged from the Start: Teaching for Epistemic Justice in Troubled Times 179
Melissa Braaten

Conclusion: Why Futures Matter: Toward a Fifth Pedagogical Stance 193
Maisha T. Winn

Notes 201

Acknowledgments 229

About the Editors 231

About the Contributors 233

Index 245

Series Foreword

by H. Richard Milner IV
Race and Education Series Editor

MAISHA WINN AND LAWRENCE WINN have assembled an intellectual dream team of experts who understand what it means to reimagine educational systems committed to the futures of our children inside and outside of schools. What could happen in teacher education and education more broadly if we were to examine questions of restoration and justice in the midst of understanding and working through institutional and systemic discrimination that maintains an equitable status quo? How might we reimagine what we believe, what we do, how we come to know and humanize others, and why we do the work we do? Winn and Winn break new ground in their book, *Restorative Justice in Education: Transforming Teaching and Learning Through the Disciplines*, as they address these important questions. Moreover, drawing from restorative justice theory and practice, the authors pose several additional interrelated questions that are often never explored in our discourse, mindsets, and practices of equity and justice in education and teacher education: "Who has been harmed in education? What are their needs? Whose obligations are these?"

The authors advance an important and powerful agenda that centers on what they call "future-oriented" pedagogies. The framework is grounded and anchored in four principles—History Matters, Race Matters, Justice Matters, and Language Matters—and a fifth and promising pedagogical stance, Futures Matter. These matterings are deeply connected within the pages of this book as the book simultaneously advances appropriately deep and broad perspectives as well as a singular goal of advancing what we know about teaching for and through transformation and restoration. Moreover, the book centers the mattering of Black Lives as society continues to demonstrate its disdain for and dehumanizing of Black bodies.

The book has important implications for how we concurrently think about and address harm and healing. Healing remains an essential aspect and phase of what is necessary for those who harm and those who experience it. How might we build teacher learning spaces that help teachers build the knowledge, mindsets, and tools necessary to prevent harm, recognize it when it emerges, and perhaps most importantly build restoration—essential to the improvement of the human condition? Tearing down and crossing disciplinary silos, the book is a potentially transformative tool for educators from preK–higher education often not engaged in the work of equity and restorative justice as well as a step forward for those who are.

A welcomed addition to the *Race and Education Series* of the Harvard Education Press, this book lays a transformative foundation for some and takes the work of justice to new levels for others. At a time when educators struggle to understand how to respond to murders at the hands of police of Black bodies such as Breonna Taylor, George Floyd, Ahmaud Arbery, Rekia Boyd, Jacob Blake, and Antwon Rose Jr., this book reminds us of the potential and importance of restoration and healing in the fight for social justice.

Restorative Justice in Education:
An Introduction

Maisha T. Winn
Lawrence T. Winn

AS WE PREPARED this edited volume for press, and COVID-19 emerged, evolved, and wreaked havoc, we were abruptly confronted with ruptures in our ways of living and understandings of "normalcy." The systemwide lack of preparedness that characterized the education landscape of the United States pointed to the glaring absence of future-oriented frameworks. Unsurprisingly, too, educational inequities were deplorably exacerbated as school systems, educators, at-home caregivers, and students in vastly different conditions and with vastly different resources and access scrambled to reimagine teaching and learning while "sheltering in place" and practicing "social distancing" in an unscripted time.

On March 7, 2020, the fifth-largest school district in California, Elk Grove Unified School District, became the first in the state to close, yet a plan for distance learning was not announced until March 23, 2020—to begin in mid-April.[1] Other districts chose to end the academic year early or had to suspend distance learning to work out technical difficulties. Yet, Andover Public Schools in Massachusetts was able to almost immediately create a "Continuous Learning Family and Caregiver Playbook," featuring resources to set up a productive learning environment at home, activities for play and mindfulness, links to websites, and information about food and resource distribution.[2] This useful playbook became a tool that may be used beyond the pandemic and in other incidences of rupture.

Inundated with the immediate, people everywhere witnessed a great divide in how learning communities were able (or unable) to respond and continue adapting to distance learning.[3] Some of this work involved tangible outcomes, such as the provision of Chromebooks and Wi-Fi hot spots, but also playing out were mindset shifts. Community needed to be cultivated in unprecedented ways; inclusion and exclusion took on new forms that gave some of us pause; a lot of thought was given to how to approach the establishment of emotional space to support children and their families; and educators were widely honored for being essential. After such an awakening, can we embrace the opportunity to radically reimagine a school system deeply committed to the futures of all children? How can teaching and learning cultivate and nurture purpose and belonging for educators and students? Can that vision extend beyond classrooms and school buildings? What paradigms are needed to engage in future-oriented pedagogies? What mindsets? What skill sets?

Award-winning novelist Arundhati Roy asserts, "Historically, pandemics have forced humans to break with the past and imagine their world anew.... [The pandemic then becomes] a portal, a gateway between one world and the next."[4] Restorative justice is a paradigm that is incredibly relevant to the current moment, as it accounts for emotional well-being and strengthens community, offering a pathway for building relationships that are affirming, inclusive, and centered on human flourishing and resilience—whether the learning community is gathered in a school building or in our own homes. Children and youth who are multiply-marginalized have long been familiar with metaphorical social distancing as an overarching aspect of their schooling experiences. The notion of "social distancing," which may more appropriately be thought of as "physical distancing," was not only metaphorical, either, for many decades, but policy and practice have segregated specific cohorts of young learners through trips to the office, forcible isolation from their classroom learning and their peers, and entanglement with law enforcement.[5]

Only a few weeks before parts of the United States called for COVID-related school closures, six-year-old Kaia, an African American girl, was placed under arrest by a police officer in Orlando, Florida—for having a tantrum.[6] While this news story was quickly overshadowed by the threat of coronavirus, the extreme nature and outcomes of this encounter felt sickeningly familiar and status quo to numerous Black students, Indigenous students, Latinx students, students with special needs, emergent bilinguals, and undocumented students.

In this edited volume, teachers, youth workers, teacher-educators, and education researchers, many of whom represent many or all of these intersectional identities, situate restorative justice as a timely paradigm that can be leveraged to spark intellectual curiosity and relational dynamics that yield transformative possibilities. The clearest pathway to this pursuit—Transformative Justice Teacher Education—is restorative justice in action across the disciplines, an equity-oriented and justice-seeking ethos and culture of teaching and learning.[7] The associated work of embracing this paradigm and related approach to teacher education reclaims the "justice" centering of "restorative justice," in intentional contrast to "restorative practice" approaches gaining traction in schools across the United States that avoid the call and urgency of undermining and eliminating pervasive inequities in education.[8] All of us who contributed to create this volume also feel strongly that "transformative" is a more appropriate naming convention for the work we describe herein, because we acknowledge that "justice" in many education contexts cannot be restored because it has never yet existed for all.

Much like schools' rush to "practice," early thought leaders envisioning and putting into action Transformative Justice Teacher Education programming nearly made the mistake of omitting "justice"—at least in the terminology of that era. In 2013, Maisha T. Winn initially asked what literacy teaching looks like, sounds like, and feels like through a restorative justice paradigm, asserting that it was possible and necessary for English educators and administrators to "grapple with tensions in classrooms and schools initiated by zero-tolerance policies and reimagine English classrooms as sites for relationship-building, peacemaking, and peacekeeping."[9] Study of a high school community committed to restorative justice subsequently demonstrated, though, that restorative justice in the context of education was essentially about "justice on both sides" and pointed to the importance of naming justice as an action that must be part of healing work.[10]

Over time, as we continued to fine-tune our ideas about how transformative justice could and should be enacted in contexts of schooling, we were inspired by scholars considering how carceral logics shape mathematics education,[11] the criticality of culturally relevant pedagogy and digital media production,[12] the role of translanguaging in "upending" colonial harm in English language arts,[13] and Wholistic Science Pedagogy.[14] In many ways, this edited volume begins where *Justice on Both Sides* ended in 2018,[15] in that the contributing authors seek to map transformative justice possibilities onto the teaching of math, English language arts, science, and social studies. The tool to get us there, Transformative Justice in Teacher Education, effectively serves as a portal through which static, top-down visions of education and related lenses of rigid, nonhumanizing classroom management and discipline are actively and rightfully replaced by future-oriented thinking that is inclusive, affirming, expansive, and justice seeking.

FROM ONE WORLD TO THE NEXT

The portal we describe is a space in which we come to be guided by complementary pedagogical stances that inform the sections and final chapter of this book: *History Matters, Race Matters, Justice Matters, Language Matters,* and *Futures Matter*. While the author-contributors certainly honor all of these stances in their work and their writing, these chapters highlight how educators and those who teach them might begin to engage specific stances as their work unfolds in diverse educational settings.

In Section I, "Why History Matters," Lopez, Duñas, and Lopez; Annamma; and Lawrence T. Winn illuminate the importance, rationale, and work of connecting histories to futures—even when students are unable to make such connections themselves. This section is guided by questions about what it means to historicize one's self in the process of imagining one's future, what educators can learn from historiographies of learning communities, and how access to history and histories can promote agency for and among students who are Black, Indigenous, Latinx, differently abled, and otherwise excluded in education contexts and society more broadly.

Section II, "Why Race Matters," includes scholars who grapple with early childhood education and math education. Souto-Manning, Chajed, Emerson, Ghim, and Nicol explore how racist ideas serve to reproduce inequities in early childhood education. The authors shed light on the power and promise of a transformative justice in education framework in early childhood education. Bullock and Meiners reveal how mathematics and mathematics education have functioned as agents of the carceral state and argue for the reimagining of mathematics education as a tool to dismantle oppressive systems. Robinson, Gholson, and Ball analyze a restorative approach to the teaching of mathematics. They address the racialized nature of mathematics and highlight the brilliance, creativity, and abilities of Black math learners.

In Section III, "Why Justice Matters," Patterson Williams, Gray, Brown, Bailey, and Rodriguez describe transformative justice as it applies to identity and sense of belonging. Patterson Williams and Gray offer a curricular model, the (W)holistic Science Pedagogy (WSP), that encourages teachers to provide historically marginalized students with educational quality. Brown and Bailey's chapter features social justice education using restorative justice practices to help students rethink their identities as troublemakers to community leaders. Rodriquez grapples with how concepts of obedience, patriotism, and personal responsibility are often associated with white children while Black and Latinx children often experience discipline and punishment. She argues that a transformative justice approach in civics education is needed to disrupt this narrative and experience.

Finally, in Section IV, "Why Language Matters," Graham, Musser, Montaño, Braaten, and Maisha T. Winn write about language as a valuable tool, resource, and asset. The authors share their experiences as classroom teachers and educators creating humanizing and transformative classrooms where students are valued, appreciated, and respected. Key to this "language work" is having the right mindset and shifting away from deficit language. The authors refuse to label students but instead redefine notions of citizenship and pursue epistemic justice. They see language as a way of cultivating bright and joyful futures.

SECTION I

WHY HISTORY MATTERS

Vanessa Siddle Walker

At a United Confederate Veterans meeting in 1919, white Georgia educator Mildred Lewis Rutherford announced a visionary plan to reject school texts that explained slavery as the reason for the war between the states, elevated Abraham Lincoln as a hero, and painted Southern slaveholders as cruel.[1] Rutherford abhorred texts that did not elevate states' rights; announcing a "crusade" for the "truths of history," she authored "A Measuring Rod to Test Text Books," recruiting likeminded white mothers to infiltrate textbook selection committees to shape the perspectives and norms children would learn. Rutherford thus helped mainstream a very particular version of history, a "celebratory American story" populated by "great leaders and great causes."[2] She undoubtedly envisioned texts akin to a Georgia history book created by Superintendent of Schools Lawton B. Evans that featured a photograph of well-kept "Negro Quarters" and explained that Negroes—not slaves—were "well treated," "free from care," and "therefore happy and devoted to their masters." They played "simple games," and white children loved to come to their quarters and listen to stories the old Negroes told in the evenings.[3]

Evans's representation and Rutherford's vision did, indeed, become foundational to the ways generations of American children were taught and learned history. "Proud patriotic citizens" could be developed, over time, as children and youth "learned about white heroes" while encountering little or no information about the strength and struggles of nonwhites.[4] *Gone with the Wind* is an exemplar of the enduring success of this lens and goal. Written one generation after Rutherford posed her plan to the United Confederate Veterans, and based on the Pulitzer Prize–winning book by the same title, this iconic film opened in Atlanta in 1939. Georgia's white political leaders declared the day of its opening a state holiday. Millions of white people attended segregated performances during its run, some wearing period costumes. For almost four hours, they celebrated the virtue of the lost cause as they witnessed the gallantry of the white South, disdain for Northern aggression, and the joy of happy Black servants.

In 2014, as the film's seventy-fifth anniversary was celebrated, Harris poll data from 2008 was referenced to pronounce *Gone with the Wind* America's "favorite movie of all time." Adjusting for inflation, *Gone with the Wind* continues to be the highest-grossing movie of all time, and the cultural impact of this production is reflected in the sentiment evoked by contemporary viewers who laud the film's great attention "to historical detail with regard to the war and the collapse of southern culture." Even individuals who acknowledge the film's problematic portrayal of racial dynamics proclaim the movie not simply entertaining but "educational."[5]

These perspectives and the film's ongoing popularity are unsurprising in the context of historical narratives in the United States. In 1939, when the film was released, the Mississippi Education Association documented the ability of a white child to go through school without learning anything about Black culture or contributions.[6] The charge is little changed today. Robin Muldor-Engram, a former Philadelphia teacher, recently noted that classrooms around the country "*still* do not have enough books that accurately depict the unsullied experiences of Black Americans."[7]

Why does history matter? When incomplete and replicated, history reproduces generational beliefs and fiercely held values that create a deeply divided America on issues related to race and equity. Historical neglect is one of the conditions that allows some Americans to be horrified by the present-day white supremacy evidenced in the language and behaviors of protestors in Charlottesville, Virginia, even as others organize and participate in a march to commemorate that day.[8] Historical neglect allows prominent patriotic citizens to express disdain for those who question representations of America that lie outside heroic portrayals of great people. Such individuals are "offended" by other Americans who bring up thorny issues and cannot understand why issues of "long ago" that remind Americans "how bad we are" must be part of current conversations.[9] Related and ongoing battles against the need to teach multiculturalism, the intervention of federal authorities in local education matters, and efforts to stop the reproduction of curricula ideologically rooted in American exceptionalism can, in fact, be understood as the latest incarnations of white sentiments and power articulated and leveraged by Mildred Lewis Rutherford a century ago.[10]

Of course, incomplete and inaccurate historical knowledge need not remain America's heritage, and another legacy points to different possibilities for children exposed to comprehensive lessons. Even as white mothers sought to create historical knowledge that would affirm the wisdom of Jim Crow, Black educators with curriculum support from Carter G. Woodson were able to use the segregated schools of Black children as spaces in which curricula and extracurricular activities infused Black history and culture into the learning experience.[11] These educators celebrated the possibilities of America's founding principles but also weaponized civics lessons so Black children would grow in their knowledge of the ways they were denied those practices. *Atlanta Daily World* rightly concluded in 1938 that after Black children had been exposed to such lessons, subsequent generations would not sit passively by and "let themselves be barred from complete citizenship."[12]

From this counter-curricular intervention marshalled by Black educators came generations of Black citizens who would keep the dream of democracy alive, not by rejecting America but by continuing to push for fulfillment of its proclamations of liberty for all. We know these changemakers as the civil rights generation, people who worked collectively to push America to fulfill its promise, and its promises, grounding their struggle in the principles of democracy and representing a sharp departure from their white counterparts who had benefitted from and internalized Rutherford's framework.

Why does history matter? Because a comprehensive portrait of America for all Americans—a narrative that crosses time periods and is representative of all the forces, factors, and people who have lived on the land and sought to fulfill democratic practices—will be critical for the American democratic experiment in the generations to come. Scholars have shown how white Americans' commitment to democracy is reduced when they exhibit attitudes of prejudice to other ethnic groups, about whom they arguably know little.[13] President of the segregated Fort Valley Industrial College Henry A. Hunt said in 1923 that history must be taught as a continuous movement and development: "The past is made to live in the present."[14] Restorative justice rightly centers the history of all peoples, embracing America's historic past as a rubric by which to unravel the complexities and harms of injustice in the present. History matters because without its inclusion, neither awareness nor justice are possible.

1

Reimagining Restorative Justice in an Ethnic Studies High School Classroom

Eduardo López, Roxana Dueñas, and Jorge López

RESISTANCE, RESILIENCE, AND REIMAGINATION. These are the essential and sequential themes born out of our Ethnic Studies course. The class, which is offered to all ninth-grade students at Theodore Roosevelt High School (RHS) and most students at the Math, Science, Technology Magnet Academy on the same campus, is an evolution of curated historical content that affirms students' histories and identities. Over the five years we've been teaching the course, we've made changes to meet the identities and needs of our students and to reflect our growing understanding and embodiment of humanizing and culturally sustaining pedagogies.[1] We view the foundation that holds the three themes of our course together, a restorative justice framework, as a paradigm shift that influences how and why we do things, guiding our intentions and daily curricular and disciplinary practices. As social justice educators guided by critical, humanizing, and liberatory pedagogies, we have sought to develop a course that inspires our students to use their histories of resistance and resilience as a springboard to reimagine their realities and futures.

In this chapter we illustrate how restorative justice is conceptualized and woven throughout the content we teach in our pursuit to educate and provide transformative, healing experiences for our students. We do this by, first, contextualizing how restorative justice came to RHS and how this framework complements and strengthens our social justice pedagogical stance. Second, we highlight two of the community building/circle activities featured in our resistance unit on Indigenous histories. Third, we explain how we cultivate resilience in our students through processes of creative writing and documenting their histories in our annual anthology book project. Lastly, we describe supporting our students' engagement in youth participatory action research that provides them with opportunities to reimagine and embody in their own lives the concept of "justice." Ultimately, we seek to share practitioner perspectives regarding some of the powerful ways restorative justice underpins the content, relational dynamics, and transformational justice approaches and experiences that characterize our Ethnic Studies course.

RESTORATIVE JUSTICE AT THEODORE ROOSEVELT HIGH SCHOOL

In 2013, the Los Angeles School Board District passed the School Climate Bill of Rights (SCBR). This resolution came to fruition after a lengthy campaign by students, parents, teachers, and community organizations to end school leaders' ability to suspend students for "willful defiance," a practice that has disproportionately impacted students of color, English language learners, differently abled, and special education students.[2] SCBR states that students "will attend schools with climates that focus on safety, teaching and learning, interpersonal relationships, and the institutional environment that influence student learning and well-being."[3] To create a positive school climate, SCBR calls for the implementation of restorative justice on all campuses, an undertaking that has come to represent "an alternative to zero tolerance policies [that] uses programs that use peer support groups and group agreements to resolve conflicts between students, and students and teachers."[4]

The year SCBR was approved, RHS became one of the first schools in Los Angeles School Board District to pilot/adopt restorative justice practices. With a supportive administration that secured funding, faculty and staff at RHS were paid to attend a mandatory year-long professional development program on restorative justice. RHS hired a phenomenal restorative justice coordinator, Dr. Michelle Ferrer, to lead the campus through a paradigm shift whereby faculty and staff were exposed to alternative approaches to mainstream zero-tolerance discipline policies. According to criminologist and restorative justice theorist Howard Zehr, restorative justice "begins with a concern for victims and how to meet their needs, for repairing the harm as much as possible . . . [and] involves a reorientation of how we think about crime and justice."[5]

During the first phase of this schoolwide effort to initiate a restorative justice paradigm shift, and prior to addressing any discipline issues, RHS faculty and staff sat in circle and participated in training related to the first tier of restorative justice: building community.[6] Faculty and staff learned how to build community through the active pursuit of healthy relationships with students and their families, a core component of restorative justice at RHS. When discipline issues eventually arose on campus, faculty and staff were encouraged to think restoratively and implement approaches explored during their training. The mindset goal was to shift from punitive measures and instead focus on repairing emergent or existing harm in student-to-student and/or student-to-teacher relationships.[7] Unsurprisingly, this transition was not a smooth campuswide process, yet school faculty and staff were collectively committed to embracing and implementing restorative justice, which at its core is about sustaining positive relationships through which youth are treated with dignity and respect.[8]

The restorative justice mindset naturally complemented the social justice pedagogical stance that grounds our Ethnic Studies curriculum. Taking into consideration how History Matters as "an opportunity to access painful histories collectively and to address historical wrongdoing in education and in school communities," we began to reimagine what freedom and justice for our students and ourselves would look like.[9] To achieve this goal, we embraced in our daily teaching practices a range of restorative justice paradigm practices, including "restorative justice discourses" wherein participants share individual and collective histories to portray "who they are and their positionality in the world."[10] Taking a critical approach in our teaching that included a restorative justice paradigm meant we committed to challenging the dominant narrative and hegemonic structures that exist in our society. Initially, though, we were unsure about the path our class discussions would take, and we worried about the harm and trauma that could or would surface in engaging in a liberatory curriculum. One way we addressed this concern was through weaving restorative justice community-building circles and practices into our classroom norms.

Resistance

How do we teach resistance in our classroom? Our work is inspired by many theoretical frameworks, including critical pedagogy,[11] tenets of Ethnic Studies,[12] critical race theory,[13] Latina/o critical race theory,[14] and culturally sustaining pedagogies.[15] Before we investigate the ways in which oppressed groups resisted and continue to resist oppression, we establish a foundation based on knowledge of self. We create space for students to explore the histories of their families and their communities. The semester begins with a unit entitled "Building Community, Identity, and Knowledge of Self." To build a strong sense of community within the classroom, students engage in a series of ice breakers, community-building circles, and writing projects.

After students spend a few months investigating and reflecting on their identities, community history, and positionality in society, we shift our attention to Indigenous epistemologies and histories. Essential questions we ask students are *"What do I know about my Indigenous roots?"* and *"What are Native values and practices?"* Whereas traditional school curricula typically begin the history of Indigenous people in the Americas with colonization, we seek to merge past and present to ensure that both history and culture are understood to be dynamic, fluid, and sustained. We are intentional about teaching our students about Indigenous people before settler colonialism and identify and use circles as a practice that allows for greater understanding and appreciation of Indigenous ways, noting that some scholars suggest that circle practices arose in Indigenous communities throughout Canada, New Zealand, and the US as a tool to promote healthy dialogue and discussion, and as an intervention to restore harmony.[16] Our 5-Value Activity is a lesson that invites students to participate in a community-building circle grounded in Indigenous values and beliefs that resonate with many of our students, particularly those who begin to identify or deepen their identification to Indigenous ancestral roots.[17]

By this point of the semester, students are familiar with using a talking piece, the significance of a centerpiece, core guidelines, and the anticipated series of activities and questions when in circle. The 5-Value Activity is introduced after students have read and analyzed an array of American Indian values grounded in fundamental beliefs shared across tribes from the US and Canada. These values, beliefs, and attitudes include veneration of age, wisdom, and tradition; careful listening; generosity and sharing; respect for nature; and group harmony.[18] Often, students compare these values with Western values and begin to question why Indigenous beliefs are not promoted in schools and in Western society at the same level as Eurocentric ideals. This community-building circle then becomes an opportunity for students to identify and present the five most important values up to that point in their lives that they feel stem from Indigenous epistemologies. There is also an artistic component to this activity; students sketch their hand on a sheet of card stock and within each drawn finger write one of the five values they identify with.

During the 5-Value Activity circle, all students are given an equal voice to share and explain the relevance of the values they selected. At the end of this circle, students' hand art pieces are placed on classroom walls to remain as visible reminders of the values students want to live up to, and also to remind them of ancestral knowledge they continue to promote in their daily interactions. Circle practice, in this instance, does a few things, introducing new ways of looking at old customs as students share in ancestral wisdom and collectively listen to each other's stories, growing as a community of learners who share knowledge and experiences. This is powerful. Students, sometimes for the first time, look at their own and others' ancestral pasts as forms to enrich or sustain their own cultural lifeways as they recognize how Indigenous values benefit their contemporary lives.

After establishing an understanding of the life and values of Indigenous people prior to contact with European colonizers, our students begin to engage with the development and impacts of colonization. Our ninth graders typically come into the classroom describing colonization as something explorers did, long ago, to find trade routes, fabrics, and spices. They often see colonization as a singular event from a long-past era, in a faraway place. Most see themselves as detached and unaffected by legacies of colonization. For this reason, we have students engage in a mock trial Socratic seminar called "The People vs. Columbus, et al."[19] Because we supplement this activity with a number of primary and secondary sources, our objective is to ensure that students understand the enduring legacies of imperialism and colonization on First Nations people, in the past and in the present.

In this character-driven mock trial Socratic seminar, students grapple with the essential question, *"Who is responsible for the genocide of the Taínos?"* Students must take into consideration the points of view of the Taíno, the King and Queen of Spain, the sailors, and Christopher Columbus. They are introduced to the ideology known as the System of Empire, according to which success is connected to owning as much property as possible (capitalism), and shown how foreigners and non-Christians were not seen as human. Simulation exercises offer many opportunities for students to analyze and interpret uncomfortable histories and narratives of racism, xenophobia, and religious oppression, among other patterns, that they may not have learned previously. Students usually become inquisitive and curious about what else they have been miseducated about, as a result. After all, most of our students come in with the understanding that Columbus was a hero who discovered America. Beyond shedding light on atrocities committed in the name of colonization, this coursework also asks students to question curricula they were previously exposed to.

We introduce students to the "Seven Pillars of Colonialism," from a teaching resource guide entitled *Teaching for Change*.[20] Colonialism fundamentally changes the ways societies are organized through systemic violence and oppression associated with grabbing the land, growing for and developing Europe, consuming colonially, hatching hierarchies, killing cultures, and exploiting the land. By introducing and analyzing these concepts, we create opportunities for students to understand systemic oppression and think beyond the various forms of interpersonal oppression they are most familiar with. When students begin to understand the pillar of "killing culture" in the context of Columbus and the Taíno, they can subsequently identify and name this pattern in other historical and contemporary contexts. We believe this is critical in making history matter for our students, many of whose families were pushed out of their home countries in Latin America as a result of colonization, as well. We want students to wrestle with these abstract concepts and historical events in order to move closer toward humanization, agency, and restorative justice.

This unit does many things, allowing students to explore resistance on multiple levels. For one, we are collectively resisting the erasure of Indigenous perspectives through our curriculum. The simulation centers Taíno narratives, theories, ways of being, resistance, and resilience. Learning that resistance and resilience can take the forms of running away, preserving cultural and spiritual traditions, collective care, defensive violence, and other subtle and subversive actions that allow for survival, students come to see that there is no singular way to survive and respond to oppression. After the students debate and discuss *"Who is responsible for the genocide of the Taíno?"* emotions are high, and some students are typically confused and critical about arguments presented during the simulation. Allowing students to access and express those feelings of frustration about injustices experienced by others is important. Irrespective of which group or individual(s) they represented in the simulation, students often describe feeling that their historical figure or group was misunderstood or silenced—and victim to larger, systemic structures and conditions. Sometimes students feel guilty about the point of view they were asked to defend. Feelings of injustice and invisibility are real and relatable; we have all been silenced or had our needs unmet. Understanding and connecting to these realities and emotions—and potentially feeling empathy for others facing similar structures and conditions—are why History Matters.

We end this unit with a timed written reflection the day following the trial, giving students an opportunity to put their feelings, arguments, and analyses into a structured writing piece. We ask them to answer *"Who is responsible for the Taíno genocide?"* and, pointing out that we cannot erase the past and must continue to move forward, also ask them: *"What do you think needs to happen to make things right for everyone involved?" "How should we hold everyone involved accountable for their actions?"* Our instructions stipulate that death and jail are not options, pushing them to generate more restorative and humanizing scenarios to hold people and institutions accountable for harm and legacies of harm. Students tend to struggle to imagine such scenarios because they mostly know justice as a form of punishment and shame—the discipline model we have implemented in US society, schools being no exception.

Because History Matters as a means of restoring historical and contemporary institutional and interpersonal harm, this unit seeks to allow students to reflect on the root causes of various harms, as well as the unmet needs of those affected. When they understand the cause(s) of the harm and the unmet needs, they can better imagine scenarios that might benefit most of those involved, while reducing humiliation and shame. Students generate scenarios such as Columbus and his sailors giving back the land they took, Spanish colonizers learning and practicing Taíno ways and values, establishing truth-telling practices around Columbus and his actions and impacts, and not celebrating his holiday. These are just a few examples, but we can see the possibilities of decolonization as a form of restorative justice when we frame inquiry questions from a restorative lens. Though the students are not introduced to the term *decolonization* in this unit, they imagine it into existence through this simulation. By thus guiding students' participation in this seminar and engagement with uncomfortable histories and alternative discipline frameworks, we create conditions to "educate children for (collective) freedom."[21]

Resilience

"Resilience is our ability to bounce back—like moss after we've stepped on it, or to find our intactness again. It is our ability to come back to ourselves, to connectedness, and to positive vision, even when the experiences and conditions are difficult."[22] After we conclude our unit on Columbus and colonization, we move on to case studies of civil rights movements that represented active resistance against ideological, institutional, interpersonal, and ideological oppression. We frame resistance as resilience coupled with strength: the ability of our ancestors, families, and communities to struggle, survive, and thrive.

To remind us of the joy and magnitude of surviving colonization and oppression, we have students engage in a creative writing process in collaboration with the nonprofit organization 826LA. We want students to end the course embodying a sense of hope and humanity, and the knowledge that they are already whole and complete and good, just as they are. Many of our students and their families have survived intergenerational trauma, among other obstacles and injustices. We ask them to write about the surviving, thriving hope and joy of it all.

Throughout the years, we have provided students with various writing prompts and possibilities for this project. They can write open letters to their future or past selves, using Ta-Nehisi Coates's *Between the World and Me* or James Baldwin's *An Open Letter to My Sister, Angela Davis* as inspiration and example. They can write to family members, friends, or even institutions to raise grievances or complaints. They can write poems or short essays, essentially anything they can imagine, so long as it touches on the content of the course and highlights the themes of resistance, resilience, and/or reimagination.

Given that we define resilience as one's ability to come back to oneself,[23] this writing project creates space for students to reflect on and celebrate their survival, histories, and experiences, regardless of how mundane or mortifying we may find them. We invite them to come back to themselves through self-reflection, storytelling, and sharing. In the process of writing, drafting, and editing, our students have opportunities to experience and explore vulnerability, and to feel seen and validated. Upon sharing their stories, students often realize they are not alone, finding new connections to peers who have shared similar experiences. The writing process, too, can be healing, and can offer opportunities to acknowledge uncomfortable personal and collective histories that need righting.

Students occasionally share harm they have experienced at the hands of family members, friends, and institutions. This is an opportunity for us to listen to the needs of our young people, and is another example of how and why history and restorative practices matter. Indeed, in asking our students to write about themselves, their ideas of resistance and survival, and/or emerging critical consciousness and new ways of seeing the world, we are "establishing a paradigm that views all children as valuable as worthy"—worthy of being seen and celebrated, and worthy of justice.[24] The pieces our students write are edited into an annual anthology that is printed and published through 826LA. Our school then buys a class set of the books, so students the following year can read the stories of their peers and learn through the point of view of young people much like themselves. Each student who has their piece published also receives a copy of the book. We have a book signing and reading celebration, inviting families and friends to come and listen to students read their pieces aloud.

We thus celebrate our young people's resilience through story sharing. Their voices become part of future curricula, documented as evidence of cultural and personal resilience. This project, then, builds relationships through the editing process; nurtures students' voices and imaginations; engages students in dialogue with self, peers, and readers; sustains culture and community knowledge; and contributes to collective healing. If we define resilience as coming home to ourselves and our connectedness, then Ethnic Studies and restorative justice are complementary pathways to cultivate resilience in our young people.

Reimagination

Our year-long course culminates with the theme of reimagination. Throughout the year, students learn about systemic oppression and the ways marginalized groups have resisted and shown resilience as they challenge and transform conditions within and/or around their communities. As educators, we think it is important for students to spend time imagining and writing into existence the ways they want their lives and communities to exist beyond oppression. Reimagination as decolonization is how we frame the process of having our students engage in thinking about what a liberated life in their community might look and feel like. We bridge learning units about Indigeneity, colonization, and decolonial liberated future realities using the tool and power of imagination.

Tapping into young imaginations can generate visions and realizations that youth have the power to change conditions in the world and can also inspire students' will to pursue a more hopeful and desirable world. One way we seek to facilitate such outcomes is by engaging our students in a six-week summative youth participatory action research

(YPAR) project. An undertaking of "youth driven collective research and action with adults," YPAR can be leveraged as a tool to empower youth to respond to societal injustices.[25] YPAR projects position youth as agents of inquiry and social change whereby youth participants often envision new realities.[26] In our collective effort to pursue justice through the History Matters stance, we thus value this pedagogical practice because it highlights and exposes students to strategies to "collectively ... address historical wrongdoing in education ... in school communities" and lets them practice creating space for reimagining a more just society.[27]

YPAR also demonstrates our commitment to restorative justice, given that we support Maisha T. Winn's claim that "the concept of 'justice' in restorative justice is the purposeful attempt to disrupt cycles of injustice and inequality."[28] This restorative justice tenet is evident in the work students produce while engaging in youth participatory action research. Students become empowered as they lead the research process and present their findings about issues they find meaningful and relevant to their peers and school community.[29] Topics of research students have chosen have included gentrification, immigrant student rights, gender discrimination, sex education, food deserts, mental health, restorative justice, and racial profiling/criminalization of youth. These topics motivate and inspire our youth to use their research to disrupt inequities and dismantle racial and other injustices they see in their lives.

Often, after presenting their research, students begin to identify as transformational resistors. Scholars have suggested that youth who identify as transformational resistors are individuals motivated by social justice who critique social oppression and engage in resistance as a political, collective, and conscious act that can bring about social change.[30] We see our students' YPAR projects as a form of resistance when they leverage their voices to raise critical consciousness about social and racial injustices in their lives and in their communities.[31] Our approach to teaching history is consistent with conceptualizations of justice that recognize the classroom as an appropriate site to cultivate transformational resistance among young intellectuals capable of producing knowledge for change. We aim to support youth as they transform current realities and reimagine a world in which everyone is treated with dignity and feels a sense of belonging.

CONCLUSION

The urgency to transform education through restorative justice cannot be overstated, especially considering the US context of hyper-incarceration and criminalization in/through schools, which particularly (but not exclusively) impacts Black and Latinx students. What is needed is a revolutionary overhaul of public education. Schools should be caring and humanizing spaces for all students. We can begin to achieve such conditions by promoting a transformative justice teaching framework that approaches teaching as "a justice seeking endeavor and learning as both a civil and human right for all students."[32] At the granular level, one precursor to this type of teaching and learning is the cultivation of positive human relationships—hence the need to embrace restorative practices in schools to build community and collectively repair harm and heal together.

For us as Ethnic Studies educators, our development of a year-long curriculum with an intentional sequence of resistance, resilience, and reimagination, guided by a restorative justice framework, reflects our commitment to honoring the full humanity of each of our students. This pedagogical stance to teaching history centers our students' identities, cultures, and lived experiences as essential components of our curriculum. Our aim is to provide students with intellectually stimulating learning environments that value and develop their critical voices and foster healthy relationships, allowing students to see restorative justice not merely as an alternative to discipline but as a way of life.

Our hope is that courageous studies of painful historical trends often side-stepped in traditional history classes will facilitate a process of naming, bringing into focus, and personalizing historically unmet needs related to the exploration of histories excluded from our textbooks. When our students learn, analyze, and empathize with these untold stories, we note that they begin to imagine concrete and symbolic ways to restore justice.[33] Empowered with a knowledge of self and an understanding and embodiment of resistance and resilience, students can, in fact, imagine collective freedoms into existence.[34]

2 DisCrit History Matters: An Intersectional Exploration of Injustice and Resistance

Subini Ancy Annamma

TRANSFORMATIVE JUSTICE IS the commitment to enact justice at both the individual and systemic level, recognizing that to move society toward justice requires that we go beyond shifting individual circumstances to change societal structures.[1] Ruth Morris reminds us, "Transformative justice takes into account the past, and it recognizes distributive injustice."[2] The integration of History Matters as a pedagogical stance is thus an essential part of committing to transformative justice—and there can be no doubt that conceptions of justice are made more robust and more applicable when there is solid understanding of how historical contexts impact moments and patterns in the present.

For educators, the History Matters pedagogical stance provides "an opportunity to access painful histories collectively and to address historical wrong-doings in education and in school communities."[3] In particular, educators who recognize painful collective histories and underlying historical wrong-doings have opportunities to highlight the individual and collective resistance of multiply-marginalized populations, those at the intersections of multiple forms of injustice.[4] The process of incorporating a History Matters stance can involve altering curricula, pedagogy, and relationships, offering several entry points for educators and scholars seeking to shift their entire classroom ecology.[5] Consequently, History Matters as a pedagogical philosophy has the power to transform classroom discourse and practices, as well as the underlying ideologies that imbue those norms, ultimately moving individual relationships and systems of education toward justice.

A commitment to History Matters is especially important because curricula have been shown repeatedly to be steeped in white supremacy, resulting in epistemic violence.[6] Tadishi Dozono notes:

> By presenting white European ways of knowing and being as universal, educators conduct epistemic violence. Epistemic violence refers to the harm done when educators privilege certain bodies of knowledge as the norm and universal, in turn disregarding other bodies of knowledge as insufficient or illegitimate.[7]

Several educators and collectives have illustrated a substantive commitment to integrating History Matters into curricular frameworks and decisions, refusing the epistemic violence Dozono identifies. *An Indigenous Peoples' History of the United States*, *Teaching for Black Lives*, and *A People's History for the Classroom* are examples of curricula designed to very intentionally link history to current inequities.[8]

With respect to pedagogy, Mexican American studies, ethnic studies, and race-conscious pedagogy are examples of critical instruction similarly committed to explicitly connecting historical inequities to modern contexts in the classroom,[9] challenging whiteness as the continued hegemonic center of pedagogy in schools.[10] For example, Cheryl Matias and Janiece Mackey note, "Because of the emotional nature of racism, sexism, heterosexism, and other isms, we . . . build race literacy through pedagogically teaching about whiteness."[11] Such pedagogical approaches seek to decenter whiteness through the thoughtful integration of more nuanced and more accurate historical contexts.

Relationships in school settings often focus on the social control of youth through a combination of labeling, surveillance, and punishment.[12] While less punitive relationships in the classroom are sometimes imagined as shallow attempts to love everyone by ignoring differences, an approach known as aesthetic care,[13] bell hooks reminds us, "There can be no love without justice."[14] She also states: "[A]buse and neglect negate love. Care and affirmation, the opposite of abuse and humiliation, are the foundation of love."[15] hooks points to the dysfunction and injustice that prevail when students face abuse, neglect, and humiliation from systemic oppressions that animate relational moments in their lives. Microaggressions take the form of youth being harassed by police on the way to school for jaywalking, surveilled in schools that increasingly look and feel like prisons, and reprimanded about dress code compliance instead of asked about their lives and well-being, and the accrual of such slights—even if none alone clearly constitutes abuse—creates a constellation of messages that imply *you are not welcome here.*[16]

In light of the persistence and negative impacts of such patterns, relationships built with students in the classroom must be constructed with an understanding of the ways oppression operates from a historical lens and how oppression informs students' lives. Can educators who do not have historical grasp of stop-and-frisk, Columbine, and zero tolerance understand how mainstream "prison nation" norms have become, and the extent to which policies and narratives problematically focus on surveillance and control of Black and Brown bodies and minds?[17] How can educators who do not know about the adultification of Black girls understand that calling a Black girl "fast" or "loud" repeats and reinforces messaging that negatively attributes characterization of and holds Black girls accountable for their actions as if they were older than they are?[18] Knowledge of history informs how we approach and engage relationally with multiply-marginalized children, and relationships matter. Kids who report trusting their teachers have lower levels of defiance and increased cooperative behaviors.[19]

Many practitioners have begun conceptualizing radical relationships between teachers and students utilizing hope, authentic caring, and solidarity.[20] Recognizing that History Matters, Maxine McKinney de Royston and colleagues practice a relational approach they call "politicized caring," which they describe as follows: "politicized caring allows us to recognize that certain teachers acknowledge the ways schools reproduce racialized and gendered stereotypes, and seek to cultivate relationships with marginalized students that acknowledges their oppression and their developmental needs as children and learners."[21] Awareness that History Matters, enacted in this way, shifts relationships because educators can recognize students, instead of acting out, as engaging in strategic resistance toward interpersonal and systemic injustices, and this robust perspective changes the ways an educator is inclined to respond.[22] In sum, then, the temporal pull of history is a crucial and foundational element of critical curricula, pedagogy, and relationships, refusing to silo the present from the broader arcs and layers of history.

At times, and for a range of reasons, history is imagined and articulated as a unidimensional narrative, focused specifically on race, gender, or class.[23] Indeed, a great many critical scholars and educators do not engage an intersectional lens or miss the multiple marginalizations oppressed people face. Issues of dis/ability, furthermore, are frequently ignored as relevant to an intersectional historical lens, and are thus often and problematically left out of critical conceptualizations of curricula, relationships, and pedagogy.[24] Intersectionality, the concept that multiple oppressions converge in unique ways for particular social groups and individuals, can be helpfully articulated with a historical stance that links multiple struggles.[25] Intersectionality can also be leveraged to address the absence of a lens to discuss or deconstruct ableism, and clarify how ableism intertwines with racism.[26]

In this vein, I now turn to an exploration of Disability Critical Race Theory (DisCrit) and how this theoretical framework is helpful for (re)building intersectional understandings that acknowledge historical figures in their full humanity. Using the lives and teachings of Ella Baker and Rosa Parks, I explore how stories about their lives at times miss intersectional commitments, limiting the ways we recognize and can learn from the power within their fights for transformative justice. Finally, I argue that disability can be reconceptualized as a political identity and engaged by intentional educators to advance intersectional ways of thinking and teaching about injustice and resistance. Ultimately, I make the case that DisCrit History Matters can be a bridge for educators to establish connections that strengthen the movement toward transformative justice.

INFUSING DISABILITY CRITICAL RACE THEORY WITH HISTORY MATTERS

An intersectional focus rooted in DisCrit "foreground(s) the *historical contexts and structural conditions* of ways racism and ableism intersect" [italics added for emphasis].[27] Consequently, DisCrit framing allows focus on how History Matters from a DisCrit lens, exploring the interdependence of racism and ableism in historical fights toward justice. Drawing on scholarly work from Disability Studies and Critical Race Theory, the DisCrit framework explores how processes of racism and ableism position unwanted bodies and minds outside the category of "normal," to justify their exclusion and segregation in education and in society.[28]

Fiona Kumari Campbell argues that ableism engages both "the notion of the normative (and normal individual) and the enforcement of a divide between perfect humanity (how humans are supposedly meant to be) and the aberrant, the unthinkable."[29] Said differently, ableism is the ideology that there is a norm that all humans should be judged against and that those who are imagined as abnormal are not worthy of resources. When intertwined with racism, that normal human is imagined as white. Gloria Ladson-Billings notes, "[I]n a racialized society where whiteness is positioned as normative, *everyone* is ranked and categorized in relation to these points of opposition."[30] Consequently, it is the interdependence of racism and ableism that position all people of color as less than normal.[31]

It is important to note that positioning people of color as "less than" is not simply a way to build a hierarchy but is also a way to allocate resources based on that hierarchy; marking people of color as less than allows resources to be funneled away from them, securing the property rights of whiteness for a small few.[32] For example, when it is continually determined that students of color do not belong in gifted education or advanced placement classes, these students lose access to rigorous curricula, engaging pedagogy, and smaller teacher-to-student ratios that allow for more substantive relationships.[33] Hence, students of color miss out on a host of resources allocated to students deemed worthy of gifted and advanced placements. Meanwhile, an overrepresentation of youth of color in special education has existed for at least forty years.[34]

Often, special education labeling for students of color is a double-edged sword wherein resources are allocated, but there is also social stigma; a lack of positive outcomes, including graduation and college entrance; and a host of negative outcomes, including higher suspensions and arrests.[35] Moreover, students of color with disability labels are more likely to be put in segregated settings than white peers with the same label.[36] Hence, being labeled as less than has deep impacts on students of color overall, and students of color with disabilities specifically. Even so, disability is not simply a thing to be discarded, an unwanted label for students.

Using the life stories of two well-known civil rights leaders, Ella Baker and Rosa Parks, both of whom experienced chronic health issues, I show how perspectives on these leaders' lives are enhanced by a DisCrit lens. The goal here is not to say that these Black women were definitively disabled and claim identities for them, but to share how chronic illness and understandings of disability influenced their lives and their activism, and why this is important.

Ella Baker

Ella Baker witnessed the acute and chronic illness of her mother, Anna Ross Baker, and herself experienced sustained health issues.[37] In an oral history recorded in 1977, Baker recounts experiencing a "severe case of typhoid fever" when she was about six years of age.[38]

> Between 1900 and 1920 blacks died of typhoid fever at roughly twice the rate of whites.... Because typhoid was usually transmitted through water tainted by sewage, the construction of water and sewer systems helped reduce typhoid rate.... To the extent cities failed to install water and sewer mains in black neighborhoods, or did so with a long lag, this would explain the differential in black and white typhoid rates.[39]

Baker's case of typhoid occurred in approximately 1909; though she did not die, she describes a long and difficult recovery.[40] Her experience highlights how illness and disability often hit Black communities harder because of structural racial discrimination, pointing to racism as a specific cause of illness and disability.

Yet disability, whether it is a condition one is born with or a condition acquired due to discrimination or activism, often influences how activism is enacted. Baker notes in her oral history that, for her, civil rights activism meant caring for others who had been discarded:

For instance, there were times when an incident like, I'll call it, the town drunk might be arrested and beaten up. Well, that didn't matter. But part of the message that we were carrying was that it did matter, because to the extent that he was demeaned, your rights were therefore decreased.... It was a period in which there was kind of a new surge of identity among some of the people who were not class people, but who recognized that there were inevitable links between those who had and those who had not, because any black could be subject to the same treatment.[41]

Baker's explicit connection of care for those impacted by addiction and helping others see how their struggles are linked was a coalition-building mindset and approach that cut across class and ability. A permanent fixture in Baker's activism, this pattern of engagement highlights how Baker understood Black people experiencing chronic addiction, illness, and disability as oppressed.

Baker remained committed to bringing services to Black people impacted by disability throughout her life. She teamed up with Kenneth and Mamie Clark, whose Northside Center for Child Development provided "social work, psychological evaluation, and remediation services for youth in Harlem since there were virtually no mental health services in the community."[42] Historical documents show that Baker worked behind the scenes to ensure that people working for organizations like the Southern Christian Leadership Conference secured sick days, holidays, and other worker's rights.[43]

Baker's own health problems were a lifelong constant. She suffered from acute back pain and "was stretched out on her living room floor when she heard the shocking news of [Martin Luther] King's stabbing."[44] Despite this, Baker rushed to the hospital that night and committed to stepping in for Dr. King, giving speeches and making appearances over the months it took him to recuperate.[45] Baker also had chronic asthma and eyesight that worsened over the years due to cataracts. While she ignored her health for long stretches and "sometimes joked with friends that she was entirely too busy to get sick," chronic health issues impacted how and when Baker engaged in activism from the 1960s through her death in the 1980s.[46] Despite constant obstacles to her personal well-being, Baker continued to build coalitions across struggles, writing in a 1959 memo,

> The more I think of a unique role for the Southern Christian Leadership Conference, Inc., in the present struggle for human dignity, the more I seem to focus on the phrase "Crusade for Citizenship." The word CRUSADE connotes for me a vigorous movement, with high purpose and involving masses of people.[47]

Baker's concept brought those previously left out into the movement. She built her crusade vision from the ground up, recruiting pastors to labor for voting rights, women to organize literacy drives, and young people to develop into leaders. When recognizing that movements needed fewer heroes and more engagement, Baker was influenced by understanding the ways different people could play different roles based on their lived experiences. She attributed her commitment to organizing to her mother, whose own illness was such an impactful part of her reality.[48]

What does it mean that we typically erase Baker's chronic health issues from discourse and writings about her advocacy? What does it teach students when we talk about various civil rights that she fought for but do not address the ways class and race impacted her activism and impact, and the wellness of those she fought for? I suggest that we miss important aspects of how philosophies are developed and enacted and goals pursued when we ignore the full humanity of ancestor leaders.

Baker argued that we need to know the distinction between mobilizing and organizing.

Charles Payne writes,

> Organizing, according to Ella Baker, involves creating ongoing groups that are mass-based in the sense that the people a group purports to represent have real impact on the group's direction. Mobilizing is more sporadic, involving large numbers of people for relatively short periods of time and probably for relatively dramatic activities.... The distinction between organizing and mobilizing has become increasingly muddled. Young people looking back at the movement

tend to see the mobilizing but not the organizing. They see the great demonstrations and the rallies and take that to be the movement. They do not see the organizing effort, often years of such effort, that made the grand moments possible. They do not see organizers going door to door for months on end trying to win trust, overcome fear, and educate people to the ways the movement might connect with their lives.[49]

Payne's argument affirms that History Matters when we teach young people about the distinctions between mobilizing and organizing, a distinction Baker found important to articulate. I add, too, that Ella Baker's *full* history matters. Experiences with her mother's and her own chronic illnesses impacted the ways and whys she organized and mobilized. In a 1970 interview, Baker stated,

> Every time I see a young person who has come through the system to a stage where he could profit from the system and identify with it, but who identifies more with the struggle of black people who have not had his chance, every time I find such a person I take new hope. I feel a new life as a result of it.[50]

Here Baker reminds us that all people have the chance to be part of a movement toward transformative justice. When we study her philosophy on organizing, mobilizing, and movement building, we must remember to understand the context in which those ideas developed. Ella Baker developed practical strategies for changing individual situations and broader social norms in no small part *because of* her lived experiences with racism, classism, and ableism. In our engagement with History Matters, we must seek to name all the ways Baker's experiences informed her work.

Rosa Parks

Many scholars and educators with a commitment to History Matters remind us that Rosa Parks resisted oppression all her life and was a radical thinker and organizer prior to refusing to give up a seat on a Montgomery bus. In her own papers, Parks writes about staying up all night with her grandfather to make sure the KKK did not come into their house. "He kept his shot gun within hand reach at all times," Parks wrote.[51] In the 1930s, she raised money to defend the Scottsboro Boys, nine young Black men falsely accused of raping two white women.[52] Parks and her husband Raymond both worked with the NAACP throughout the 1940s and 1950s.[53] Parks's history of thinking and organizing against white supremacy was, in fact, consistent and persistent throughout her life.

Still Rosa Parks is best known for refusing to give up her seat when a bus driver demanded she do so, a refusal that launched the Montgomery Bus Boycott. Parks's role in that successful activist undertaking has enshrined her in national history books. What is rarely discussed, though, even by those who recognize her role as a key architect of the civil rights movement, is that Parks struggled with chronic illness throughout her life as a result of medical racism and her resistance to injustice. As a child, Parks was often sick with chronic tonsillitis, and her mother had to save money for years before she could get her daughter a tonsillectomy when she was nine years of age.[54] Parks's experiences with childhood sickness illustrate structural inequities in the medical field that shape access to health care for Black people in the United States, often exacerbating illness until it becomes chronic.[55]

Rosa Parks received repeated violent threats after she refused to give up her seat, yet it is not well known that Parks developed both chronic insomnia and stomach ulcers as a result, illustrating how one can acquire chronic illness for resisting oppression.[56] Parks's autobiographer emphasizes, "The third theme that comes through poignantly in her papers is the depth and toll of the poverty and health issues that resulted from Parks's bus stand."[57] Parks's own writings point to these harmful impacts in various ways. A year after the 1955 action for which she is best known, Parks wrote,

> Hurt, harm, and danger
> The dark closet of my mind
> So much to remember[58]

Hence Parks's own words remind us how resistance against systemic injustice can take often-hidden emotional and physical tolls on multiply-marginalized people, causing or exacerbating chronic illness.

Parks's resistance to segregation also impacted her employment. For five weeks after her refusal to give up her seat on the bus, coworkers at the department store where Parks worked never spoke to her, and she was then let go. Her niece describes the hurt Parks felt,

> She got a lot of attention for that arrest. . . . She was disheartened that her black co-workers did not want to speak to her. If you were doing anything for change you were an outcast. Jim Crow conditioned black folk to think this was the best life they were going to get. People just stopped speaking to her until she was let go.[59]

Parks's Black coworkers were, of course, extremely aware that they could also lose their jobs and be subject to threats if they socialized with Rosa Parks. Parks's experience reminds us that systems of inequity condition people to respond negatively when others refuse to accept the oppression.

How can the physical, emotional, and economic toll of resistance on Parks be ignored? How are the power and implications of the story limited if we do not talk about the ulcers and insomnia that plagued Parks after she was threatened by whites and unsupported by many Black people within her immediate community?

Even with the harassment she experienced, Parks remained steadfast in her beliefs. In 1956, she wrote about a moment during childhood when she stood up to a white child who harassed her. She stated, "I would rather be lynched then to be mistreated, then not say 'I don't like it.'"[60] While Parks refused to be coerced into silence, like Ella Baker, she often hid the ways responses to her resistance had impacted her health. Parks's biographer noted,

> Sometime in the 1990s, Rosa Parks appears to have filled out a self-help marketing questionnaire about health and personal traits, marking one of her attributes as the tendency to conceal [her pain] from others making light of even the most trying circumstances.[61]

It is essential that all youth learn the full story, though, because it helps situate the many ways history connects to the present. The toll Parks paid for resistance should not be ignored. "Though the righteousness of her actions may seem self-evident today, at the time, those who challenged segregation were often treated as unstable, unruly, and potentially dangerous by many white and some black people."[62] When we describe Rosa

Parks as a hero whose actions were celebrated by all, her humanity is stripped and we lose a deeper teaching and learning moment.

As we pursue transformative justice, the incredible cost Parks paid for her resistance should be noted—and also linked to the ways students today pay similar prices when they push back against oppression. We need to talk about how those of us who resist are situated as unstable, difficult, and dangerous, labels that fill the cumulative files of many multiply-marginalized students of color.[63] Moreover, students of color who are not thus branded but are rewarded for their own compliance can learn what it costs their labeled peers and themselves when they acquiesce to white supremacy and other harmful, unjust social norms.

When educators ignore the physical and emotional toll Parks paid for fighting discrimination, they inevitably miss how Parks was intentional about healing. Professor Stephanie Y. Evans has revealed that Parks regularly practiced yoga later in her life. Her niece, Sheila McCauley Keys, recalled,

> Well into her senior years she has only recently begun practicing yoga. Splendid silver hair gives her away as the oldest student in most of the classes she occasionally attends with family, but she doesn't care. She's reached a point when she considers herself a student of life.... Eventually, she learns the movements and yogic principles well enough to practice alone in her home.... Inner peace and clarity have always been important to her.[64]

Drawing attention to Parks's personal yoga practice, which Keys beautifully described as "poetry in her motion," is *not* a call for educators to prescribe yoga for every multiply-marginalized disabled and/chronically ill person who experiences oppression. This truth can, however, shift our understandings of how "the mother of the civil rights movement" approached life and learning, and how she was active about caring for herself, even though she did not often share her pain with others. Parks knew systemic oppression and the harassment she experienced from her resistance to that oppression continued to harm her physically and emotionally. She also knew she needed to tend to what was happening to the world and take care of herself.

Honoring the value of reflecting on Parks's legacy with a fuller understanding of her humanity, Stephanie Y. Evans wrote,

> When I recently discovered the previously unpublished 1973 picture of "Rosa Parks practicing yoga at an event" in the [Library of Congress] digital archive, I recognized it is a poignant illustration of how Black women's healing traditions are historical, spiritual, creative, and political.[65]

Consequently, Evans reminds us that Parks's yoga practice, then, was more than just exercise or a prescription for others to follow; it was part of Black women's lineage of resistance.

When we teach toward transformative justice, we need to share with students how political philosophies are formed and maintained. An intersectional DisCrit approach to History Matters allows us to better identify and describe interlocking systems of oppression and how such systems have historically impacted leaders and movement builders, and currently impact leaders and movement builders today. Consequently, DisCrit History Matters because the injustices Ella Baker and Rosa Parks experienced caused or contributed to their chronic illnesses and, at the same time, shaped their philosophies on and enactments of resistance.

CONCLUSION

The lives of Ella Baker and Rosa Parks remind us that living with and resisting systemic racism, ableism, and other oppressions deeply impact human health and well-being. Thus, educators who adopt a DisCrit History Matters stance as part of their pedagogical philosophy must consider how navigating systemic racism and ableism is linked with microaggressions in curricula, pedagogy, and relationships.

Regarding curricula, chronically ill and disabled Black, Indigenous, Latinx, and Asian people have always been part of movements toward justice. Yet their health experiences, many of which are caused or exacerbated by experiences of and resistance to systemic injustice, are often absent from the curriculum. I have written that "If dis/ability were engaged with as an important political identity, instead of a thing to remediate, the curricular response would be something much more engaging."[66] Educators with a DisCrit History Matters stance actively seek to uncover and include such instances by presenting movement members as whole people, keeping their stories and experiences intact. Among the many benefits of this approach is the opportunity for disabled students to witness themselves reflected in the curriculum and for nondisabled students to resist ableist perspectives about disabled people.

With respect to pedagogy, it is typically the case that educators determine a student is failing and focus on remediation, a word that describes students trapped in a learning ecology focused on fixing difference.[67] I have argued that "If dis/ability were imagined as a political identity with material inequities and resistance tied to it, instead of a biological failure, the pedagogical response would be vastly more productive."[68] That is, instead of focusing on fixing the student, educators could aim to fix the student's learning ecology, creating access to a DisCrit History Matters curriculum. Such a shift supports a classroom ecology wherein educators and students alike view disabled students not as burdens, but as learners who have ways of understanding the world that nondisabled people do not. A DisCrit History Matters stance teaches nondisabled students that they are not better than their disabled peers, that they have things to learn from disabled students, and that disability is a political identity.

Lastly, educators need to approach relationships with the recognition that our students are often navigating violent systems in and out of schools, and such conditions impact their emotional and physical health. Many of our students and members of their families and communities navigate chronic illness as a result of systems that limit their access to clean environments and medical care. Additionally, students must often stand up to teachers who enact white supremacist ableist practices in their classroom curricula, pedagogies, and relationships. Resistance costs them physically and emotionally. "If dis/ability were conceptualized as a welcomed political identity, instead of a thing to punish for failing to meet standards, the behavioral response would be something much more loving."[69] Because bell hooks already established that there is no love without justice, DisCrit History Matters in relationships must continually link students' behaviors with the systems and contexts in which those behaviors are rooted. This does not mean we let students act any way they want; it means that we as educators seek to better understand and articulate the roots of student behaviors, to change our responses from punitive to loving. Connecting actions and systems is the pathway through which our commitments to transformative justice are enacted.

The socio-political thoughts of Ella Baker and Rosa Parks and many of the actions they took aligned their praxis with their lived experiences with systemic and interactional oppressions.[70] Both leaders developed inclusive philosophies and enacted them by consciously seeking justice in a myriad of ways for both others and themselves. We can learn from the lives of Baker and Parks that chronic illness and disability can be reconceptualized as political identity, and intentional educators can engage with the full humanity of these and other historical figures to center intersectional ways of thinking and teaching about injustice and resistance. In this way, DisCrit History Matters allows educators to help students make connections that strengthen our pursuit of transformative justice.

3

The Whole Story Matters: *Building Historical Capital with Youth*

Lawrence T. Winn

> We don't have any place to go to teach us about us, or talk about slavery, and things like racism. They won't let us talk about these things in school or teach us about the system. Here we get to talk about what we want and things that matters.
>
> —Prince, BOND Participant, Age Fifteen

IN JANUARY 2016 members of BOND were planning for their upcoming research presentation at the 3rd Annual Cities United convening in Birmingham, Alabama. Cities United invited eight youths to share their research on educational inequities with over three hundred mayors, youth, and city leaders from throughout the United States. The trip to Birmingham for the youth participants was a big deal. For many of the youth, it was their first time leaving Madison (other than going to Chicago) and/or flying on an airplane. Just six months earlier, I had asked BOND members where they wanted to go for their upcoming 2015–16 field trips. Several of the youth yelled out "water park," "laser tag," "Bucks versus Bulls game," and "out to eat at the Cheesecake Factory at the mall." Prince, hiding his twisted locks under his hoodie and placing his chin in the palms of his hands, waited patiently while his peers shouted out their requests. When it quieted down, he said, "I want to go down South. I want to go visit where we are from. I want to learn about my people." The room was full of laughter. Pryor remarked, "Stop being funny, we [are] not taking a field trip to the South." I looked at Prince and said, "Let's make it happen. Let's figure out how we can travel to the South. What city do you want to visit?" Prince responded, "I don't know, maybe Atlanta but not where Emmitt Till was murdered." I said, "Yes, Atlanta is oozing with Black excellence. It has a Black mayor, Black businesses, Black millionaires, Black colleges and universities." Prince said, "Wow, Black everything! I see."

Prince's dream of visiting the South to learn about where his people are from (he was referring to Black families' Great Migration from southern states to northern cities such as Philadelphia, Detroit, New York City, and Chicago) was described on a Wednesday in September of 2015.[1] On this cold, snowy Midwestern January in 2016, Prince and his BOND peers—Pryor (who is Prince's brother), David, Kevin, Kendrick, Paul, and Gregory—were reviewing data for their research project. Prince was also holding court and expressing his frustration with his high school teachers' failure to provide him and his peers the curriculum, facts, and space to discuss historical events that currently impact his community. Prince eagerly wanted to talk about the upcoming 2016 election between Donald Trump and Hillary Clinton, and why his community's trash had not been collected in over two weeks. He also wanted to learn more about Emmitt Till and how his death was similar to the murders of Sandra Bland and Tony Robinson. Melissa, the Supervisor of Youth Programs from the City of Madison, and Parker, a local police officer, joined the group circle conversation of Ta-Nehisi Coates's *Between the World and Me*.[2]

Intrigued by Prince's enthusiasm and command of historical facts, Melissa asked Prince why he and his peers consistently come to the Spot and not to local community-based youth organizations such as the Youth Club. Without hesitation, Prince spoke about how schools and afterschool programs prohibited him from being himself and not teaching him the "whole story about history." According to Prince, the Spot served as a place where youth "get to talk about what we want and things that matter." The Spot is a learning place—a community room housed in a local housing complex in the Westbrook community—where teachers and other educators are invited by youth participants to engage in conversations about history, race, and education. It is their opportunity to make connections between present injustices and past social movements. These young people read the life stories of Marcus Garvey, Fred Hampton, and Assata Shakur. They were also introduced to Black enterprises, redlining, mass incarceration, Jim Crow, and Black Wall Street. They were curious about understanding history and how it impacts their present and future.

The prevailing question for youth of color residing in communities encumbered by underperforming schools, overpolicing, and a plethora of additional racial inequities is where they can go to express their concerns, see Black excellence, learn about the history of oppression, debate politics, and share ideas about social transformation. Several studies have revealed that classrooms and youth development programs steer away from historical, political, and social conversations about racism, police brutality, or any topic that may be deemed too controversial for some cohorts.[3] Many of these classrooms or learning programs instead employ neoliberal educational programs.[4] According to Ms. Yvette, a Westbrook community parent, "Kids don't have anywhere to go to learn what it means to be African American or Black." She was a staunch advocate of the youth transforming the community room into a learning space where youth bonded over social issues.

In this chapter, I explore the ways in which Black males who have been alienated and sidelined within the traditional K–12 classroom develop critically conscious learning spaces to share, engage, and debate topics that are not discussed at school or community-based youth organizations.[5] The focus of this study is on BOND, a Black youth collective led by youth and supported by educators and city officials. I found through participant observations and interviews that the Spot served as an alternative classroom that was humanizing, restorative, and engaging.[6] In this context, youth shared their experiences, learned about African

American history, explored race, celebrated their accomplishments, and laughed at each other's jokes. The time they spent together and with educators helped cultivate their critical consciousness, which provided them with historical capital, defined here as knowledge and facts that help an individual understand how historical patterns and occurrences are connected to present-day events and issues. Like social capital, as described by Pierre Bordieu, historical capital is resourceful and allows an individual to engage others in ways that create pathways to career, educational, and social opportunities.[7]

I begin this chapter with a historical synopsis of the social and economic conditions under which BOND members and many African American families live. Using an ethnographical method employed by W. E. B. Du Bois in the *Philadelphia Negro: A Social Study*, I offer a historical overview to describe the milieu that shapes the youth participants' frustrations, frames their critical consciousness, and demonstrates their pursuit of opportunities and "connections."[8] As Du Bois suggests, provision of a historical context does demonstrate that youth's so-called "problems were rooted not in heredity but rather in their environment and social conditions that confronted them."[9] In addition to using field notes and thick description, I cite data and use descriptive statistics to provide quantitative support to the in-depth interviews and observations presented in this chapter. Following the historical synopsis, I review and examine conversations from BOND sessions, interviews conducted with participants, and archival materials produced by the youth. The analyzed data demonstrate the youth's desire and need for a separate space where they can cultivate their critical consciousness and invite educators who engage and share their histories with the group.

THE HISTORICAL ROOTS OF THE MADISON'S "PROBLEM AND TROUBLE"

The Spot is a modestly furnished community room with two offices set in the back, a kitchen and bathroom for public use, and a long wooden table surrounded by ten to fifteen mismatched chairs. The table and chairs are placed in the center while cushioned benches beckon along the low-installed windows; a hanging multicolored cultural art piece is placed on the center wall adjacent to the whiteboard. This is the place many of the youth have come to call their classroom. The Spot provides a humanizing learning experience where their life stories are valued, their histories are appreciated, and their futures are hopeful. It is a restorative space in the midst of the punishment and discipline they experience at their schools and in Madison.

Since the 1980s, African American families who migrated to Madison from cities such as Chicago, Illinois; Milwaukee, Wisconsin; and Gary, Indiana, moved to Westbrook before relocating to other sections of the city.[10] Many of these African American families moved to Madison for opportunities and better schools.[11] For example, Ms. Ruby, a community mother and local organizer, said, "I followed my daughter who moved from Evanston for a job and to grow her family. Then my other daughter moved here. Now all of us are here." Pryor described his journey to Madison as a chance for better schools. He stated, "My mom moved from Chicago to change the scenery. She wanted us to go to better schools, too." A common recurring theme that emerged from the interviews and observations suggests that many of the youth's families relocated to Madison and other cities in Dane County for opportunities and to improve their life chances of breaking cycles of generational poverty caused by systemic social and economic barriers. The new families moving to Madison caused panic within the liberal white community. Many elected politicians, teachers, and residents often suggested that the new families were "coming up here and bringing their problems," and "schools are underperforming because of the people from Chicago." Many of these new arriving families who relocated because of opportunities made the Westbrook community their first home.

Westbrook is physically bordered by highways to both the north and the west, several miles of preserved marshlands cut off the south section, and a middle-class to affluent neighborhood marks the east end. The neighborhood is divided into three county zones, making it difficult for new residents to feel part of a singular neighborhood. To add to the confusion, local high school students living within a one-mile radius tended to be enrolled in at least three different schools. Of the nine youths I focus on for this study, five attended the same high school (Beacon High School); the other four all attended different high schools. Since many of the students were relocating from Chicago, teachers and other community members referred to the newcomers as "poor families from Chicago." Chapelle decodes what being from Chicago means: "Just because we are from Chicago they think we are trouble and from the projects."

Westbrook is a food desert; it is without a grocery store. Residents' only option for food, drug prescriptions, or household items was the national pharmacy Drug-Mart (pseudonym), which closed in the summer of 2014, to the dismay and uproar of the community. Local leaders protested to Madison's City Council and wrote letters to Drug-Mart's shareholders, to no avail. BOND members also believed that the closing of Drug-Mart was unjust and a direct attack on the Black community. During one BOND session, the youth contemplated making the closing of the pharmacy the focus of their youth participatory action research project:

PRINCE: Drug-Mart is all this community has. The old people get their prescriptions and medication from there.

DAVE: Why are they closing it? They don't care about us. They can do what they want.

PRINCE: What can the mayor do? Nothing! He told us he has no power.

MONICA: What do you think y'all can do? What action will y'all take?

PRYOR: Chad [city council representative] won't help us. He still did not get us our basketball court.

PRINCE: The Brook has no grocery stores and now they closing this. Shit, we barely have a bus that runs through here.

There is an abundance of cultural community wealth within Westbrook.[12] Most notably, Ms. Ruby and Ms. Love frequently led community residents in organizing efforts to improve the quality of life in the community. Ms. Love stated, "I care about my community. People can say what they want about us, but we do our best and want the best for our kids just like them [white people]."

Leaving Westbrook and driving under the highway heading toward the Isthmus is another story—a tale of two Madisons. If you are Black living in Madison, you experience higher rates of incarceration, school suspensions, poverty, and unemployment. If you are white, on the other hand, Madison is a great place to live. In 2013 the Wisconsin Council on Children and Families released *Race to Equity: A Baseline Report on the State of Racial Disparities in Dane County*.[13] The report highlighted profound and entrenched racial disparities, contradicting everything the liberal community is known for being: progressive, highly educated, opportunity rich, racially harmonious, and equity-centered. The majority of the African American families represented in the *Race to Equity* report reside in four to five heavily populated low-income communities.[14] According to *Geography of Opportunity, Capital Region, Wisconsin* report data, too, Westbrook lacks access to quality health care, employment, transportation, and food options—and ranks "very low" for the "Childhood Opportunity Index."[15] These profound data suggest that Westbrook is not only racially isolated but also socially marginalized by both geographical location and placement. Pryor knew all too well of these disparities: "Everything in the *Race to Equity* report we already know. It is nothing new! The same thing happening to us here happened to us in the past and happening to Black people everywhere." The youth knew the data not only from analyzing it but also from their lived experiences. Pryor connected the data to the problems and issues plaguing Black families throughout the United States in the present and also the past. According to Prince, "The shit is fixed. I have been telling y'all this that the system is working just fine. I'm woke man."

The paradox of Madison's liberal culture and progressive politics coexisting with the economic hardships and racial inequities experienced by African Americans caused anguish and mistrust for BOND participants. The youth were fully aware of the two Madisons, and cognizant of their lack of access to resources and opportunities outside the community. For example, the following conversation between Kevin and Paul gives insight into their understanding of racial inequities:

KEVIN: White boys at my school get warnings. Black students get suspended. When a Black student comes to school and even smells like weed, they get sent home and suspended. But when a white swimmer comes to school wasted or blasted,

>   the teachers give them eye drops and tell them to go to the bathroom to wash up.
> PAUL: Yeah, remember we went to that white party with those white girls. The police came and smelled weed coming from the bathroom. The police told them [white students] that he was going to come in and told them to flush the weed down the toilet. We were like wow. We would have been given tickets and suspended.

Kevin and Paul recognized how school staff and police officers treat Black and white students differently. Throughout interviews and discussions, it became apparent that the youth felt that being Black males made them targets of the police and by their teachers. Racial inequities present many challenges for BOND participants, and the *Race to Equity* and *Geography of Opportunity* data illustrate specific economic and structural barriers these and other youth must overcome. The following sections explore the Spot as a youth-led counterpublic that allows youth to develop and sustain critical consciousness and build historical capital.

"I CAN TALK FREELY . . . IT FEELS LIKE HOME."

Although viewed by some passersby as "just a community room" with a wooden table and mismatched chairs, the Spot was "the" destination for Black males in the Westbrook community. They arrived every Wednesday to debate and discuss issues that mattered most to them. It was also a place where they came to talk about the milieu of Madison, question why poverty continued to exist in predominately Black communities, challenge visiting "system workers" about their roles in systemic racism and opportunity barriers, and strategize to transform their community. Catherine Squires refers to a public sphere or counterpublic as a set of physical or mediated spaces where historically marginalized Black, Latinx, and Indigenous individuals and groups gather and share information, debate opinions, and tease out their political interests and social needs with other participants.[16] The Spot functioned much like the barbershop or stoop in the Black community. On any given day, both the barbershop and/or the stoop would be full of active bodies talking about sports, politics, and social issues.[17] David explained the Spot's relevance to Melissa. He stated, "We come to learn what the schools don't want to teach and we can talk about things that are important—stuff like race." David exclaimed that the "Spot was the only place where I can talk freely and I can learn from adults who care and will look out for me. It feels like home." David made a clear distinction between feeling unwelcomed at school while feeling free and comfortable at the Spot.

The Spot was nothing like school; it was the complete opposite. For many of the participants, school was not enjoyable, and some even suggested that their schooling was not applicable to their everyday lives. David recounted his experience, "The teachers don't care for us. We are treated differently. And the police harass us. All we got is each other." Many marginalized youth of color living in urban communities, especially African American males, see their stories statistically represented in data reports. For example, *Civil Rights Data Collection* shows that "Black K–12 students are 3.8 times as likely as white students to receive one or more out-of-school suspensions and 1.9 times as likely to be expelled."[18] So it is not at all shocking to hear David's statement that he values an environment where "I can talk freely and I can learn from adults who care and look out for me." The "can talk freely" contrast implies that he and other youth are reluctant to speak in class out of fear the teacher would reprimand them or dismiss their answers or questions.

Kevin shared a similar experience that happened with his teacher. He explained that after learning about Jim Crow at the Spot, he was excited to share his newfound knowledge with his history class.

> I raised my hand and asked the teacher if she could explain why we are talking about the Civil War and we have not talked about slavery or Black people. She just said we would get to that and thank you. See, that is why I don't and won't talk in class.

Kevin was disappointed that the teacher refused to engage him and failed to notice he was eager to contribute to the class discussion; now he refuses to participate in class. My participants' interviews and conversations about their teachers suggest that most of the youth feel teachers "don't engage" or "don't care" about Black students. BOND participants constantly described their educators as "not engaging," "not teaching," "not learning," "not caring," and "not listening to us." "Not," a negative, represented their learning experiences in school.

Making the case that teachers need to consider a critical pedagogy that is engaging intellectually and applicable to the lives of the students, Jeffrey Michael Reyes Duncan-Andrade and Ernest Morrell propose that teachers design a model of education that prepares students to face the economic and social barriers and inequities in their life.[19] Maisha T. Winn similarly argues for restorative teacher education, a teaching method that emphasizes classroom culture based on restorative justice principles such as building relationships and community and discussing how issues impact students' communities, foundations that encourage student participation and reduce the possibility that students will come to be suspended.[20] Both pedagogical approaches emphasize the crucial intersections between teacher, student, and critical thinking.

Gloria Ladson-Billings suggests that effective teachers working with students of color understand the importance of culturally relevant pedagogies.[21] In a similar vein, H. Richard Milner posits that teachers have a responsibility to build knowledge and discourse around race or societal curriculum sites because students experience these complex issues in their communities and read about them on social media.[22] Providing the example of Natasha McKenna, Michael Brown, Travyon Martin, Sandra Bland, Freddie Gray, and Philando Castile losing their lives to violence by police officers between 2012 and 2016, Milner suggests that these deaths and the pattern they point to impact the daily lives of marginalized youth of color, and are one of many reasons teachers should create learning environments that promote discourse about race and social issues. Although BOND participants read and discussed these deaths and other social issues on Facebook, Snapchat, and with their friends, interviews and observations showed that none of the aforementioned pedagogical approaches or issues were being employed in their classrooms.

Figure 3.1 illustrates topics that were discussed at the Spot, and/or in schools, or in neither setting. For each topic, I asked the group whether they had discussed the issue or relevant related issues at school.

The figure highlights that only three of the nine topics were discussed in schools, among these were the *Race to Equity* report, which was a

FIGURE 3.1 Social justice and history discussions chart

TOPIC	DISCUSSED IN THE SPOT	DISCUSSED AT THEIR SCHOOL
Racism	✓	
Police Brutalities	✓	
School Discipline	✓	
Slavery	✓	
Race to Equity Report	✓	✓
Tony Robinson	✓	✓
Oscar Grant, Michael Brown, Sandra Bland, and others who lost their lives to violence by police officers	✓	
Black Lives Matter	✓	
Election (Donald Trump and Hillary Clinton)	✓	✓

popular local publication, and a presidential election that was underway and dominating the news. Tony Terrell Robinson, Jr., was an unarmed nineteen-year-old Black man fatally shot by a police officer in Madison, Wisconsin, on March 6, 2015. Many BOND members knew him and were impacted by his death. Several community marches and memorials were held in his honor, and his death sparked a community movement against the use of police force. Although these three topics were widely discussed, BOND participants' K–12 classroom teachers neglected to talk about issues of racism, school discipline, or police brutality.

Favorite discussion topics at the Spot were community policing and the system of oppression. BOND participants wanted to know how to prepare themselves and be safe. For example, when interviewed about his experience with racial disparities, Prince brought up his encounters with the police: "We are targets. They try and get us for nothing. I know I am Black, but damn. The police be on us for nothing." He referenced Michelle Alexander's *The New Jim Crow* and talked about mass incarceration. When I asked if he had read the book, he said, "No, just heard about it."[23] Other youth participants talked about "overpolicing," "surveillance," "tracking," and "lack of rights." The youth encouraged each other to know their rights but also believed police could deny them their rights at any time. Monica, a BOND supporter and mother of one of the participants, suggested that a presenter from Milwaukee discuss community policing and citizen rights, but BOND members held opposing views about the speaker teaching them about their rights.

MONICA: Do you want a speaker from Milwaukee to come in to discuss knowing your rights?

PRINCE: What rights? Man, we don't have no rights when it comes to police. They can check you for whatever reason they want. Y'all remember what happened to us after the last guy came to tell us about our rights. Police asked could we check you? No sir. They checked us anyway and proceeded to ask us to empty our pockets. No rights. Nothing changed. We no have right in schools. We get suspended for asking questions, any little thing.

MONICA: That was my concern. The backlash that happened last time.

KENDRICK: When you speak up, you get popped [murdered]. *[He starts to mention police killings]* ... we want to make it and do right. We want to be citizens, but it seems the more we know, the worse it is for us. The less we know, the better we are.

Youth gravitated to the Spot because it was a public space that enabled them to be agentic, vocal, and critical. The Spot served as a place where young people developed "an awareness of how institutional, historical, and systemic forces limit and promote the life opportunities for particular groups."[24] Black males became "woke" at the Spot. David often mentioned, "They don't like us to know the truth. Always telling us about their history. Nothing about us."

"I AM WRITING A LETTER TO OBAMA TO TELL HIM HOW I FEEL ABOUT MY SCHOOL EXPERIENCE."

In my observations and interviews of these youth and educators, I learned that youth came to the Spot to discuss issues with one another but also because they enjoyed building relationships with Lance, Monica, and me, as well as the other adults. Kevin stated, "We don't get a chance to talk to adults because they always talking at us. Here we get to learn and have fun and be ourselves in front of y'all." Paul claimed, "We come here and we get to think and they [adults] push us to think more. At the Youth Club, it's the adults versus the kids." Kevin and Paul both mentioned how the Spot differed from their classrooms at school. One difference is everyone gets a chance to speak and speak what is on their mind. The group sits in a circle for discussion, but the talking piece that is sometimes used to give the speaker the floor never really works at the Spot. The circle (around a square table) instead allows youth and adults to build natural conversations that are free flowing.

Kevin and Paul's perception of the Spot as a community space of free-flowing conversation without the control of adults is best illustrated in a discussion from February 10, 2016, about Beyoncé and the water in Flint, Michigan.

PRYOR: Did y'all see Beyoncé at halftime?

KENDRICK: They are trying to do her dirty because she was speaking the truth. She had on black leather like the panthers, the sistas [sic] had on black berets, and they made the X in the middle of the field. The white folks are going crazy. She was like power to the people. Folks are straight racists for hating on her. She is proud to be Black and what's wrong with that?

PRINCE *(interjects)*: But did y'all see all the heat Cam Newton is getting for not speaking to the media after the game. But the white governor from Michigan refused to talk about the lead water in Flint, Michigan, and no one ain't saying nothing. That's the system.

TORRY: Prince, you keep saying it's the system. What do we have to do?

KEVIN: Be like Malcolm X.

PRYOR: King didn't work, they killed him. X didn't work, they killed him. What do we do? Man, I was thinking if I should

	run for governor and then free all the Black people. I think King and X died for nothing.
LANCE:	What do you mean died in vain? You don't think anything changed?
PRYOR:	I think they did all they could, but they keep changing the game. They keep making it harder and nothing is changing. I think I would make the same sacrifice to change things for my brothers and sisters.
PRINCE:	I am writing a letter to Obama to tell him how I feel about my school experience. Some of the other students are writing to senators and Scott Walker. People told me that he will respond, but he ain't going to change anything I want change. What do you think, Lance?
LANCE:	Prince, I think that is a good start. I think you should write the letter.
PRINCE:	Cool. I'm going to need your help.

This conversation is an example of an unstructured and uncontrolled discussion with adults that flowed freely and lasted thirty minutes. It began with Kendrick and Pryor giving their commentary about the Super Bowl and the backlash Beyoncé received for paying tribute to the Black Panthers and Cam Newton received for not speaking to the media. The issues they highlight are racism and cultural imperialism.[25] This led Prince to bring up the water crisis in Flint, Michigan, and how wrong it was for the governor not to speak. Prince's focus is social injustice and the ongoing devaluing of Black lives in Flint. Then the conversation moved to a discussion about Dr. Martin Luther King, Jr., and Malcolm X and whether it is worth sacrificing your life for change. The youth shared their knowledge of historical Black leaders, and an exchange emerged between Lance and Pryor regarding the meaning of sacrifice. As illustrated, the adults participated in the conversation by asking questions but never attempted to control the dialogue. The whole time, youth and adults alike were analyzing and discussing pertinent issues and asking each other about possible ways to change the system. No one had the right answer. Everyone was encouraged to participate. All participants' thoughts, ideas, and experiences were valued and appreciated.

This conversation also highlights bonding between Prince and Lance. Lance is a former police officer, and BOND youth saw him as part of the system. I observed for over a year how the youth used coded language to mock Lance with words such as *crossing guard, mark, intel*, and *the system*. However, Lance kept coming back and eventually became an adult ally. Lance made the following statement about his reasons for coming back to the Spot:

> I care about the guys. I share a similar story, growing up in Milwaukee. The system is just waiting for them to make one wrong move. Although they tried to run me away, I kept coming back because I want the best for them and care about them. They're just kids responding to the conditions of their environment. Can't blame them for not trusting too many people, especially the police during these times. I get it.

Lance used the word *care* twice to describe his reason for coming back. As previously discussed, *lack of care* is a theme that emerged from youth as they shared their experiences with the teachers and police officers. Lance insists that he cares for the youth and wants the best for them. Prince's appeal to Lance to help him write his letter to President Obama signals that Lance is now an adult ally.

After Lance attended BOND sessions for over a year, he used his "connections" to help the youth find employment. He met with Chappelle several times to prepare for interviews and accompanied him to meet with prospective employers. On one occasion, Lance showed up to Chappelle's job at the car wash and left him a significant tip. Chappelle shared with the group his appreciation of Lance: "Man, I made more money from that tip than washing twenty cars. Lance was looking out. I need him to come every day." Beyond helping the youth stay "woke," my findings suggest that the Spot was valued as a free space where youth and adults could overcome their past problems or perceptions of each other and talk about issues that matter. The youth and Lance repaired harm that framed their relationship and began to build faith in each other.

THE "WHOLE STORY" IS WHAT MATTERS

Prince, David, Pryor, Paul, Kevin, Kendrick, Gregory, and the other BOND members created a space that gave them a platform to learn about their past, present, and future. In May of 2016, they presented their research findings to over three hundred mayors in Birmingham. They spoke with passion, confidence, and mastery of the issues and facts. They toured Birmingham and saw Black businesses, met the Black mayor, and visited several civil rights monuments. When they returned home, despite being marginalized and counted out by their local schools, these young people continued to cultivate relationships with teachers, police, and educators. "Histories Matter" more to these youth than their teachers ever knew.[26] Indeed, historical capital provided them the confidence and knowledge to converse with educators, and motivated them to change their community and stay "woke," an expression Black community activists and social media users adopted from R&B singer Erykah Badu's 2008 record *Master Teacher*. Critical consciousness and historical capital led and equipped these youth to stand up for Trayvon Martin, Tanisha Anderson, Tamir Rice, Oscar Grant, Sandra Bland, and Tony Robinson. Their only hope is that these same conversations can happen within K–12 classrooms where all students have opportunities to share their story—and their histories are valued. Youth are interested in "the whole story" or a history that embraces the harms of racism and discrimination, sacrifices of immigrants, accomplishments of women, the legacy of excellence of African Americans, the failures of society, and the beauty of diversity.

SECTION II

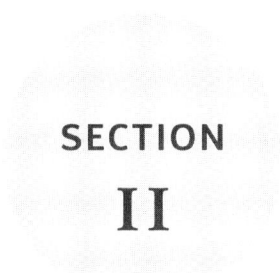

WHY RACE MATTERS

Tyrone C. Howard

The racial uprisings and protests of 2020 will go down as one of the nation's hallmark moments for racial justice and equality. Under the banner of the Black Lives Matter movement, a cross-section of multiracial and mixed-aged people with diverse gender identities converged nationally and internationally around not only racial justice but also racial justice for Black folx. To see hundreds of thousands of people come together amidst the COVID-19 pandemic was a moment in time that many advocates for racial justice thought could never happen in these United States. So, what next? Was this a moment or a movement? Important shifts in our dialogues regarding ending racism and dismantling anti-Black racism were intriguing, but will these broader conversations inform collective action?

While protests in 2020 brought unprecedented attention to the salience of racial inequality in the United States, those who have been engaged in scholarly inquiry on race and racism at the K–12 and higher education levels have examined these issues for decades, if not longer.[1] As calls for racial justice have echoed louder in the mainstream, it should be noted that these calls have been a constant for quite some time among Black scholars, practitioners, and advocates. Thus, to be clear, race still matters in the United States. Race matters in US life, law, ideology, policies, and practices. Race matters when it comes to opportunities, advantages, and privileges, and to be abundantly clear, race matters when it comes to education opportunity and access.

Yet, any contemporary analysis of race would reveal that race still remains the elephant in the room, our societal taboo, our refusal to truly acknowledge that this nation's original sin is an overwhelmingly large part of what stands in the way of creating a much more just, equitable, and humane society today. Scholars such as Anna Julia Cooper, Ida Wells-Barnett, and Carter G. Woodson have been telling us for over a century that race matters, and moreover that Black lives matter. Race remains the issue no one wants to acknowledge or discuss. However, as much as we attempt to ignore it, look around, over, and under it, the quest for racial justice remains a constant reality in our society, schools, and classrooms. Given the complexity of race, the challenges race poses, and our simultaneous national fixation on and avoidance of the matter, race in schools has become our ticking time bomb, set to explode on a moment's notice. Race is our historical lightning rod, equipped with centuries-old baggage, uninformed beliefs and ideas, and hurtful stereotypes the mere mention of which can quickly divide people who are seemingly united. Educator Marian Wright Edelman says that throughout America's history, race has been a "noose choking our capacity to soar."

The field of teacher education is not exempt from race and racism. Teachers and teacher-educators can and must play a pivotal and transformative role in how matters tied to race and racial justice become integral aspects of our work. The pervasiveness of colorblind admissions policies, race-neutral field placements, and inadequate teacher mentorship with respect to racial justice play complicit roles in the maintenance of white supremacy, perpetuating an ideology that continues to suppress race-conscious approaches to teaching and learning for youth of color. Drs. Maisha T. Winn and Lawrence T. Winn make clear to us the need for explicit and sustained focus on justice, equity, transformation, and race consciousness if we seek *to transform the disciplines through restorative justice*. This will require robust efforts to spark dialogue and action among educators and teacher-educators seeking to pursue racial justice within and through the context of analyzing schools, school ideologies, school policies, and school practices.

The following section clarifies what it can look like to pursue racial justice in early childhood education and within mathematics classrooms. The authors are bold, insightful, and timely in their ask that we reimagine race, space, and place when it comes to teaching and learning. This work matters because justice matters—and where justice is our aim, racial justice is always a core focus and starting point. Current realities demand a different way of engaging teachers and teacher-educators that centers insight regarding the racial realities that impede learning for far too many students every day in this nation. This is the time to know, care, and act with an intentional and unapologetic focus on the type of transformation and justice our students need and deserve.

4 Race Matters in Early Childhood Education

*Mariana Souto-Manning, Avanti Chajed,
Abby Emerson, Hyeyoung Ghim,
and Maureen Nicol*

> Race ... functions as a metaphor so necessary to the construction of Americanness.... Deep within the word "American" is its association with race ... American means white.
>
> —Toni Morrison[1]

IN THE UNITED STATES, young children are born into a society where racism is deeply rooted and pervasive.[2] They grow and develop in a society where whites utilize political, economic, and cultural systems to maintain power, a society where "ideas of white superiority and entitlement are widespread, and relations of white dominance and non-white subordination are daily reenacted across a broad array of institutions and social settings."[3]

In education, following the *Brown v. Board of Education* ruling in 1954, "the dismantling of legalized race segregation, Whiteness took on the character of property in the modern sense in that relative White privilege was legitimated as the status quo."[4] Early childhood education was and is no exception. Early childhood teaching and teacher education in the United States continue to be characterized by firm commitments to legitimization of the status quo of whiteness.[5] Despite a long and rich history of early care and education in Black and Indigenous communities, the early childhood curriculum "continues to reflect White, middle-class cultural norms," reifying the belief that the Eurocentric viewpoint is the most valued and valuable in educational contexts.[6]

Young children internalize "power between the races"[7] through social practices and replicate racialized power dynamics and relationships through play.[8] They learn early on, through a variety of experiences, the concept of "Whiteness as property," meaning whiteness expanded from an identity marker to "a type of status in which White racial identity provide[s] the basis for allocating societal benefits."[9] Whiteness is a formidable obstacle to transformation in US society, a cogent safeguard of indelible power dynamics. Racial segregation in US (pre)schools is a situated representation of how whiteness conserves entrenched power, and racial segregation is a dominant feature of today's early childhood classrooms. A recent *New York Times* headline denounced, "Racial Segregation in New York Schools Starts with Pre-K."[10]

Given the stronghold and harmful consequences of whiteness as property, it is crucial that early childhood educators address harms inflicted on children of color. Restorative justice can serve as a powerful pathway to ensure that children of color are "honored as human."[11] Nevertheless, the majority of early childhood educators continue to subscribe to a color-evasive racial ideology,[12] purporting the need to be neutral even as they utilize problematic, ableist discourses they insist are "colorblind."[13] Claiming that young children "don't see color,"[14] many subscribe to the belief that race does not matter,[15] ignoring how, historically, "neutral principles guaranteed that white preferences should remain undisturbed."[16] In purporting neutrality within a context marked by inequality, early childhood educators further their allegiance to whiteness as property.

Despite decades of research confirming that children are highly aware of race and experience racism,[17] early childhood educators continue to exculpate themselves from addressing race and racism in their teaching.[18] Such behaviors stem (at least partly) from "the re-production of racism in and through teacher education."[19] Early childhood education and child development textbooks employed in early childhood teacher education pervasively silence the importance of race and racism.[20] This pattern perpetuates teachers' ideology that "children are simply too young to engage in discussions about race."[21] Textbooks seldom introduce important research findings pertaining to young children and race, such as the ability of six-month-old infants to categorize people by race and gender nonverbally,[22] or the ability of two-year-old children to relate behaviors to racial categories.[23] Consequentially, early childhood teachers often lack the knowledge and resources to support the education of children of color.[24] Without tools to interrogate racism or implicit bias, teachers inflict harm and foster inequity through everyday practices that support racialized power hierarchies that preserve whiteness as property.

Recognizing the need for new tools to repair the harm experienced by young children and their networks,[25] this chapter offers a counterstory of restorative justice in an early childhood classroom. Throughout the chapter, we undertake the definition of restorative justice as "making the wrongs right, but making it right in a way that both sides can come to an agreement."[26] We hope to offer early childhood teachers an opportunity to "think about moral and ethical obligations of addressing harms and needs,"[27] to question the racialized status quo of education with young children, and to repair the harm caused in and by early childhood education. To establish the relevant context, we begin with a review of the existing literature regarding how race and racism continue to critically impact young children in early educational settings.

LITERATURE REVIEW

The values, experiences, practices, and histories of children, families, and communities of color are often measured against a white "normal."[28] This is a durable consequence of how, through the "entangled relationship between race and property, historical forms of domination have evolved to reproduce subordination in the present.... the evolution of whiteness from color to race to status to property... historically rooted in white supremacy."[29] This lens is central to understanding the exclusion and harm experienced by children of color in today's early childhood classrooms. As legal and critical race scholar Cheryl Harris explains, the right to exclude, which is central to whiteness as property, is visible in every facet of US society. In this section, we thus concern ourselves with the right to exclude in education.

Although *Brown v. Board of Education* was a landmark case widely touted for its benefits, the ruling protected and continues to protect white interests while inflicting harm on children of color. The ruling, for example, led to the mass firing of Black teachers, closure of Black schools (wherein, in many cases, Black educators taught Black children by engaging Afrocentric epistemologies), and dismantling of teacher education programs with a proven record of preparing teachers to successfully educate Black children. This ultimately and quickly ensured the exclusion of Black teachers from schools.[30] Legally established "expectations of relative white privilege" continued to serve "as a legitimate and natural baseline" post-*Brown*,[31] upholding white privileges and reifying a sense of white superiority, the ruling "declined to guarantee that White privilege would be dismantled, or even to direct that the continued existence of institutionalized privilege violated the equal protection rights of Blacks."[32] This legacy persists, as exclusion and segregation continue to characterize the experiences of children of color in US schools today.

Research confirms that children of color continue to withstand harm in schools via policies and practices that pose as neutral but were designed and implemented to protect white interests and uphold racism.[33] Three components are central to the harm withstood by young children of color: teacher demographics, teacher education, and early childhood education quality (as it pertains to curricula and teaching). We review these damaging patterns in turn.

Early childhood education is characterized by growing racial disproportionality; white early childhood teachers predominately teach children of color, who represent a growing majority of US students overall.[34] This disproportionality, combined with recent data pointing to the overwhelmingly positive impacts of teachers of color on the educational trajectories of children of color,[35] has led to calls for more teachers of color.[36] Such calls, though, overwhelmingly fail to consider the depth of harm experienced by teachers and communities of color post-*Brown*: the elimination of 38,000 African American educator positions between 1954 and 1965; a 66 percent decline in African Americans majoring in education between 1975 and 1985; and the elimination of 37,717 teacher candidates and teachers of color between 1984 and 1989, among others.[37] Although significant, these numbers are only part of the story depicting the current state of early childhood education.

How and what teachers teach matters. As such, many scholars and practitioners have been cautious against initiatives narrowly focused on recruiting and hiring teachers of color, knowing that race alone does not result in knowledgeable teachers committed to justice-oriented teaching.[38] The education of early childhood teachers, overwhelmingly marked by whiteness in terms of demographics and epistemological orientation, prepares (mostly white) teachers who continue to uphold white interests and foster white supremacy in numerous ways.[39] Although early childhood teacher education programs do not overtly communicate a firm commitment to upholding white interests, this commitment is covertly enacted via existing structures (e.g., student teaching placements, course content), racialized definitions of quality, and an overwhelmingly white faculty composition.[40]

In a 2018 literature review, Mariana Souto-Manning and Ayesha Rabadi-Raol showed that early childhood education is marked by three dominant attributes: allegiance to white interests via white supremacy, teaching practices rooted in pathological paradigms of children and communities of color, and the overprivileging dominant American English monolingualism. That is, the field centers white interests, promotes white supremacy, upholds inferiority and deficit beliefs pertaining to children and communities of color, and sees the language practices of communities of color as needing remedy. As such, early childhood education in the US systemically and continuously inflicts harm on children, families, and communities of color. It is within this context that we seek to transform early childhood education in the pursuit of justice, acknowledging the importance of history, race, justice, and language in this much-needed undertaking, and using these key factors to ground the conceptual framework we employ.

TRANSFORMATIVE JUSTICE AS A CONCEPTUAL FRAMEWORK

We engage a conceptual framework of transformative justice in education that affirms that History Matters, Race Matters, Justice Matters, and Language Matters.[41] Given that the historic consequences of enslavement and of *Brown* in whitifying the teacher workforce still matter and continue to be unavoidably visible in early childhood classrooms, as explained in our review of the literature, we regard race as perhaps the most salient pedagogical stance of transformative justice in early childhood education today. We take this view because racist ideas remain at the core of early childhood education, upholding white interests and harming children, families, and communities of color.

The transformation of early childhood education in the pursuit of justice is predicated on a paradigm shift that centers restorative justice in (pre)schools and classrooms. It is important to understand that, beyond a set of practices that can be transferred, restorative justice reflects (and requires) a deep change of mindset by all community members involved, necessary to interrupt any historical legacy of systemic oppression.

Despite its structural importance, race has remained tangential to early childhood education, even as young children of color experience harm and violence due to racist ideologies and actions every day. Just last year, Kaia Rolle, a six-year-old Black girl in Florida, was arrested for having a tantrum at school.[42] This incident points to the urgent need for school community members to demand and actively pursue a paradigm shift to interrupt racism and foster transformation in the pursuit of justice. With the goal of addressing the harm caused by the atrocities experienced by young children of color within the context of early childhood education, we employ Maisha T. Winn's framework for transformative justice in education, which describes the need to engage with concepts of race to achieve justice in all school settings. Winn links the use of force on Black youth to our country's past enslavement of African peoples and, as recent events illustrate, not even our youngest children are safe from this devastating legacy.

Although many educators see the early childhood classroom as a neutral place,[43] Winn's framework accounts for how racial hierarchies are often "reproduced in the local activities of the classroom."[44] If we are to see and support "teaching as a justice-seeking endeavor," early childhood educators must explicitly and consistently take up issues related to race in order to disrupt injustice and foster justice.[45] It is from such a lens that we ask: What happens when children, families, and communities of color are centered in the early childhood classroom demographically and epistemologically?

METHODOLOGY

Engaging critical race methodology to understand what happens when children, families, and communities of color are centered in early childhood classrooms, we focus on the race stance of transformative justice in education and centering racism in all aspects of our research.[46] This focus seemed particularly appropriate because majoritarian stories serve white interests and subordinate communities and individuals of color—or at least silence their perspectives and experiences. Our review of the existing literature specifically highlighted how consistently "teacher education programs draw on majoritarian stories to explain educational inequity through a cultural deficit model and thereby pass on beliefs that students of color are culturally deprived."[47] We thus organized our data as a counternarrative act of resistance, building on longstanding traditions of storytelling in communities of color.[48]

Because of the centrality of race to our conceptual framework and methodology, the purposive selection of an early childhood classroom was of utmost importance. The focal classroom was selected because it was an early childhood classroom where all teachers were persons of color located within a center where all administrators were persons of color. The prekindergarten (preK) classroom had one full-time teacher of color, one part-time paraprofessional of color—both identified as AfroLatinx women—and fourteen three- and four-year-old children (thirteen were children of color—Black, AfroLatinx, and Mixtec). The center where the preK classroom was located received Head Start funds in addition to New York Pre-K for All funds, and thus employed federally identified income guidelines regarding student enrollment, which meant that all of the young learners therein were members of families with low or no income.

To create our counterstory of early childhood teaching, we draw on field note, artifact, and interview data collected via participant observation over the course of one academic year in this public preK classroom in New York City. We organized data in packets according to event, and focus here on the data packet that focused on race most saliently, per consultation with the lead teacher in whose classroom data was collected. Once we identified the most relevant packet, we drew on previously introduced data from the existing literature on race in early childhood education, as well as our own professional and personal experiences as early childhood and elementary educators committed to racial justice for learners across the spectrum of racial identity (i.e., Asian, Black, AfroLatinx, white, etc.).

We read, reread, and analyzed the data via a layered and iterative process. We created composite characters representing the focal teachers (Yamilet and Karina), parents (Carmen), and children (Citlalli, RJ, Juan, and Marcus), constructing a counterstory dialogically. Our aim with the dialogue we constructed was to "critically illuminate concepts, ideas and experiences" that illustrate how race matters in early childhood education.[49] We used our voice and communicated our experiences in the form of collective narration.

RACE MATTERS IN EARLY CHILDHOOD EDUCATION

Carmen entered her son's preK classroom in New York City and greeted the teacher: "Buenos dias, Yamilet," giving Yamilet a hug. Yamilet had a close relationship with her students' family members and often greeted them with a hug. While Juan, Carmen's three-year-old son was hanging his backpack, Carmen whispered to Yamilet: "You know, Juan is worried about this new boy. He said he's big and scary." Looking confused, Yamilet asked, "RJ?"

CARMEN: Sí. Creo que este es su nombre.

YAMILET: Oh, he just joined us.

CARMEN: Maybe I should keep Juan home a few days?

YAMILET:	That won't be necessary. We will talk about during circle time and come up with a plan.
CARMEN:	You sure? Do you think the kids are safe?
YAMILET:	I know RJ is bigger than the other kids, but we must remember that he is four. Sometimes four-year-olds are frustrated and communicate their frustration in their behaviors, you know? RJ left another school and he seems to be upset. And, because he is bigger, his behavior may look more scary.

The conversation was disrupted as other children arrived in the classroom.

RJ was a large four-year-old Black boy who had cornrows and often wore sweatpants and untied shoes. He had entered Yamilet's classroom after leaving two prior preKs, in November (shortly after the date enrollment was counted, determining the amount of preK funds awarded to programs). We know it is important to note RJ's race; young Black children often experience disproportionate harm as they attempt to communicate their feelings. Black students have been disproportionately disciplined; a 2018 US Government Accountability Office report showed Black students are 23 percent more likely to be suspended and expelled than their white peers.[50] Recent events, including the previously mentioned arrest of six-year-old Kaia Rolle, add arrests to the harms withstood by Black children during their (pre)school experiences. To be sure, "Orlando Police Department officials said Rolle was one of two children Turner arrested that day, the other was 8 years old."[51] Yamilet knew of the punitive impact of racism on Black children and on Black boys.

YAMILET:	You know, I feel sorry for RJ. This is his third preK. I can only imagine how being a large Black boy impacted him leaving the two other preKs. They cannot even be boys. Play. Move around. Throw tantrums. Before long, they are seen as violent. And they learn that. Se dan cuenta de que son víctimas del racismo de esta sociedad. Solo por ser quienes son. No tienen que hacer nada.

Yamilet knew that RJ had been harmed by the durable legacy of racism and needed to be better understood by his peers. She knew it was her obligation to facilitate and everyone's obligation to render RJ a full and valuable member of the community. There was much at stake. Although she was not fully aware of the specific experiences RJ and his family had been part of within the context of his prior preK classrooms, she was acutely aware of Black males' historical depiction as violent and the long history of dehumanization in the US.[52] As such, she was committed to bringing all community members together to address the harm RJ was experiencing, especially when it became clear that even three- and four-year-olds had already absorbed a paradigm that situated RJ as a threat. In response, Yamilet skillfully worked to disrupt that mindset and support her students and their parents in a collective "paradigm shift."[53]

Soon, Yamilet started singing as she assembled and conducted a human choo-choo train that took the children to the rug area, where they formed a circle. Yamilet sat right next to RJ. She was holding a plastic toy microphone as a talking piece.

> YAMILET: You know, RJ just joined us and we didn't take the time to really welcome him to our community. Welcome to our community, RJ. It's great to have you here. I feel like I don't always know how to communicate with you yet, but I am learning. I hope you will help me.
> *(She passed the mic to RJ.)*
>
> RJ: Okay. But sometimes I get so angry I don't know what to say. In my old classroom, Ms. White yelled at me, "Stop! Get out!" She grabbed my arm and got me out. It hurt. So, when I get angry, I throw my shoe. Then no one hurt me.

RJ had thrown his shoe the day before and ended up hurting Yamilet physically when she tried to mediate a situation where two children, including RJ, wanted to play with the same toy. Yamilet always took an approach to conflict that fostered "justice on both sides."[54] While Yamilet didn't know at that moment how deeply harmed RJ had been, even at age four, she was well aware of the need to create an opportunity for him "to heal and put right the wrongs."[55]

When it came to Juan's turn, he said, "Welcome, RJ. I was afraid of you. I told my mom you are big and scary. But I didn't know your teacher hurt you. My teacher never hurt me."

CITLALLI: Teddy bears are big. And they are loving. I think you are loving, RJ. Wanna be my friend?

Although it wasn't RJ's turn to talk and the talking piece proceeded clockwise, RJ looked at Citlalli and nodded his head. When the talking piece reached Karina, the paraprofessional, she said, "It is great to have you here. We love you. We promise not to hurt you. We won't throw you out of the classroom. You belong here."

After this experience welcoming RJ, every child present realized that RJ had been excluded from their classroom community in various ways, and they made a plan to redo their bulletin board with photos that included RJ. Though the bulletin board was titled "Our Community," none of the photos featured RJ. The children also decided they would take turns being RJ's special friend, showing him around and answering questions. RJ was part of these responses developed by the community. Before they transitioned, Yamilet asked the children if they had anything else to say.

MARCUS: You know what, Yamilet?

YAMILET: ¿Que mi amor?

MARCUS: When the police stop my daddy. My daddy said it's cuz he must think he scary jus cuz he a Black man.

And just like that, the stereotype of Black boys and Black men as threatening started being problematized by three- and four-year old children in this preK classroom who had identified societal harm that had been inflicted and were working to repair such harm. The implications of racial injustice were present in Yamilet's pedagogical moves, yet she did not explicitly raise the topic of race. Many educators are concerned that race is not developmentally appropriate in the early childhood context, but it was a child, Marcus, who explicitly addressed race. Race is already a feature of early childhood educational contexts and on many students' minds; Yamilet simply created the space where race could be brought to the fore and gave students an opportunity to reflect on and restore justice.

CONCLUSION AND IMPLICATIONS

During their circle time, the children had collaboratively developed plans, established a renewed sense of community, and addressed concerns while recognizing each other's humanity—experiences that build understanding and trust. Yamilet had convened a circle where everyone was respected, everyone had a voice, and no one was interrupted. Emotions were acknowledged and welcomed. It is important to know that Yamilet had been part of a justice-centered teacher education program, advised and predominantly taught by faculty of color. She was familiar with the critical role of such circles in addressing harm; she had experienced the power of this technique in her teacher education classes. As such, Yamilet knew the potential of restorative justice to address conflict and foster peace building, and she was prepared with relevant tools and the necessary mindset to facilitate restorative justice processes and practices with her students.[56]

Everyday counterstories unfolding in preK classrooms stand in stark juxtaposition to dominant narratives of Black boys as behavior problems. The counterstory highlighted in this chapter shows, furthermore, that race matters in early childhood classrooms. There can be little question that efforts to transform early childhood education without explicit commitment to addressing the needs incurred from harms inflicted on children, families, and communities of color will inevitably continue to uphold white interests, dehumanize children of color, and cause further harm. Early childhood teachers (and those who teach early childhood teachers) must thus embrace their responsibility to cultivate a "restorative impulse," address the harm caused by the durable impacts of racism in all facets of US society, and work restoratively to foster justice in and through their daily classroom practices.[57]

5

Abolition in and Through Mathematics:
Three Radical Reimaginings

Erika C. Bullock and Erica R. Meiners

> If unfinished liberation is the still-to-be-achieved work of abolition then at bottom what is to be abolished isn't the past or its present ghost, but rather the processes of hierarchy, dispossession, and exclusion.
>
> —Ruth Wilson Gilmore[1]

MATHEMATICS ACHIEVEMENT HAS long functioned as an indicator of individual intelligence and signified a person's value to the state.[2] Critical mathematics education, a subdomain of mathematics education, endeavors to address how some facets of power operate in and through mathematics and mathematics education. However, scholars who align with critical mathematics education have not established a connection between mathematics or mathematics education and the school–prison nexus.[3] This lack of attention is likely due to the fact that scholars in mathematics education, and arguably in other content domains, primarily position the school–prison nexus as a policy or disciplinary issue rather than an issue relevant to "content." Mathematics educators further distance themselves from the carceral state by relying on the perceived neutrality and objectivity of mathematics. Whereas a US history or literature class could, for example, teach the linkages between chattel slavery and targeted criminalization, most mathematicians would argue that algebra class content does not lend itself to discussing such issues and connections. It is, however, unduly arrogant to position mathematics and the teaching and learning of mathematics as outside the carceral apparatus that shapes our schools and communities.

Elsewhere, we have argued that mathematics and mathematics education largely operate as agents of the carceral, or punitive, state.[4] Through, for example, the creation of algorithms used in flawed predictive policing tools or mathematics curricula and assessments that divest targeted communities from higher education, mathematics becomes what Micol Seigel describes as "violence work" as knowledge workers "make real . . . the core power of the state."[5] Far from neutral, the ways the field is defined, valued, and taught perpetuate a sense of objectivity used to order, sort, and classify nations and people. Those who consistently use mathematics (e.g., physicists, mathematicians, statisticians) may perform calculations and create models, but they cannot claim to be removed from how their labor circulates. For example, as Seigel argues, "Defense and weapons researchers labor at the thinnest remove from the soldiers who end up plying the products of their design."[6] There is power both in the ability to do mathematics and in numbers themselves. Neglecting to attend to both of these forms of power nullifies reform efforts in mathematics education oriented toward equity and social justice.[7] Therefore, discussions about how Black, Brown, queer, migrant, poor, and other people have been marginalized by mathematics require looking beyond issues of identity and representation to interrogate and ultimately disentangle the layered connection between mathematics and carceral logics and practices.

Prevailing logics still suggest that mathematics is apolitical, ahistorical, acultural, and asocial, and these frameworks are amply reproduced in K–16 contexts, leading most people to question whether and how social and political considerations should show up in mathematics classrooms. Numbers are considered objective. The axioms, theorems, and algorithms taught in mathematics classrooms over time carry with them an immutable and antiseptic character that renders them impermeable to outside concerns. Even critical mathematics educators who invest in creating pedagogical models that promote equity and social justice, and see mathematics as a cultural and political product, find it challenging to let go of this way of seeing mathematics as timeless, static, essential, and, above all, neutral. In addition, both critical and noncritical mathematics education circles enforce a value system wherein mathematics is not only an exceptional good, but is necessary, and all children must thus learn mathematics.[8]

We do not dispute the value of mathematics in the world and that young people should learn some mathematics. However, we question what this deification of mathematics does to our world. Rejecting prevailing assumptions, we note that the reproduction of mathematical mythologies—mathematics as apolitical, ahistorical, acultural, and asocial—functions to deepen and reproduce carceral logics. Our question is thus, *How could mathematics and mathematics education be mobilized to create alternatives to the carceral state?*

LIMITS OF EQUITY AND TEACHING MATHEMATICS FOR SOCIAL JUSTICE

In recent years, scholars have begun to question how "equity" operates within mathematics education circles. Yet, given the more than three decades of equity-speak within mathematics education, scholars and practitioners are finding that all of the effort expended in the name of equity has resulted in negligible achievement progress for Black, Latinx, Indigenous, and poor students. In fact, when considering the experiences these students tend to have in mathematics classes, proliferation of standardized testing and other accountability measures has made their mathematics experiences worse.[9]

The pattern of worse outcomes despite "progressive reforms" is not unique to mathematics. All too often, social and political movements move toward the reform strategy that *promises* progressive change in short order over hard, longer-term struggle for radical shifts. Yes, change can be incremental and slow, but we must not settle for reforms that, at best, simply tinker around the edges. As educators, theorists, and organizers, we are invested in paradigm shifts that can build sustainable, radical (or root) changes. We are looking for "non-reformist reform," to use Marxist André Gorz's term from 1964, or reforms that delegitimize violent structures and systems, and/or make material differences in the lives of those oppressed.[10]

The history of imprisonment and policing is a story of reforms, sometimes based on good intentions, that purport to make a "bad" system better but generally expand the underlying logic and reach of the carceral state. As an example, we consider the "new technologies" that dominate current criminal legal reforms. In the wake of recorded and widely circulated police killings that fueled multiple uprisings, numerous jurisdictions moved toward mandating that police officers wear body cameras. This reform, which has not addressed the racial violence of policing, now funnels even more resources to equip police with even more surveillance technology, which continues to be used against the targets of policing. Electronic ankle monitors, advanced as a bipartisan "alternative" to imprisonment, not only turn prisoners' homes into prisons and families into jailers but are increasingly being deployed *after* people serve their sentences behind bars as a condition of probation and parole. Rather than shrinking the number of people under state control, or reducing our reliance on punishment, these new e-carceration tools thus expand the prison–industrial complex. The reach of prisons now expands beyond prison walls and prison terms, predictive policing now criminalizes people based on algorithms, and digital surveillance and recognition programs are now able to track virtually everyone.

Equity-oriented reforms in mathematics education reflect a similar reformist character. Achievement gap logic has created a narrative that establishes white students as the norm to which all other students, particularly Black students, should aspire.[11] Mathematics is an anchor to this normative thinking, which reinforces a paradigm of inferiority in which Black children are considered inherently inferior to white children and will only find success insofar as they strive to meet standards of whiteness.[12] The psychic violence this way of thinking exacts on Black children is staggering. They are consistently treated as a problem to be fixed. The source of any lack of "success" that they experience mathematically is situated within them, leaving mathematics education and educators without fault. Equity reforms organized around this logic focus on finding the perfect pedagogical apparatus to "fix" what is "wrong" with the children who create the gap.

Equity discourse in mathematics education has focused narrowly on issues related to teaching and learning with some attention toward student experiences in out-of-school spaces. Identity and beliefs of both teachers and students have been central. The focus has been internal to the system of mathematics education, with the intention of improving pedagogy, curricula, and, to a lesser extent, policy in order to close "the achievement gap." What equity research has not done is look at how mathematics and mathematics education participate in creating and maintaining broader social inequities; there is no external focus. Therefore, the impetus for reform in mathematics education—including, but not limited to, equity-oriented reform—has largely come from within, typically when test scores are low or groups voice dissatisfaction about tracking practices. Outside pressure that has spurred mathematics education reform has come in the form of nationalist calls for increased attention to mathematics in schools in order to make the nation better equipped to compete with other nations (e.g., the National Defense Education Act, *A Nation at Risk*).

REIMAGINING MATHEMATICS EDUCATION

Both a politic and a practice, abolition demands that we cultivate ways of thinking that are not grounded in violence, punishment, and surveillance. Yet abolition is not simply about what we need to challenge and dismantle, but what we need to build. For theorists Stefano Harney and Fred Moten, the object of abolition is "[n]ot so much the abolition of prisons but the abolition of a society that could have prisons, that could have slavery, that could have the wage, and therefore not abolition as the *elimination* of anything but abolition as the *founding* of a new society" [emphasis ours].[13] Given that carceral logic is entrenched in the US psyche and governs notions of educational reform and change, the abolitionist position requires a radical reimagining of a new mathematics education. To this end, we offer three cases—one in the classroom, one in policy and curriculum, and one outside of school—as entry points for such an outcome. One of these examples is from a real-world context, and the other two are speculative. We draw from fiction "to confront mathematics education from a radically different cultural location" that allows us to challenge "common sense" notions of what constitutes "good" mathematics education.[14] As scholar and poet Gloria Anzaldúa reminds us, "Nothing happens in the 'real' world unless it first happens in the images in our heads."[15]

An exercise in freedom dreaming is an opportunity to manifest our internal desires for a mathematics education that neither harms nor kills.[16] A fictional case allows us to create an alternate reality that operates outside of present constraints and to see a different mathematics education. However, the alternate reality that we imagine here is not entirely detached from our present reality. It presumes some form of school and some space that is outside of school; it also presumes roles of teacher and student and the support of public dollars. While the school we imagine is not governed by the rules of schooling prevalent today, we acknowledge that it would be possible and potentially favorable to imagine mathematics education unattached to schools.

In the Classroom

There are seventeen students in a large classroom working on a project. Nine are in Ms. Jones's algebra class, and the remaining eight are enrolled in Mr. Whitaker's art class. They are all analyzing geographic data they collected about their community when they left school premises with GPS software to map community features such as schools, liquor stores, places of worship, pawn shops, parks, and grocery stores. They quickly noticed that while alcohol is plentiful in their community, good food is in short supply. "Don't they know you need to eat while you drink?" one student questioned. He concluded his question with "Funny. Not funny." As Ms. Jones moves around the room listening to conversations and helping students with data analysis, Ms. Easton enters the room with her social studies class, another eight students who disperse throughout the room to join their teams, eager to share new learnings about the mini lesson Ms. Easton just taught on redlining.

Ms. Jones, Ms. Easton, and Mr. Whitaker were implementing a semester-long project about community resources grounded in the school's focus on interdisciplinary cooperative learning. Each day, a three-hour cooperative learning block allows students to engage in project-based learning with a cross-disciplinary teaching team focused, in this case, on how mathematics, history, civics, and art intersect. Through periodic "fictional school" exercises, students are encouraged to submit requests for topics they would like to cover during this learning block. When the teaching team agreed that community resources were an excellent topic choice, they set out to help their students understand how points of disciplinary intersection can help residents identify, articulate, and address issues within their own communities. The semester began with a discussion of resources, assets, and liabilities, after which students began to take walks around the community to identify community resources. They would later discuss what could be done with the data they collected, what messages they would like to craft, and how they could compose that messaging.

Yesterday, the students had been sitting, bewildered, wondering why their community looks as it does. Ms. Jones, Ms. Easton, and Mr. Whitaker had decided to split up the class the following day. Ms. Easton would take a portion of the group and talk with them about redlining and its effects for a portion of their three-hour cooperative learning block. Then those students would rejoin their research teams, share what they had just learned, and initiate group discussion.

Two students in a group who had not learned about redlining with Ms. Easton became fascinated with the idea and went to the computers on the side of the room to do some research about their city. They found images of their neighborhood nearly fifty years in the past showing a thriving shopping area and lots of white faces. They learned that the jail that now sits behind the city's municipal office building was once an open-air market. Some students began to argue, and Mr. Whitaker, the art teacher, approached them to see what was going on. The students told him they wanted to find a way to show changes in their community from past to present in order to highlight how processes such as redlining cause community blight. The argument was about how they could show these things without making their community appear to be a hopeless place. Mr. Whitaker pulled out his iPad and showed the students pictures of protest art, which prompted conversation about what it means to tell the truth and how truth telling can be both beautiful and sad, at the same time.

When class was over, the three teachers sat down for their planning time. They decided to coordinate two mini lessons the next day: a mini lesson on measures of central tendency, because one of the groups had been unsure about whether it would be most effective to talk about the mean or the median of a particular phenomenon, and a second mini lesson on art and activism to explore art as a tool for communicating complicated messages. Ms. Easton, Ms. Jones, and Mr. Whitaker then continued to plan for the rest of the week, beginning with a scan of their state curriculum standards to note which had been covered in today's work.

This vignette highlights several possibilities for an abolitionist approach to the mathematics classroom. The GPS activity was inspired by Laurie Rubel and colleagues' teaching mathematics for spatial justice work, which features projects that leverage GPS technologies to help students use mathematics to better understand their neighborhoods.[17] The fictional school approach allowed students to cocreate the curriculum; teachers designed content and coursework based on issues of interest proposed by the students. Each member of the teaching team was assigned a small class to ensure that the combined class contained fewer than thirty students. As they created mini lessons to focus on the problem, the teaching team ensured that students were learning about and through mathematics, technology, civics, history, and art, which were situated as complementary disciplines that can and often should be integrated.

The teaching team was committed to teaching course content in such a way that students could use emergent learnings and even the learning process to understand the world around them and act on those understandings. To support this endeavor, school administrators arranged for these teachers to come together for significant planning after class, and allowed them to report lesson and curricular standards alignment *after* the fact, so class time could unfold organically. As such, the vignette represents a classroom community guided by a student-directed curriculum focused specifically on using content to read and respond to the world. In addition, this vignette highlights the infrastructure needed to support such a context.

In Policy and Curriculum

Dr. Jordan, the school district's leader for secondary education, is anxious to begin the meeting. In a few moments, the cafeteria will be full of parents and other community members gathered strategically around tables, pouring over document after document. Dr. Jordan's staff knows this is a big moment. It always is. The annual curriculum review is the time the community comes together for a week to look at the successes and failures of the previous year and approve plans for the following year. The group will also reconsider the ongoing five-year strategic plan they have been using to guide their work. On the agenda: reviewing the courses to be offered at the high schools and the curriculum plans for these courses; evaluating plans to respond to changes in state graduation requirements; and making staffing decisions for the next year.

A group composed of Mr. Contreras, mathematics teacher and department chair at one of the high schools; Ms. Singh, parent of a grade 10 student; Mr. Roberts, parent of a grade 8 student; Mr. Slocum, director of high school programs at the local Boys and Girls Club; and Mrs. Clifton, retired teacher and owner of a local dry cleaners, huddled around a map of curriculum pathways designed to accommodate the state's shift in graduation requirements from two to three credits in mathematics. "I can't even read this," Mrs. Clifton lamented, as she tried to make sense of the complex graphic. Ms. Singh and Mr. Roberts nodded in agreement. The group changed gears and read through the new legislation, using the whiteboard next to their table to list the requirements. As they returned to the map, Mr. Contreras explained the document his team had crafted using an elaborate system of color coding and arrows.[18]

"This paper is really complicated to read, but there is one thing for sure ... there aren't many arrows pointing to Pre-Calculus or the courses beyond that," Mr. Slocom observed. "Kids really need that for college." Mr. Contreras replied: "Well, we wanted to provide as many avenues for students to meet the three-credit graduation requirement as possible in order to accommodate as many students as possible. Some of those pathways don't require students to take Pre-Calculus." Mrs. Clifton's brow furrowed. "But is that really the goal?" she asked. "I know that we want the kids to graduate from high school, but don't we want them to be able to do something after that?"

Mrs. Clifton approached the whiteboard and began to write. "Based on what I see here, a student could take Pre-Algebra, Algebra I, and a beginning computer science course and graduate, right?" Mr. Contreras nodded in agreement. "But there's a problem with this," Mrs. Clifton continued, "My niece is a freshman at the state university, and she had to have way more math than this and she's majoring in business. Could this student do that?" Mrs. Clifton tapped the marker on the whiteboard underneath the list of courses while waiting for an answer. "Do they have enough to go to the community college?"

"That's my question," Mr. Slocum added. "We have job programs that we connect students with who do not plan to go to college. We give them a skills test and give the scores to the programs. Those tests have geometry problems on them. This kid would be screwed."

The group continued to discuss the curriculum map. As their time drew to a close, Ms. Singh suggested they summarize their discussion and make a plan for the next day's meeting. "Well," Mr. Roberts began, shaking the map in the air, "we definitely don't approve of this map. It's hard to read, and parents and kids can't really see what their options are, so this can't go out. The other issue is that it seems like there are too many ways that this can turn out for kids."

Ms. Singh interrupted, "Yes, and remember that this whole curriculum review started a few years ago because we parents pushed the school board and the superintendent because they weren't doing right by a lot of the kids. It's been great that we've been able to remove some problem teachers and change a lot of the ways that things are done around here, but this is the first time that we get to respond to a major policy change."

"This is major," Mr. Contreras agreed. "I appreciate your feedback on our document, and I see where you are coming from about the readability. We were looking at it as a guide for us and didn't think about how other people would see it. I don't want people to feel like we're trying to pull something over on them."

"That's why we're all here. We'll make it better," said Mr. Roberts. "Why don't we start tomorrow by pulling these pathways apart." Mrs. Clifton agreed and offered to look up admissions requirements for the community college, the state university, and the local small liberal arts college for reference. "I also want to look at some of the added courses," added Mr. Contreras. "The math team was thinking about if we should fit in some consumer math and stuff, so maybe you all can help us to think about that this week, too."

Dr. Jordan thanked everyone in the room for investing in such an arduous and important process. "This process is really tough, but I feel like we start to trust each other more each year. Let's keep this momentum!"

The annual curriculum review represented in this vignette is an example of the community placing demands on the school district to make changes due to schools mistreating their children. The review process facilitated direct community input on issues related to staffing and curriculum. The group focused on graduation requirements was composed of district personnel, parents, community leaders, and business leaders who came together to vet the district's plan. It is clear from the dialogue that there was a strong sense of accountability to the community, combined with a desire for and growing sense of partnership. Participants commented on pathways that restricted opportunity and the accessibility of communications to families. Community representatives pointed out that district goals (meeting new graduation requirements) did not align with the community's goals for its children (having options after high school), and the group set out to fix this together. Time and effort spent on the curriculum review was an investment toward building trust between the school and community in order to make the school a relevant institution in which students can learn and grow.

Outside of School

In 2015, a group of young people coalesced in opposition to Chicago's "solution" to critiques regarding the ongoing violence of policing: a new $95 million police academy in a Black community on the southwest side of the city. Galvanized by a local and national political moment that clearly pointed, again, to the consistently racialized violence of policing in the US after the deaths of Sandra Bland, Eric Garner, and Lacquan McDonald, to name a few, young people organized to intervene in this proposed expansion of policing. Over many gatherings, young people demanded, debated, and analyzed budget documents. The resulting campaign and coalition, #NoCopAcademy, produced savvy political education materials centering a public and abolitionist approach to mathematics, and orchestrated some of the most creative direct action Chicago had seen in years.

Coins, Cops, & Communities: A Toolkit was created by young people—key organizations included young Black folks from Assata's Daughters and Percy Julian High School—to support popular education about city spending on policing in Chicago, and to amplify public dialogues about what communities really need to stay safe.[19] One activity in the toolkit, "A City Budget in Pennies,"[20] asks participants to use one hundred pennies, representing 100 percent of a city budget, and designate how many pennies they would allocate to each budget category. In small groups or pairs, people are encouraged to talk through their budget priorities and make decisions about what to prioritize in order to build a healthy, functioning, safe city. After the small groups finish, they share their plans and talk. The finale introduces Chicago's current operating budget, which directs approximately 40 percent of city funding to the police.

The toolkit also included calculations—produced and prioritized by young folks—showing how even a small fraction of these resources could be used otherwise. One year of Chicago's spending for substance abuse, $2,581,2720, for example, translates into half a day of Chicago's budget for policing. One year of Chicago's spending for employment services for people with disabilities, $303,070, is an amount the city spends in less than two hours for policing. This toolkit is accompanied by other largely youth-produced public education materials that work to raise awareness and provoke dialogue. For example, a youth-produced short video features young people interviewing primarily other young people in the street with the question *How much does Chicago spend on policing every day?* and following up with other questions such as *What percentage of the city budget is spent on policing?* The "real" response—*the city currently spends $4 million a day, 38 percent of the total budget*—is met not only with shock but also with great ideas about how this money could be used differently to generate safety.[21]

Across the city of Chicago, young people used the toolkit and accompanying educational materials to facilitate workshops offering political education to church groups, youth networks, and community-based organizations. As a direct result of their campaign and these educational materials, 120 additional organizations signed onto a campaign that was explicitly identified as an abolitionist campaign, agreeing that contracting the power and underlying financial resources of policing is a shared goal and vision to work toward. Even as the city voted to start construction in late 2019, #NoCopAcademy used mathematics to grow community-level abolition consciousness. Young people facilitated workshops that centered math literacy across the city, and used the tools of math in service of abolition, offering an example of young people mobilizing through radical imagination to use mathematics as a tool and pathway for political education outside the classroom.

CONCLUSION

While mathematics and mathematics education have long functioned as agents of the carceral state, we argue that all is not lost. Taking an abolitionist position with respect to mathematics education allows us to see mathematics as one tool among many to dismantle oppressive systems rather than simply an oppressive system within itself. Such a vision requires a radical imagination because the punishing logic of schools is so entrenched in our ways of thinking. The three examples presented in this chapter offer new visions for engagement with mathematics education in the classroom, in curriculum and policy, and in the community. It is our hope that these three examples will inspire additional visioning that leads toward mathematics education practices (and eventually norms) that redress, rather than reproduce, harm.

6

When Race Matters in Mathematics:
Practicing Three Commitments for Children Learning Mathematics While Black

Darrius D. Robinson, Maisie L. Gholson, and Deborah Loewenberg Ball

IT WAS THE END of a long week of mathematics learning, and as students were reflecting on the week, Ayana mused, "I used to think I was never going to the board, but now I will." This reflection stood in stark contrast to Ayana's disposition with respect to this practice at the beginning of the week. On Monday, she had recoiled at the mere mention of presenting her mathematical thinking to the class from the whiteboard that stood at the front of the classroom. "I don't do that," she told her mathematics teacher. Later, when she was given an opportunity to share her thinking at the board, Ayana politely, and decisively, declined. Yet across the week, Ayana increasingly engaged in and vied for opportunities to present her mathematical thinking at the board. On Friday, just four days later, her hand shot up at every opportunity to present at the board, and when she was given the opportunity, she presented her thinking confidently.

In most classrooms, Ayana's initial proclamation that she does not present at the board, and her subsequent refusal of an opportunity to do so, would be read as an act of resistance. Such refusals are understood as commonplace for Black learners and are often attributed to an individual- or cultural-level lack of interest, motivation, resilience, or competence. In our classroom, Ayana's stance is read differently. Her proclamation and refusal are understood to be embodiments of her relationship with mathematics, in general, and to the specific practice of publicly sharing her mathematical thinking. Rather than pointing to individual or cultural deficiencies as the explanation for why Ayana was firmly uninclined to share her mathematical thinking in a public way, we employ a relational perspective. That is, we recognize her refusals as reasonable responses to the ways being a Black (and female) child has shaped her experiences with mathematics learning.[1]

RACE MATTERS IN MATHEMATICS LEARNING

As we seek to advance justice in the classroom, a Race Matters pedagogical stance requires that we consider how racism and racist ideas impact teaching and learning.[2] In the context of teaching and learning mathematics, the notion of Black intellectual inferiority underscores what Danny Martin describes as a racial hierarchy of mathematics ability wherein Black learners are located at the bottom.[3] Research examining the phenomenal realities of Black children shows how this notion, rooted in anti-Blackness, traverses macro-, meso-, and micro- levels to enact various forms of violence—epistemological, symbolic, and even sometimes physical.[4] Many conversations about Black learners and mathematics learning begin with a default assumption that Black learners lack characteristics key to mathematical success. As a result of such discourse, the policies and practices that shape mathematical learning environments, including those aimed at equity and inclusion, frequently construct Black learners as deficient and in need of intervention, remediation, and repair.[5]

Mathematics education researcher Kara Jackson demonstrates how this notion operates and flows through multiple levels to impact the learning of Black children. In her study of the mathematical learning experiences of two Black children and their families, Jackson documents how a local discourse about Black children and their (in)ability to do mathematics shaped schoolwide curricular decisions and the pedagogy of its teachers. Guided by an assumption that the local Black children did not enter middle school ready for success with grade-level material, one school sought to remediate Black learners by devoting their entire first year to reviewing content from the prior grade. This lack of instructional rigor was compounded by classroom participation structures that limited students' access to recognition as mathematical beings. Jackson describes one teacher's use of an instructional routine that narrowly constructed competence in mathematics as a function of speed and accuracy. Each day, students were given ten math problems to complete. The student who completed all problems correctly the quickest was recognized as the math king or queen for the day. Due to the highly competitive nature of this routine and its closed conception of mathematical performance, many Black children were further pushed to the margin of mathematics as they were unlikely to earn recognition as math royalty. The combined construction of Black children as deficient and the narrow conception of mathematics success also led to interactional conflicts. Jackson documents how one Black girl, Nikki, who was very successful in this routine, began to draw the ire of her peers. As a result, Nikki chose to dampen her visibility as a successful mathematics student in order to alleviate interactional turmoil.[6]

Other research within mathematics education shows that these types of pedagogical choices structure the learning environments of Black children writ large. Black children experience subpar mathematics instruction characterized by overly "proceduralized" content,[7] limited participation structures, and few opportunities to be recognized as mathematics knowers and doers. It is against this backdrop, that we hear Ayana's assertion that she does not go to the board. It suggests to us that Ayana's sense of self as a mathematics knower and doer does not include her making public presentations of her mathematics thinking. Moreover, we understand that it is likely that Ayana arrived at this conception as a result of racialized mathematics learning experiences, like the ones detailed by Kara Jackson.

Along with performance and competence, recognition is considered an integral component of a learner's identification as a member of a learning community.[8] Recognition requires seeing oneself—and being seen by others. Unfortunately, and all too often, Black children are not recognized by others as mathematics knowers and doers. This lack of recognition creates conditions that limit their chance to perform mathematical competence. Ultimately, this pattern leads to poor images of oneself as a mathematics knower and doer. Having been socialized into the notion that they are not mathematical beings, Black children, like Ayana, become even more reticent to engage in mathematical performances. This vicious cycle is often allowed to run in perpetuity, with some Black learners being pushed further and further to the margins of the discipline of mathematics, resulting in the unjust foreclosure of potential mathematical futures. Left unchallenged, Ayana' sense of self in relation to presenting her thinking at the board is likely to have a negative impact on her learning. If she never goes to the board, she misses out on valuable learning opportunities, making it even harder for her to see herself as a knower and doer of mathematics.

What is needed to disrupt this cycle? We contend that space must be made within mathematics learning environments to repair harm and restore students' mathematics identities. Previously, we advanced a curricular approach as a form of mathematics therapy designed to begin the process of repairing the types of harm we have highlighted.[9] This chapter complements that work by describing an approach to mathematics teaching in which the central aim is to affirm Black learners as knowers and doers of mathematics.

A JUSTICE-ORIENTED APPROACH TO MATHEMATICS TEACHING

Our vision of justice in the teaching and learning of mathematics centers around an imagined future in which Black children do not develop mathematically in environments shaped by notions of their intellectual inferiority. Reaching that future requires acknowledging and repairing the harm such environments have caused Black children, as well as transforming mathematics learning environments to prevent such harm from recurring. Key to this transformation are pedagogical approaches that reject the notion that Black children are subpar learners of mathematics. Guided by this vision of transformative justice in mathematics teaching, we advance three pedagogical commitments that create space for Black learners to meaningfully participate, learn, and identify with mathematics: (1) asserting, showcasing, and celebrating the brilliance of Black learners; (2) centering the mathematical identities of Black learners; and (3) honoring student agency while supporting students to enact different forms of participation in mathematics. These commitments work in concert to confront the phenomenal realities of being a Black child in mathematics contexts and undergird an approach to mathematics teaching that seeks to intervene on the unjust foreclosure of mathematical futures for Black learners.

PEDAGOGICAL COMMITMENTS IN ACTION

In the remainder of this chapter we discuss each of the commitments and illustrate them with examples. The examples come from our observations of a mathematics class that was co-taught by Darrius and Deborah. Guided by the pedagogical commitments outlined in this chapter, they endeavored to provide thirty fifth graders, many who, including Ayana, identified as Black and evidenced a tenuous relationship with mathematics, with a learning experience that affirmed them as competent knowers and doers of mathematics. Working collaboratively, we culled through video recordings of this class to identify examples of each of the three focal pedagogical commitments in action.

Asserting the Mathematical Brilliance of Black Learners

Research on the racialized nature of mathematics for Black children demonstrates the need for mathematics teaching pedagogy that starts with a different assumption about the mathematical ability of Black learners.[10] Following Danny Martin and colleagues, this commitment establishes the mathematical brilliance of Black children as an axiom from which all pedagogical decisions stem.[11] A wholesale rejection of deficit discourses, this commitment entails recognizing and valuing the mathematical ideas that Black learners bring to the learning environment, and building on those through instruction. This commitment stands in contrast to orientations that conceptualize Black children as needing repair, and results in different instructional decisions.

For example, consider how this commitment shaped one decision about instructional content. As a formative assessment, students had completed the task in figure 6.1.

As we looked over students' responses, just over half (51 percent) of the students answered 2/6, the correct response. In many classrooms serving Black students, these data would lead to the interpretation that almost half the students had not mastered the material and would likely lead to a period of reteaching and remediation until the pressures of limited instructional time (or a belief that those who have not yet mastered the content will not be easily able to do so) would propel instruction forward. Guided by our commitment to recognizing the brilliance of Black children, we were compelled to explore alternative explanations. Combing through student responses, we noticed a pattern in the incorrect responses. Among the incorrect responses, 2/5 was most common and was typified by the student work presented in figure 6.2.[12]

Starting with the assumption that Black children are brilliant, our analysis began by asking what this student's work showed regarding their understanding of relevant mathematical ideas. We could see in this response important understandings of key ideas related to identifying fractions. The student recognized that the entire shape needed to be partitioned into equal pieces, that the number of those equal pieces named the size of each piece, and that the number shaded represented the quantity

FIGURE 6.1 Naming fractions formative assessment

What fraction of the rectangle below is shaded blue? _____

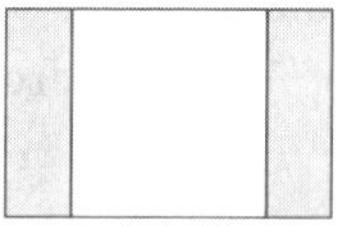

Explain how you know: _____

FIGURE 6.2   Student response to naming fractions formative assessment

What fraction of the rectangle below is shaded blue? _____$\frac{2}{5}$_____

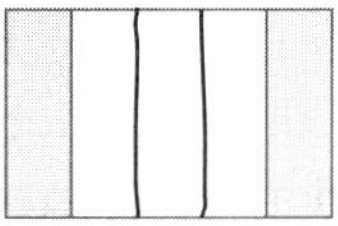

Explain how you know: ____How I know it's $\frac{2}{5}$ is because there is 2 shaded in and there was a big space so I made them into equal parts.____

that answered the question. This led us to an alternative interpretation of the data. The issue did not lie with students' level of understanding, but with the representation of the problem: the size of the model made it difficult to discern between fifths and sixths as appropriately sized pieces. Rather than leading us down a path that suggested remediation, our commitment to seeing the brilliance of Black students enabled us to recognize their competence, and to see that their responses were connected to a representation we used, rather than erroneous understandings. We saw all that these children knew and saw our own contribution to the conditions that led them to mislabel the fraction.

Centering Black Learners' Mathematical Identities

In the course of teaching mathematics, teachers make many instructional decisions that structure classroom interaction. Examples include deciding who gets called on to share their mathematical thinking and reasoning; who gets assigned which roles during group work; and whose contributions are publicly encouraged, noted, and acknowledged. In addition to influencing the conception of mathematics and mathematical competence that students develop, these decisions communicate messages about who is capable of knowing and doing mathematics.[13] Left unexamined, such decisions and resultant interactions often result in patterns that suggest Black children are inferior knowers and doers of mathematics.

One way we saw this commitment in the video records was through the management of classroom discussions. While classroom discussions are a rich site for student-driven learning, they also can be sites of great risk. During one discussion about fractions, one of our Black students presented an incorrect solution to the mathematics task. Although his solution was incorrect, the student's work raised an important mathematical idea, one that was essential to propelling the class toward the correct solution. The risk in this situation is that the student and his classmates might focus only on the incorrect solution, reducing his status as a knower of mathematics. Our commitment to centering his mathematical identity led us to keep track of this important contribution and to remind the class of its significance at the end of the problem. By doing so, we hoped to affirm for this Black boy, and for his peers, that he, as well as every other Black student in the classroom, is a knower and doer of mathematics and that his contributions are essential to the learning environment.

A commitment to centering the mathematical identities of Black learners seeks to prevent and eliminate those patterns by enacting the work of teaching mathematics with careful attention to the way Black learners are positioned in relation to mathematical knowledge and activity. Pedagogy guided by this commitment requires teachers to acknowledge that many interactions occur in the course of learning, and each interaction has the power to do good or cause serious harm. The commitment to centering the mathematical identities of Black learners compels us as teachers to act with intention to facilitate interactions that bolster Black children's status as mathematical knowers and doers and to intervene on those that challenge this status.[14]

Supporting Participation and Honoring Student Agency

The activity structures that students participate in during mathematics learning play a key role in shaping the mathematics they learn and their conceptions of mathematical competence.[15] In response to the literature documenting this pattern, recent mathematics education reform efforts have centered around changing mathematics instruction from teacher-driven to more student-centered approaches. Classrooms characterized by this approach ask learners to engage in classroom activity structures, such as classroom discussions, that require them to adopt new forms of participation in order to be successful.

A commitment to supporting Black learners' participation in such structures involves acknowledging the racialized risks and vulnerabilities associated with adopting new forms of participation. Black learners routinely learn mathematics in environments characterized by participation structures that limit their opportunities to engage in sense making, and these histories limit their chance to identify as sense makers. Based on these experiences, Black learners are unlikely to participate in new structures without targeted supports that encourage their participation. Given that their identities are at stake, this pedagogical commitment includes honoring student agency by making space for Black learners to modify participation opportunities in ways that reflect their current sense of self in relation to mathematical activity.

To illustrate this commitment, we return to the story of Ayana. On Tuesday, the second day of instruction and a day after her declaration that she was not the type of person who presents her thinking on the board, Darrius noticed that Ayana had a key insight that he wanted her to share during the ensuing discussion around the problem. However, when he asked Ayana if she would like to present her insight at the board, she declined immediately. Given the current emphasis on mathematical practices and equal distribution of opportunities to learn,[16] one could imagine a well-intentioned teacher insisting that Ayana present her thinking. In some contexts, such as "no excuse" charter schools, which are attended by many Black children, instructional philosophies such as "no opt out"[17] would make Ayana's refusal unacceptable. In a classroom guided by this philosophy, Ayana would have to share or accept a consequence for refusing to do so. This approach, rooted in logics of control, ignores the racialized risks and vulnerabilities of the interaction and the collective weight of Ayana's prior experiences, her history-in-person, which likely informed her refusal.[18]

Guided by a commitment to honor and respect Ayana's agency, Darrius decided not to press. However, his acceptance of this refusal did not mean Ayana would never present her ideas at the board. Our shared commitment to supporting Black learners in enacting different forms of participation led us to instead explore under what conditions Ayana might become willing to present at the board. Later that day, Deborah noticed that Ayana again had a mathematical contribution that would advance the group's discussion. When asked to share her thinking with the class, Ayana again declined an invitation to contribute at the board. This time, Deborah offered a modification. Noting that Ayana had worked collaboratively to arrive at her contribution, Deborah asked if Ayana would be willing to go to the board with her partner to share their collective thinking. This invitation Ayana accepted, allowing her to try on the identity of one who presents at the board.

As a result of this modified opportunity, Ayana began to see herself as someone who enacts smartness by going to the board. Not only did Ayana reflect fondly on the experience (see figure 6.3), but she also began to seek out opportunities to present at the board by convincing her groupmates to present collectively. In time, she also began seeking opportunities to present at the board without the support of groupmates.

FINAL NOTES

Who or What Requires Repair?

The three pedagogical commitments that we advance in this chapter are focused on dynamics of repair and restoration, transformation, and the reimagination of Black children's mathematical futures. However, if we are not careful as teachers, even with the pedagogical commitments outlined above, we may misconstrue the work of teaching as repairing, restoring, or transforming Black children.[19] When our gaze falters and

FIGURE 6.3   Ayana's end-of-class reflection

Write one thing that you did that was smart today.
  go up to the Board and raised my hands.

settles on these children as change-worthy or we aim to close achievement gaps, increase advanced mathematics enrollment, or prepare the future workforce, we problematically fall into a set of pedagogical commitments centered on achievement. Danny Martin caricatures two types of mathematics teachers who hold achievement-based commitments: missionaries and cannibals. Missionaries, in Martin's construction, are attempting to "save African American [or Black] children from themselves and their culture,"[20] whereas cannibals subsume (or consume) Black children under mathematics, maintaining a willful, narrow focus on mathematics practices that exclude the Black child as a person.[21] Achievement-based commitments have been historically harmful to and for Black children in mathematics classrooms, so different commitments are thus warranted.

According to Martin, the alternative to achievement-based commitments is premised on experience. Experienced-based commitments focus on repairing, restoring, or transforming Black children's *relationships* to mathematics and mathematical activity structures, *not* repairing, restoring, or transforming the child. Within pedagogical commitments based on experience, the Black child is seen as whole and perfected—brilliant. Focus on the experience compels a teacher to question mathematical tasks undertaken by children and the activity structures in which children operate. Of course, experience-based commitments are steeped in a Race Matters stance, which recognizes the importance, relevance, and salience of Blackness as fundamental to the pedagogical approach. Achievement-based commitments, on the other hand, are unsurprisingly steeped in stances (or ideologies) that call for colorblind orientations that fundamentally obfuscate, obscure, or minimize race and racism.[22] The distinction between repairing, restoring, and transforming the child versus repairing, restoring, and transforming their relationship to mathematics may seem slight but has deep implications for the mathematical futures of Black children.

Children's Mathematical Agency Is Relational Work

As Ayana's reflection at the end of the week suggests, the promise of an experienced-based pedagogical approach is that Black children come to view themselves more positively in relation to mathematics and mathematical activity, forging pathways to different mathematical futures. Ayana shifted how she thought about herself as a mathematics practitioner and contributor. Her relationship to going to the board to present her mathematics thinking transformed from being a practice that she was opposed to participating in to one in which she sees her potential for continued engagement. In this, we see Ayana embracing more of her mathematical agency. We understand agency, in this context, as children's capacity to transform their own lived experiences. Romanticizing Ayana's agency would place this transformation entirely within her ten-year-old, Black-girl body, situating her as an individual child who changed her own mathematical world. Romanticizing the work of teaching would attribute Ayana's transformation entirely to Darrius and Deborah. The pedagogical commitments exemplified in this chapter, however, importantly illustrate a relational dynamic in which a child's mathematical agency is "socially and relationally produced; it is in other words an outcome of social relations, rather than essential quality of the individual child [or children]."[23] A relational approach thus highlights the web of connections formed between the children, teacher(s), and content in and beyond the classroom setting.

Attending to this web of relations, and the ways that they are influenced by race, lies at the heart of our vision of justice in mathematic teaching. Guided by a restorative impulse, we endeavor to manage the interactions in our classrooms in ways that promote the development of mathematical agency for Black learners while acknowledging the harm done to them in the course of their mathematics learning. We offer the pedagogical commitments of (1) asserting, showcasing, and celebrating the brilliance of Black learners; (2) centering the mathematical identities of Black learners; and (3) honoring Black learners' agency while supporting them to enact different forms of participation in mathematics as starting points for embodying a Race Matters stance in mathematics teaching. This stance is critical to intervening on the unjust foreclosure of Black learners' mathematical futures.

SECTION III

WHY JUSTICE MATTERS

Danfeng Soto-Vigil Koon

Justice matters because the world is profoundly unjust and young people know this. Who could miss the expanding tent cities,[1] the nearly one in thirty-one adults imprisoned or surveilled,[2] the criminalization of immigration,[3] or images of worldwide mass flooding that we are told will double this decade?[4] The suffering and death caused by the COVID-19 pandemic predictably layered inequalities upon inequalities,[5] and the rise of state and nonstate white terror will directly impact many young people and indirectly touch many others.[6]

When we as teachers consent and contribute to twelve years of mandated seat time in which we pretend the world is fair and we are marching toward progress, the brightest and boldest of our young people are left with no other choice but to push back, opt out, or self-destruct.[7] Our legitimacy, as teachers in the classroom and adults in schools, is eroding. We have, at most, a frail claim to having gotten anything right. The world our students now face is a world that adults have, to varying degrees, built, participated in, or turned a blind eye to. While individuals and collectives have always resisted and built alternatives, these other pathways have not been enough to slow the multiple ways greed, consumption, and exploitation have permeated our institutions and left us at an uncertain crossroads.

In these times of dizzying human and ecological devastation, teaching without centering justice in our curriculum, pedagogy, and relationships fails to prepare students for adulthood at these crossroads—or for the transformative work needed to lead us beyond them. And yet decades of educational policies have hitched classrooms to an industry of nationally devised standards, curricula, assessments, and textbooks that reify and justify dominant racial, social, and ecological relational dynamics.[8] Even student supports, interventions, and discipline are increasingly externally produced, packaged, and sold to schools so that educators and administrators might better "manage" unruly students.[9] Through these policies, hyper-capitalism that often targets communities of color has reshaped education and severely constrained content, pedagogy, and discipline. Students rightfully ask, "Why do I have to learn this?" with the teacher responding that "They," meaning the district, standard writers, textbook companies, test-makers, college admissions staff, and/or their future bosses, say so. In these classrooms, teachers pretend to teach, and students pretend to learn.

How do we instead, as teachers, look into the eyes of our students and teach in ways that recognize the truth of how we got here, the ways unequal social relations and ideologies imprint themselves on our lenses and expectations, and actively transform our curriculum, pedagogy, and classroom cultures to prepare for the evolution of society?[10] How do we use language to open new possibilities and dissect and understand the machinery of injustice in the content of what we teach and the disciplines we deem the common core? How do we teach in ways that build on, rather than subtract from, the critical pedagogies that exist in families and communities as stories of migration or sit-down talks from parents when the world breaks their children's hearts? How can we, as educators, grow and cocreate with those in critical youth development spaces that are outside or alongside traditional schools—pedagogical spaces that are a means of education, survival, and personal and social transformation for our students?[11]

The following chapters offer concrete examples of practices that restore and transform the educational process so young people and educators can emerge more fully human. Each author builds on the work of researchers and scholars who have identified theories, principles, values, and practices that recognize the role and responsibility of educators to support young people in understanding, critiquing, and transforming their world—even, or perhaps especially, within state ideological apparatuses such as compulsory schooling.[12]

In chapter 7, Alexis Patterson and Salina Gray outline a (W)holistic Science Pedagogy that recognizes students and teachers as whole beings and encourages science teachers to engage in critical self-reflection, relevant real-world learning, and pedagogy that supports students to become active agents of science rather than mere consumers of it. Their framework also notably stresses the importance of attending to students' social-emotional well-being though relationship building and restorative practices.

Bryan Brown and Karega Bailey provide in chapter 8 an intimate case study of a transformative restorative justice circle following a fight between two boys. The dean of discipline elevates the conversation from right or wrong narratives and instead listens to the children. He affirms their positive identities as "Kings" and invites these students to step up into leadership roles as older children on the school playground. In this way, disciplinary practice encourages two young boys to transform themselves from "troublemakers" to community leaders.

Finally, Noreen Naseem Rodríguez in chapter 9 describes in rich detail how a teacher's centering of voices from communities often deliberately silenced exemplifies a transformative justice approach to civics education. Using as examples the voices of Toni Morrison, Sylvia Mendez, and Aki Munemitsu, Rodriguez explains that transformative civics education for young children intentionally centers the stories and experiences of Black, Indigenous, and People of Color, rather than continue to enforce obedience, patriotism, and personal responsibility and center only dominant narratives and voices.

Teachers today have the daunting task of teaching for a future we do not know, for a future that often keeps us up at night. Paolo Freire has long reminded us that "Education either functions as an instrument which is used to facilitate the integration of the younger generation into the logic of the present system and bring about conformity or it becomes the practice of freedom, the means by which men and women deal critically and creatively with reality and discover how to participate in the transformation of their world."[13]

Read in the light of today, integration into the logic of the present system is clearly insufficient. Curricula and pedagogies that fail to recognize this nation's racist history, the complex diversity of its current people, and the everyday lived consequences of an exploitative economy continue to alienate students whose immediate lives teach them a different truth and lead them to seek different answers—and these young people exist in poor white communities, as well as in communities of color. Even students who do succeed, by school standards, memorizing content and following rules, are not being equipped within or through the present system to understand, intervene in, or improve the actual world that surrounds them. Justice, as we are talking about it here, or the recognition of injustice and the interruption and reparation of it in our schools, is a first step. Transforming the world is the goal.

7 Promoting Equity and Justice in Science Classrooms via (W)holistic Science Pedagogy

Alexis Patterson Williams and Salina Gray

RECENT SURVEY DATA suggest adults in the United States identify various reasons for the underrepresentation of Black and Hispanic/Latinx individuals in science, technology, engineering, and math (STEM) careers; chief among those reasons are lack of encouragement to pursue studies in STEM and lack of access to quality education in preparation for STEM fields (see figure 7.1).[1] Recent STEM degree and certification data paint a similar picture. Analysis of the nearly 667,919 STEM degrees and certifications awarded in 2015 highlights disproportional representation of White (63.6 percent), Black (8.6 percent), Hispanic (12.1 percent), Asian (11.6 percent), and multiracial (3.3 percent) students.[2] Racial/ethnic enrollment and outcome disparities related to STEM begin well before college. The most recent National Assessment of Educational Progress data for science highlights parallel performance gaps between traditionally marginalized and nonmarginalized students in science.[3] While these data points may not capture the entire story, they do draw attention to problematic teaching and learning trends in education.

Disparities in STEM education quality and participation encouragement are emblematic of centuries of injustice and inequity experienced by

FIGURE 7.1 Perceived reasons more Black and Hispanic/Latinx people are not working in STEM

Percent of those in science, technology, engineering and math jobs who say each of the following is a major, a minor or not a reason why there are not more blacks and Hispanics working in STEM jobs in this country

Reason	Major	Minor	Not a reason
Less likely to have access to quality education to prepare them for these fields	52%	25%	22%
Not encouraged to pursue these subjects from an early age	45	25	28
Less likely to think they would succeed in these fields	34	36	28
Face discrimination in recruitment, hiring and promotions	32	30	37
Lack of black and Hispanic role models in these fields	32	36	31
More are being trained in these fields, but the process is slow	25	42	32
Just less interested in STEM fields than others	19	25	54

■ Major   ■ Minor   Not a reason

Note: Respondents who did not give an answer are not shown.
Source: Pew Research Center, Survey of US adults conducted on July 11–August 10, 2017, "Women and Men in STEM Often at Odds Over Workplace Equity."

Black and Latinx communities. Noting that the scientific and technological divide has a long legacy in the United States, Shirley Malcom points to diverse perspectives in scientific scholarship as a means to address historic and ongoing injustice.[4] This chapter offers a curricular model, (W) holistic Science Pedagogy (WSP),[5] that encourages teachers to provide all students the quality science education they deserve and are due.

(W)HOLISTIC SCIENCE PEDAGOGY

WSP requires five commitments from the teacher, as commitment encourages teachers to move from beliefs about equity to dedicated action toward just and transformative science teaching. As Souto-Manning and

Winn argue, commitments ensure teachers "can reflect on and commit to the active pursuit of transformative justice."[6] (W)holistic Science teachers use strategies and tools to ground students' content knowledge in critical awareness of structures and institutions that create and maintain the racial, gendered, and economic hierarchies that characterize society. A (W)holistic Science teacher recognizes the connection between students' lived experiences and their participation and achievements within the domain of science. Students and teachers are encouraged to envision deeply relevant and useful learning practices.

Commitment 1:
Commitment to Ever-Developing Self-Awareness

Critical reflection and critical consciousness are the two components of self-awareness. Effective teachers take risks and engage in constant self-reflection that extends beyond pedagogy and practice, acknowledging that who they are influences and impacts their students. Teacher development depends heavily on self-awareness: the process of getting in touch with one's feelings and behaviors.[7] To be self-aware, teachers must reflect on their words, their behaviors, and the impact on students.[8] While reflection can lead to change, and possibly to improved instructional practices, it is not inherently critical. Critical reflection "lays bare the historically and socially sedimented values at work in the construction of knowledge, social relations, and material practices ... it situates critique within a radical notion of interest and social transformation."[9]

The (W)holistic Science teacher is aware of prevailing stereotypes about youth of color, women, and other underrepresented groups within science. These stereotypes are challenged, deconstructed, and replaced with more accurate and inclusive representations and paradigms. This radical form of pedagogy requires a critical and historically sound reconstruction of what has become the canon of science inquiry, research, and scholarship. To create spaces where both traditionally marginalized and nonmarginalized students can thrive, teachers must first engage in rigorous and critical self-reflection.

How is self-awareness relevant to science instruction? In science classrooms, teachers are challenged to instill in all students reasonable understandings of science content and process, and train and create future generations of highly skilled science practitioners. Self-aware teachers recognize the various ways their own personal experiences, biases, and values inform instructional practice, and their beliefs impact curricular choices, norms, and expectations related to academic rigor, and even expectations about who is and who can be a scientist. Students' science identities are informed by who and what they believe themselves to be, as well as who others recognize them to be.[10] Mainstream systems of science education present and teach science from a highly Eurocentric and Westernized perspective, leaving many students from marginalized groups feeling disconnected, unable to identify with, or develop an affinity-identity for, science (or a science affinity-identity).[11]

What does the (W)holistic Science teacher need to do to be ever developing self-awareness? (W)holistic Science teachers must be actively self-aware to change and improve their pedagogy. To do so requires they be critically reflective and critically conscious, recognizing their own privilege and position of power in society and being mindful of how the social and political constructs of gender, race, ethnicity, and class inform school and educational culture.[12] While the teacher's pedagogical style is central to instruction, ideologies are the belief systems that provide the value premises from which decisions about practical education are made.[13] Because values and ideologies influence instructional approaches, teachers must constantly revisit and question the premise and foundation of their own belief systems. Specifically, do they believe science is an elite system of knowledge limited to an exclusive and specific type of student? Do they believe science instruction must focus only on the enduring canonical topics? (W)holistic Science teachers interrogate their beliefs and values and, upon finding values that are steeped in oppression or white supremacy, do the work required to deconstruct these problematic mindsets.

As such, the teacher committed to ever-developing self-awareness is critically reflective and commits to

- understanding self, including core values, beliefs, and motivations;
- understanding self in relation to others;

- learning about identity development and intersectionality;
- acknowledging how structures and systems influence self and others; and
- recognizing their own positionalities and privilege in society.

The teacher is also critically conscious and commits to

- understanding the history of the covert and overt oppression and privilege of various historic and contemporary groups;
- understanding the impacts of covert and overt oppression and privilege on various groups; and
- understanding the role of scientists and the use of science in creating, maintaining, and justifying the covert and overt oppression and privilege of various groups.

Commitment 2:
Commitment to Science and Its Practices

The purpose of science education has remained the same since the inception of formalized schooling in science: to provide students with insight into the material world, as well as opportunities to develop the ability to think and rationalize like scientists. Teachers committed to science and its practices will thus engage their students in science learning that encourages the use of science to make sense of the world and is also reflective of scientific habits of mind.

What does it mean to be committed to science and its practices?
An increasing number of science educators have been calling for more authentic, dialogic science instruction, arguing that more authentic instruction would incorporate reading, writing, and hands-on activities while engaging students in ways that help them practice arguing from evidence, making reasoned explanations after engaging in critical conversations about their findings.[14] Classroom teachers committed to this epistemological approach to science education facilitate students' coconstruction of scientific knowledge and processes of inquiry. Students in such learning environments are expected to assess alternative perspectives by weighing available evidence, assessing the viability of the scientific claims, and constructing an argument for their chosen viewpoint.

Teachers committed to WSP and the practice of science will constantly expand their own content and pedagogical knowledge, utilizing up-to-date content and optimal practices to make clear connections between their classroom pedagogy and the real world so their students come to see the world through the lens of science and scientific thinking. Mass media, a dominant source of public science understanding, provides people with topics of discussion in a social forum where "citizens judge controversial science."[15] Given that mass media outlets now frame so much of what we all learn about science and provoke so many controversial conversations, using popular media in the science classroom can be an effective pedagogical strategy for teachers to enhance their students' scientific literacies. Students' attitudes and perceptions about controversial science topics related to biotechnology, genetics, and even environmental science tend to be shaped at least as much by popular culture as by classroom science, so the (W)holistic Science teacher will capitalize on the power and limitations of media and incorporate into their science instruction issues such as fake news and ways to gauge the accuracy of scientific information and reasoning being presented.

What does the (W)holistic Science teacher need to do to develop this commitment? The development of more hands-on, inquiry, and problem-based science learning opportunities requires culturally informed, dynamic instruction. A more expansive array of teaching styles can help teachers connect science content and scientific practices to real-world issues, and the teacher committed to science and its practices must

- continuously develop their own science literacy through reading, watching the news, etc.;
- pursue professional development opportunities for science teaching;
- be willing to teach in ways that align with contemporary standards and research in science education;
- seek opportunities for students to apply science content in real-world contexts; and
- make science content and science practices relevant.

Commitment 3:
Commitment to Science as a Transformative Agent

Science and technology have literally transformed our lives. Vaccines have saved millions, improving the life expectancy of our species,[16] and machine inventions sparked our society's transitions from agricultural to industrial and beyond. Scientific enterprise and scientific developments are powerful, sometimes transformative agents of change that impact the cultural forms and health and well-being of humankind.

Science has also been used to create and maintain taxonomies, value systems, and social hierarchies to distinguish perceived racial groups,[17] transforming the lived experiences of humans around the world. Science became a particularly powerful hegemonic force in and beyond Europe, as scientists espoused and reified notions of hierarchical structures based on race, class, and gender, justifying prejudice and mythological paradigms that rendered European males superior to all others. Notable, prominent scientists of the day canonized racist ideologies, elevating these beliefs to claims of scientific fact.[18]

The ramifications of these narratives have shaped science-related identity development and social interactions. Science engagement and the cultivation of an identity in science can embolden and empower students to critically evaluate the world around them, transforming their personal lives.[19] Yet, science engagement and identity development can be more tenuous for women, English language learners, and students of color. Narratives that have shaped traditional science curricula and pedagogy normalized science and science identity as belonging to a very specific, narrowly imagined "type" of person. We must create new narratives and classroom norms that include diverse learners in the ongoing practice of science.

Invariably, those who have education and skill become decision-makers and gatekeepers at every level of society. Robin Millar and Rosalind Driver argue that "[j]ust as a personal knowledge in science empowers pupils to act in their everyday lives, so a critical appreciation of the way scientists work empowers them, as future citizens in a participatory democracy, to query, question and seek alternative views on scientific and technological decisions which affect their lives. Interpreted in this way, science in schools has an enabling rather than an alienating function and has a critical role to play in a liberal education."[20] Scientific literacy is critical to the formation of students as productive and thoughtful citizens, able to meaningfully interact and potentially use the content and process of science to transform the world around them.

What does it look like to teach science in transformative ways? (W)holistic Science teaching is a paradigm of inclusion, rather than tolerance. As agents of transformation, science teachers must provide more diverse conceptions of the content, processes, and practitioners of science. Effective and transformational science pedagogy goes beyond the traditional science canon to purposefully include the innovations, scholarship, and other relevant contributions of individuals and groups outside the dominant majority.

What does the (W)holistic Science teacher need to do to develop this commitment? Science instruction can and should be transformative. This type of instruction includes teachers engaging students in discourse around the historical impact of science in shaping public opinion and ideology on issues of identity, race, class, and gender. Since much of the public's ideological framing comes from media and popular images, these cultural models must be deconstructed. Through meaningful and critical conversations, the (W)holistic Science teacher must consider

- how the canon of science education has perpetuated the notion of science as a prerogative and domain of European men;
- how teachers can implement pedagogical practices that are inherently more liberatory and just for all students; and
- how educators can provide space for oppositional voices and ideas outside mainstream science to thrive.

Discussion around these issues is critical to scientific literacy, speaking directly to the socio-historical and cultural interactions between science and society.

Commitment 4:
Commitment to Your Students' Social and Emotional Well-Being
Transformative Science teachers often present students with examples and data highlighting systemic or local injustices, requiring students to

confront inequity created by science and/or understood using the lens of science.[21] While these may be powerful learning experiences that are meaningful, motivating, and deeply relevant, they may also trigger students and make them vulnerable to sorrow, hopelessness, and frustration.[22] Any teacher utilizing a transformative approach must also be committed to monitoring, encouraging, and supporting students' social-emotional well-being. Mr. Hall, a science teacher, paid attention to students' social, emotional, cognitive, and behavioral state in his class with the aim to build relationships with his students.[23] According to this science teacher, monitoring and ensuring students' social-emotional well-being showed care for his students, which led to opportunities for transformative teaching and learning.

What is social-emotional well-being? The ideas of well-being and wellness are complex constructs that have been discussed extensively.[24] They are often described as individuals' assessment of their own psychological and physical functioning. Richard Ryan and Edward Deci define well-being as optimal psychological functioning and experience,[25] while Reuven Bar-On describes it as a subjective state that emerges from a feeling of satisfaction with one's physical health and oneself in general, one's close interpersonal relationships, and one's occupation and financial situation.[26]

Isaac Prilleltensky describes well-being as occurring at the individual, relational, and collective levels—allowing us to consider how one might assess the wellness of a classroom full of individual students. Well-being may be defined as "a satisfactory state of affairs for individuals and communities that encompasses more than the absence of disease. Many aspects of the psychosocial, economic, political, and physical environment influence the state of well-being; while many aspects of well-being reach beyond health into the realm of values, thriving, meaning, and spirituality."[27]

Robert Phillips similarly defines healthy communities "as homes, schools, and neighborhoods where all citizens experience physical, mental, and social well-being."[28] Based on these theories of well-being, healthy classrooms are positive spaces where students are thriving socially and emotionally while experiencing physical safety and making meaning of classroom content. Students' ability to learn is incumbent on the overall health and safety of their classroom community and the teacher's ability to foster such an environment.[29]

How is social-emotional well-being relevant to science instruction? Teachers must consider how their pedagogy may harm and disrupt students. This is particularly true when we take on culturally relevant and/or social justice approaches to learning. Take, for instance, Ms. Lindahl, a high school science teacher who provided her students with statistics from national and intercultural cancer databases. Her goal was to help students see how corporate and government policies, pollution, and racism were connected to incidences of cancer and mortality rates across low-income communities and communities of color. Ms. Lindahl believed this approach would "arm [her] students with the tools and knowledge to face this disease and to consider the kind of social changes necessary to address both its causes and effects."[30] She came to realize that these lessons evoked fear, sadness, and pain in her students that she was not addressing, so she began to incorporate activities that highlighted solutions to various causes of cancer with the hopes of promoting activism and hope in her students.

While science was being used as an empowering tool and lens to understand injustice, Ms. Lindahl's students learned that science and scientists had also created and ignored injustice, and learning about these layers of injustice caused some students distress. Learning about Henrietta Lacks, the Tuskegee syphilis experiment, how doctors experimented on enslaved women, and other such grave injustices can trigger distrust, frustration, and bewilderment, so teachers must recognize that the potential for such content to (re)activate trauma from direct or indirect experiences of harm and distress. Students whose backgrounds are similar to scientists who have acted in such heinous ways may also experience guilt and shame. Because both types of emotional distress must be addressed, (W)holistic Science teachers take an active role in monitoring the social-emotional well-being of their students, taking action to address harm created by the lesson.

Shawn Ginwright has argued that effective programming will support students to "act upon their environment to create the type of communities in which they want to live. By integrating issues of power, history, identity, and the possibility of collective agency and struggle...."[31] The (W)holistic Science teacher must be committed to developing students' social-emotional well-being as part of teaching for justice and also to addressing the distress that justice-related topics can create for students. Teachers committed to the social–emotional wellness of their students will

- cultivate relationships with their students and get to know them;
- validate students' experiences and stories as connected to science learning;
- assess and build on students' prior knowledge;
- engage the community (including parents) as valuable partners in student learning;
- actively work to flatten social hierarchies within the classroom;
- construct meaningful, heterogeneous groupings that work together equitably;
- integrate lessons that present science content and practices from diverse perspectives;
- develop their understanding of trauma-informed practices; and
- teach their students about trauma, emotional wellness, brain functioning, and so on as part of the curriculum.

Commitment 5:
Commitment to Using Restorative Practices

Restorative practices originated in the legal system. The earliest documented case of restorative justice in school first appeared in Australia in the 1990s.[32] Restorative practices in schools are an approach to discipline that seeks to address and repair harm to individuals and to the community and an alternative to ineffective punitive measures that have disproportionately impacted students of color and students with disabilities.[33]

One of the central tenets of restorative practices is creating peace, for both the individual and larger community within and outside the classroom.[34] The science classroom is a community of learners who are often collaborating and communicating in ways unique to science. Restorative classroom management practices are a means to create and maintain a safe, healthy, and engaged community.

How is restorative practice relevant to science instruction? In an engaging science classroom, students are discussing, building, constructing, and exploring in ways that are not passive or inactive. The potential for students being off task may feel heightened due to the level of independence and freedom that may characterize a science lab or hands-on activity. Clear and explicit expectations, as well as fair and consistent teacher responses, are crucial to maintain a sense of community in which all students feel equal. The (W)holistic Science teacher makes sure students are not unfairly reprimanded or unjustly penalized along lines of gender, race, ethnicity, or any other identity marker. When discipline is necessary, the teacher gives students time to reflect on their behavior, think about harm they've caused others, and contemplate how to undo that harm so they may reenter the classroom community. Restorative practices are used so that patterns of harm can be broken, rather than breaking a student who caused harm. The (W)holistic Science teacher understands that all students are valuable members of the learning community and knows that when students act out the action is often a cry for support.

What does the (W)holistic Science teacher need to do restorative practice? (W)holistic Science teachers understand that many students have experienced harm by virtue of their identities, and acknowledge the harm many students from marginalized groups experience due to dominant narratives in the world around them. One salient assault is that for millennia science has been presented as the domain of European and European-descended males, excluding the contributions of females and people from non-Western societies, an idea perpetuated in large part by mainstream media.[35] As a cultural transmitter, media provides opportunities for information and debate but also harm. Students' conceptions of themselves and others as scientists (or not) can be informed and influenced by what they see and hear in the media.[36]

Restorative science pedagogy capitalizes on a more radical view of science learning that extends beyond narratives that dominate media and curricular coverage. Facilitating conversations to deconstruct and disrupt harmful, unjust, and inaccurate ideologies is an undertaking foundational to restorative practices in the classroom.

A commitment to restorative practices in science requires that the (W)holistic Science teacher

- understand the disproportionate punishment in traditional measures of discipline;
- acknowledge the harm classroom community members can cause each another;
- ask "what has happened to them?" rather than "what is wrong with them?"
- provide narratives and counternarratives to offer more robust and comprehensive understandings of the scientific enterprise; and
- facilitate regular conversations to restore justice and repair harm caused by individuals and groups in the classroom, by science/scientists, and/or by society.

CONCLUDING THOUGHTS

Students are whole beings, socialized through multiple experiences, interactions, and levels of awareness. As such, educators must move far beyond the notion of overly scripted socially and culturally irrelevant curricula if they are to create meaningful, real-world learning. The approach must be holistic, responding to students' mental, physical, and emotional needs. Increasing diversity, global diffusion of knowledge, and dependence on science and technology warrant the differentiation of our teaching practice. WSP is a framework that begins to equip teachers to leverage science and scientific thinking as tools of liberation, healing, and transformation. Given that this is unfamiliar territory for most educators, we offer two key considerations for teachers interested in embracing this framework.

First, we recommend that teachers, irrespective of their own personal backgrounds and identities, consider using this approach with all their students, including those who are white and affluent. While many common examples of equity-informed curricula come from low-income or underserved communities, it is a misconception to believe that white and wealthy students will not benefit from a justice-based approach to science. To the contrary, these students may face "the steepest learning curves" when it comes to instruction on issues of injustice, inequity, bias, and discrimination.[37] Moreover, white and wealthy students may have ample power and privilege to leverage against issues of inequity in the present and in the future. As Maxine Greene has shown, some students (and parents) do not notice or recognize injustice, so the role of the teacher is "to argue the cause of justice and persuade others of the importance of moving beyond self-interest to a consideration of their responsibility as members, as citizens."[38]

Second, we recommend that teachers make a personal commitment to the five principles outlined in our framework. It has been our experience that (W)holistic Science teachers must engage in the work of constructing their positionality and developing a restorative way of being while sustaining their own wellness as transformative agents of science. For example, supporting and encouraging the social-emotional well-being of one's students can be particularly challenging when a teacher is struggling to maintain personal social-emotional wellness. Sharron Chubbuck and Michalinos Zembylas provide an example of how therapy, classes on nonviolent communication, and relationship building with students helped one novice teacher committed to a justice curriculum overcome self-imposed pressure to save her students, negative self-talk, and the "debilitating effects of her strong sense of moral compunction and the accompanying sense of guilt."[39] Ultimately, this novice teacher was able to be just and empathetic and approach teaching for justice with joy; she noted that "kids need to play and to connect with you through other elements than just the sorrow of, the sadness of social injustice."[40] This example also highlights how self-awareness allowed this novice teacher to recognize that her own deteriorating well-being was negatively impacting her students. Indeed, like the other commitments, social-emotional wellness starts with the teacher, so teachers must establish and develop these commitments within themselves before they can effectively engage in this work with their students.

WSP provides teachers with a framework that encourages commitment to a nexus of experiences that engages and reflects students' whole selves, points of reference, and interests. Rather than attempting to work exclusively within existing constructs and the narrow, problematic structures of traditional curricula and pedagogy, we offer (W)holistic Science Pedagogy as a pathway to radically transformed science teaching and learning.

8 Building Queens and Kings: *The Restructuring of Identity Through Transformative Restorative Justice*

Bryan A. Brown and Karega Bailey

THREE STUDENTS WERE in trouble. They knew they did something wrong, but none of these young men wanted to talk about it. I was engaged in a conversation with my coauthor, Brother Karega Bailey, when he was called on, in his capacity of Dean of Culture, to address an emergent disciplinary situation. What followed was a prime example of the profound potential of restorative justice practices in a K–6 school. In response to what most schools would identify as a punitive and violent incident, leaders in a school dedicated to social justice offered something beyond punishment. Attempting to support all the students involved, Brother Karega responded by identifying the humanity of those involved, asking for accountability, and redirecting them toward empowerment.

A RESTORATIVE JUSTICE CIRCLE VIGNETTE

As the boys walked into the room, they sat in a restorative justice circle to talk about the incident. They knew the process well. Each student took turns sharing a slightly different version of the same narrative.

Emmanuel explained that while he was playing on the playground, Derrick ran up to him and slapped him on the back of the head. After chasing Derrick for a while, he attempted to punch Derrick.

Tashaun's version of the story was different. He was not directly involved with the fight but was instigating the fight between Emmanuel and Derrick. He explained that Emmanuel constantly plays pranks on him and Derrick, and tried to punch Derrick as part of a game. He explained that today Tashaun was tired of Emmanuel's antics and decided to punch Emmanuel hard enough to let him know he was not playing.

Derrick's account of the story connects the other two versions. Derrick claimed that all three boys were playing a game of daring the others to perform pranks. He explained that Tashaun had dared him to punch Emmanuel as part of the game. He was angry with Emmanuel because he claimed Emmanuel plays the game all the time but gets mad when other people hit him. He alleged that Emmanuel punched him back hard after he playfully punched him as a part of the game. Derrick's claim was that, while he was merely joking and playing a game, Emmanuel was trying to hurt him, so he had to defend himself and a fight ensued.

While the transcript of this conversation is unavailable, the interaction was captured through a digital voice memo. Building on the basics of restorative justice conversation described here, a skillful example of restorative justice process emerged, rooted in three vital steps: identifying participants' *humanity*, asking for their *accountability*, and *redirecting and empowering* those involved to take on a new role.

Table 8.1 documents the boys' conversation with Brother Karega in the restorative justice circle. They are discussing what transpired to start the fight and attempting to determine a way to resolve this situation between three students.

After allowing the young men time to apologize to each other and to take responsibility for their own actions, Brother Karega added another layer to the conversation by issuing a challenge for these students.

Building Queens and Kings • 121

TABLE 8.1 Restorative justice circle conversation, *part one*

LINE	SPEAKER	QUOTE	ANALYTICAL NOTE
1	Brother Karega:	Have you ever seen grown men playing fighting games?	Teacher establishes a new standard for behavior: men.
2	Students:	No	Students answer his question.
3	Brother Karega:	If adults played fighting games, like slap boxing, what would happen?	Teacher asks for a rationale for adult behavior.
4	Derrick	They would get hurt.	Student provides a rationale for the group.
5	Brother Karega:	If there were adults around when you were playing this game, what would they have done?	Teacher returns to the adult standard of behavior; asks students about the standard.
6	Tashaun	They would have broken it up.	Student offers a reasonable adult action response.
7	Brother Karega:	Tell me why, King?	Teacher asks students to offer a rationale and affirms their identity by calling them "King."
8	Emmanuel:	The adults are supposed to keep everyone safe.	Student offers a standard expectation of behavior: safety.
9	Brother Karega:	As community members and leaders, it's not just the adults' responsibility to keep everyone safe. It is a community responsibility. You know how this works! We have a community responsibility for protection. If I was with you, would you play the same game with me? Would you hit me?	Teacher offers a new community standard based on the students' own reasoning.
10	Students:	No.	Students reply.
11	Brother Karega:	Why not?	Teacher requests additional reasoning.
12	Derrick:	'Cause you're a grown man.	Student offers a reason.
13	Brother Karega:	I thank you for your presence here in this space. Young Kings, you have the same responsibility as I do. You are not just a community member. You have the responsibility to be a community leader and protector. Our space is too special for any type of violence to be here. We are protectors and leaders.	Teacher redefines the role of the community and the value of the space. He attempts to offer a new vision for these students' roles and identities in the community: "protectors and leaders."

TABLE 8.2   Restorative justice circle conversation, *part two*

LINE	SPEAKER	QUOTE	ANALYTICAL NOTE
14	Brother Karega:	Brothers, you are third graders. You have these kindergarteners looking up to you. If they see you doing this [fighting], they will follow your lead. Is this something you would want them to do?	*Teacher shifts the students' role to make them leaders in the community, essentially elders.*
15	Students:	No.	*Students respond.*
16	Brother Karega:	You have a responsibility out there. From now on if you see anyone arguing or anyone fighting, you need to be a leader. You need to get over there and make sure everyone is safe and this place is a place of peace. You have been the leaders on the playground and teaching the younger kids that we protect each other. For the rest of this week, I want to see you all monitoring the other kids. You think you can handle that, young King?	*Teacher gives the students a new role and a specific responsibility.*
17	Students:	Yes.	*Students accept their new responsibility.*

This vignette points to the intersections of theory and practice in restorative justice approaches to discipline. While involvement in a fight is always constructed as a disciplinary problem, this was a situation in which a skillful school administrator chose to understand the actions of those involved, request their personal accountability, and provide them with an opportunity to redirect subsequent actions in an empowering way. Consistent with the basic tenets of restorative justice pedagogy, the approach highlighted in the vignette centers students over shame and attempts to offer young people an opportunity to use missteps as a platform to become community leaders.

TROUBLEMAKERS TO LEADERS

In a mainstream school, these boys would likely have been suspended in keeping with zero-tolerance policies that have been adopted as a widespread approach thought to make schools safe spaces.[1] Unfortunately, these culturally insensitive policies lead to increased suspension rates that disproportionately impact African American boys and girls.[2]

The zero-tolerance approach to discipline focuses on shaming student "offenders" by removing them from the classroom.[3] While the educational consequences of being removed from school for one's mistakes have proven to be disastrous,[4] in most instances this would have been the outcome for young Emmanuel, Tashaun, and Derrick.

At the heart of the focal interaction, on the other hand, is a careful recrafting of the right or wrong binary. Although these three youths were involved in what was clearly a fight, there is no discussion of right and wrong. Brother Karega operates beyond the binary. Instead of discussing who was wrong and who needed to apologize, every student is provided an opportunity to tell their story. In framing this opportunity, each student is allowed to be understood and, perhaps more importantly, hear how their actions impacted the community. Every student listened and understood how their actions impacted their fellow students. Everyone listened, shared, and was asked to understand each other.

Instead of starting with a focus on the right or wrong of the situation, Brother Karega asks the students a sequence of questions to get them to rethink their standards of behavior (lines 3–7). With a simple set of questions, he helps the students refocus their understandings of who they should be by introducing a new standard. Brother Karega moves their focus from "things kids should do" to a focus on "things adults do." He starts by asking them (line 1), "Have you ever seen grown men playing fighting games?" In a strategic move, Brother Karega never answers the questions he raises, instead allowing the boys to answer each question. He follows his first question with a second question that asks the students to recognize why adults choose not to play the types of games that initiated their conflict. He asks (line 3), "If adults played fighting games, like slap boxing, what would happen?" Taking the same approach, he allows the boys to answer the question by providing their own rationale. What emerges as even more powerful is the way he asks (line 7) "Tell me why, King?" In this exchange overall, two interesting insights emerge. First, Brother Karega indirectly brings into focus a new standard of behavior without explicitly saying so. He offers the standard of adulthood but asks the students to provide reasoning regarding why adults would avoid the focal behavior. Second, he subtly sends the young men a message of identity by referring to them as "King." The norms of restorative justice are evident here: students are asked to be active listeners in their circle but also challenged to conceive of themselves as adults in their own community. This is a powerful opportunity for third graders.

This vignette is also a disciplinary conversation that would be completely unfamiliar in most school settings. Yet, the literature indicates that a focus on shaming children for their mistakes often damages students' sense of belonging to school and hinders their academic performance.[5] Being labeled as a bad student because of a fight or disciplinary incident can negatively frame how students see themselves as belonging to school.[6] In the vignette situation, on the other hand, students involved in a disciplinary incident were simply asked to provide an explanation of why they believe the incident happened. These explanations were not evaluated, but the students were instead praised for their transparency. The Dean of Culture specifically thanks the students for being present in the trusted space of the restorative justice circle (line 13). The conversation does not simply identify victim and culprit. On the contrary, the collective responsibility approach assumes mutual accountability and allows each student to consider their role in the incident. Finally, the restorative justice circle involves a three-stage process of identifying participants' humanity, asking for accountability, and redirecting and empowering students to change their behavior for the better.

Identifying Participants' Humanity

The initial stage of this community circle involved allowing students to find their humanity. Research on sense making tells us that when students offer explanations, even wrong explanations are deeply rooted in logic.[7] Students apply what has worked for them before in a new context. Allowing students to tell their stories without judging them for their logic creates space to recognize the sense making and logic of their actions. In this specific case, the boys' stories of a prank game gone wrong captured the humanity of their actions. Whether one student was angry because another student hit their head, or was angry because the hit was too hard, or was angry because they perceived their friend became overly serious about a game, the logic makes sense. The students sat and listened to each other without being judged. The dean merely asked them to reconsider the game and, importantly, validated them and their participation in the space by saying (line 13), "Thank you for your presence here in this space." Beyond removing opportunities for young people to grow, a community of zero tolerance assumes that children are using irrational thoughts to operate. By contrast, a transformative restorative justice approach to education that is rooted in understanding students and their community norms begins by recognizing the humanity of students' thinking and actions.

Asking for Accountability

Although recognizing the humanity of the students helps circle participants identify their own and others' thinking and reduce the shame of traditional disciplinary approaches, the strategy used in this vignette still centralizes accountability.[8] A hallmark of the interaction was the skillful approach Brother Karega used to frame community accountability. In a traditional disciplinary approach, students would be punitively disciplined for involvement in a fight and reprimanded for not recognizing the way their actions impacted the community. What Brother Karega does is help the students understand that their actions do not merely impact them alone, and that student actions help to define and (re)frame the learning community. He explained (line 13), "You are not just a community member. You have the responsibility to be a community leader and protector." This framing of community roles moves the students from seeing themselves as being accountable for themselves toward a shared vision of themselves as community leaders. The Dean of Culture does this by asking these students to adopt a position of leadership in relation to younger students, explaining (line 14), "Brothers, you are third graders. You have these kindergarteners looking up to you. If they see you doing this [fighting], they will follow your lead. Is this something you would want them to do?" This exchange is powerful, as it helps the students reconsider relational dynamics and rethink their role.

Redirecting and Empowering

The final move in the restorative justice circle exchange, the assignment and reassignment of a new identity and role for the students, occurred when Brother Karega took an additional step after the students had the opportunity to tell their stories and provided them with a vision of collective responsibility. He asked the boys to rethink their role and assigned them a new role as community leaders and role models (line 16):

> You have a responsibility out there. From now on if you see anyone arguing or anyone fighting, you need to be a leader. You need to get over there and make sure everyone is safe and this place is a place of peace. You have to be the leaders on the playground and teach the younger kids that we protect each other. For the rest of this week, I want to see you all monitoring the other kids. You think you can handle that, young King?

In encouraging and asking the boys to take on a new responsibility as peacekeepers in the school and think of themselves as role models for younger students, Brother Karega specifically asks that they intercede if they see students "arguing" or "fighting." This vision of leadership would not arise in a traditional disciplinary model. Furthermore, instead of missing classroom time, these students are being called to contribute to and shape their community in a positive way. As these young people emerge from their mistake, they will thus have an opportunity to explore and assume a new, empowered identity as one outcome of their restorative justice experience.

The K–6 elementary school in Northern California where this vignette played out was founded to provide students with a social justice education, and social justice was thus embedded in every aspect of the school's design. Math, literacy, history, and science lessons were all intentionally structured to help students understand the social realities that shape their daily lives. This newly established charter school was located in a working-class neighborhood and served a population of African American and Mexican American students from that neighborhood, as well as students from nearby neighborhoods whose families had sought out this opportunity for affordable alternative education. Given that the institution chose to foreground social justice approaches, mainstream disciplinary approaches were rejected in favor of a schoolwide disciplinary approach grounded in the tenets of restorative justice.

WHAT IS RESTORATIVE JUSTICE?

What counts as restorative justice? Restorative justice describes disciplinary practices that aim to support just resolutions that focus on both the victim and the offender in any situation where harm has occurred. Belinda Hopkins describes restorative justice as

> An innovative approach to offending and inappropriate behavior which puts repairing harm done to relationships and people over and above the need for assigning blame and dispensing punishment. A restorative approach in a school shifts the emphasis from managing behavior to focusing on the building, nurturing and repairing of relationships.[9]

In keeping with the abovementioned (re)focus on relational restoration, a restorative justice framework centers education and educational process in the disciplinary action. Far too often, schools are places where a child's education becomes secondary to creating a hierarchical environment of strict discipline.

Moving from Zero Tolerance to Restored Opportunity

One of the most dramatic differences involved in adopting a restorative justice approach is a shift in framework. To set a standard for behavior, many schools default to a zero-tolerance approach to achieve assumed standards.[10] Educators adopting a restorative justice model, on the other hand, must engage in a paradigm shift that requires rethinking the needs and roles of all involved. Most notably, as restorative justice circles redefine the roles of victim, administrator, and disciplinarian, the role of victim is challenged.[11] Most practitioners of restorative justice find common ground is the shared assumption that removing a student from class is far from an ideal way to educate that student in their time of error.[12]

The most obvious paradigm distinction between standard and restorative justice approaches to discipline is that the former suggests that a student deserves to be punished for breaking the rules, while the latter framework centers the collective in decisions about discipline.[13] "Restorative justice practices allow schools to create individualized solutions that are manageable for the offending students to fulfill, allow victims to receive closure, and repair the harm caused by the misbehavior."[14] This reorientation from top-down accountability toward processes and outcomes that engage and center students represents a radical departure from traditional frameworks.

Whether the restorative justice approach is a circle, small group discussion, or one-on-one interaction with a restorative justice leader-mediator, the collective is core to the decision-making and the outcome. As students discuss specific challenges and/or harm incurred, victim and perpetrator alike have a voice in deciding what counts as an appropriate resolution. This upends the norm of all decisions about discipline being predetermined by school administrators, normalizing instead experiential learning processes that involve everyone impacted in collective dialogue and decision-making to identify the best pathway to closure.

Restorative justice approaches place significant value on preserving classroom time, and practitioners share a common assumption that all students involved in any incident deserve to be educated.[15] Zero-tolerance approaches, on the other hand, assume that the best way to discipline a child is to remove their opportunity for education. Yet, because students dismissed from school as disciplinary punishment often suffer academically due to lost classroom time, the focus on sustaining classroom time stands firmly at the heart of a restorative justice approach to school discipline.[16]

Another distinct characteristic of a social justice approach is the role of the community. A hallmark of restorative justice is the use of community in decisions about how to resolve conflicts. While there is little uniformity around what counts as "community" in restorative justice, the practices are similar across contexts. In some settings, a community can simply be the students involved in an incident. Others adopt mentoring models where students, their older mentors, and one or more school officials meet in community circles to work toward resolution. Sometimes family and school administrators are included in circle discussions to address classroom and schoolwide challenges. Each of these approaches, though, removes discipline from the hands of a school administrator, resituating decision-making powers and responsibilities among a community of individuals. Data accumulated over the years suggests that transitions to restorative justice (RJ) frameworks have long been intended to address how zero-tolerance policies disproportionally impact African American students:

> Schools implement RJ to address several issues. For example, it is implemented to address overuse of exclusionary discipline that can lead youth, often disproportionately youth from minority groups, from the classroom to court and prison. Some schools use RJ to address bullying in some instances; however, this is a contested approach. Bullying introduces a power imbalance that leaves the victim vulnerable.[17]

The suggestion that mainstream punitive approaches that rely on "exclusionary discipline" have disproportionately impacted "minority groups" implicates the individual(s) who make the decisions about discipline. These individuals include teachers and administrators alike. A shift toward a more community-oriented approach to discipline through restorative justice changes outcomes by changing whose voice gets heard. It is unsurprising that schools using restorative justice approaches see dramatic reductions in inequitable disciplinary action based on race.[18]

Moving from Shame to Accountability

In adopting a restorative approach, schools engage in a radical departure from traditional disciplinary structures that ask rule violators to pay a price to resolve their violation. A common price for rule violation in mainstream contexts has been out-of-school punishment or in-school separation from the student population. These exchanges, which are situated as and widely thought to be just, ultimately shame students by marking them as bad actors.[19] This shame-centered approach also silences victim voices in decisions about how to resolve conflict.

One of the subtle shifts that occurs when a restorative justice approach is adopted is a shift in focus from shame to accountability. Trevor Fronius and colleagues note, "Reintegrative shaming acknowledges the impact of wrongdoing on both the offender and those who were harmed. Shaming may materialize as direct actions (requiring a student to publicly apologize) or indirect actions, expressions of disappointment by a teacher to a parent of a student."[20] This idea that "offender" and victim alike should be cared for emerges as a unique aspect of restorative justice approaches.

Should discipline include decisions about what is best for the victim *and* the perpetrator? Should those who make punishable mistakes be asked to repent for those mistakes publicly? While answers to these questions vary considerably, the shift to a restorative justice framework requires those adopting restorative justice practices to carefully reconsider how shame and accountability can be vital factors in building community disciplinary norms.

A REVIEW: WHAT DOES THE RESEARCH SAY?

Restorative justice found its origins in the cultural norms of South Pacific and Native American cultures in which an ethos of restoration supersedes a desire for punishment.[21] As opposed to shaming an individual from their shortcomings, these cultures shared a desire to allow the "offender" to serve the community, restore their standing, and improve the community.[22] As educators in the United States began to recognize that bias was leading to disciplinary practices characterized by undeniable discrimination against African American children, many called for restorative justice alternatives.[23]

The first movement in this direction involved a rush to define restorative practices and explain their value to schools. Restorative justice practices were not perceived as mere classroom management devices; scholars suggested instead that adopting restorative justice approaches could help disrupt the school-to-prison pipeline that begins with inequitable disciplinary approaches and outcomes.[24] Recrafting how we view so-called "perpetrators" was identified as a first step in altering the trajectory of discipline:

> RJ thus treats perpetrators simultaneously as agents and as victims, a twofold lens through which to view wrongful behavior as a reflection of systematic inequalities rather than just as an expression of individual pathology. For this reason, many see RJ as particularly well suited to the task of disrupting patterns of institutional racism.[25]

As opposed to viewing students' behaviors as pathological, a restorative justice approach calls on educators and administrators to recognize the role of society in producing those behaviors and how students can be empowered to help articulate and create the type of society they would like to see. In this way, restorative justice frameworks came to be a movement to transcend a binary vision of victim/perpetrator and ground communities of change agents.

Research on the impact of restorative justice approaches to classroom discipline offers the field an unclear vision of effectiveness. On the one hand, a wealth of qualitative research points toward the value of restorative justice in changing the culture of discipline. In contrast to the many studies that point to inequitable outcomes that arise through punitive approaches, a growing body of research now shows that teachers and students believe restorative justice approaches produce a culture of fair disciplinary responses. Though most restorative justice research to date has been descriptive, a few studies suggest that restorative justice approaches positively impact school climate and school attendance.

Impact on School Climate

Restorative justice approaches tend to be interwoven with a shift in school culture.[26] Students going through restorative justice counseling, furthermore, have been shown to demonstrate growth in their social-emotional intelligence.[27] The act of taking personal responsibility and working with students to decide what counts as social justice appears to be a way for students to connect with and practice mindsets and skills associated with social and emotional competence and well-being. Traditional approaches, by contrast, punish students without enabling or encouraging them to practice working with peers and other community members to achieve a healthy resolution. In one study of school-district-level implementation of restorative justice disciplinary approaches, for example, "two-thirds of staff perceive the RJ program as improving the social-emotional development of students, and 70 percent of staff reported that RJ improved overall school climate during the first year of implementation."[28] Given that over three hundred administrators and leaders were involved in this restorative justice initiative, these are significant perceived outcomes.

Importantly, though, a second thematic research finding has been that restorative justice programs often fail when isolated. Programming appears to be largely ineffective if educators attempt to embed these unfamiliar alternative approaches in their work without parallel embeddedness in a larger schoolwide policy on discipline.[29] Researchers have thus suggested that schools that integrate restorative justice into the school's overall philosophy and operational framework are likely better suited to establishing a program that works and lasts.[30]

Impact on Attendance

Another pattern among the early research findings on restorative justice outcomes and impacts relates to connections between restorative justice and absenteeism and attendance.[31] Findings from a study documenting a three-year restorative justice implementation undertaking show that student tardiness decreased 64 percent and absenteeism decreased 50 percent.[32] Perhaps one of the most resounding implications of instilling restorative justice disciplinary frameworks, then, could be the many benefits accrued through the additional classroom time students experience when a disciplinary approach that alters how students and classroom time are valued ends up changing how a lot of students enact a new perspective about the value of school.

A RETURN TO THE VIGNETTE

Revisiting the vignette, we can now better understand how the small group of students sitting in their restorative justice circle and discussing the implications of their own actions were engaged in a healing process. These students were a part of a school culture that welcomed and valued this experience, and the Dean of Culture offered an effective application of restorative justice. As he initiates his exchange with the children, a subtext serves as the foundation for the interaction: Brother Karega never discounts the logic the students used regarding getting into a fight, and he never discredits their decision-making or chastises them for their actions. Instead, he uses the students' own logic as a starting point to help them find a healthy and community-oriented vision for moving forward. He challenges them to move from being young boys who may fight because they feel mistreated to seeing themselves as growing boys who have a clear and important community leadership responsibility. Children make mistakes. As an advisor to this group, Brother Karega lets the students know that although they are children, the expectation is that they will soon become more like adults. Brother Karega helped them see themselves on a pathway to adulthood by framing their trajectory as headed toward community leadership. In this way, what began as a shared incident of violence ended with individual and collective responsibilities of protection.

Asking for Accountability

Another dimension of the vignette that offers an exemplary model for restorative justice is the way Brother Karega asks the students for accountability. He approaches accountability on two levels. As Dean of Culture, he asks the students to be accountable to the larger school community, using the standard of community responsibility to ask the students to shift their focus from protecting themselves to seeing their role as protectors of the community. This is a prime example of how students and teachers can renegotiate their roles in restorative justice circle contexts. On another level, Brother Karega challenges the boys to take personal responsibility. Each boy was redirected to see himself as a role model for the younger students, and they were subsequently asked to adopt a vision of themselves as role models, community leaders, and protectors. While these roles might seem abstract, the boys agreed to assume the role of yard supervisor for the lower playground. This approach to accountability proved to be dynamic in that it offered the boys new self-expectations that were specific and aspirational. Ultimately, then, the vignette offers a telling case for how restorative justice spaces provide opportunities for students to enact accountability for their actions.

The students also had a chance to redirect their identity in an empowering fashion, not as young boys in an elementary school, but as current and future "Kings." Brother Karega carefully reassigns these students a new way of seeing themselves, a new identity, by referring to them as "Kings." He never provides them any opening to shift this new narrative about who they should be. That is, even in their mistakes, he sees and names them as kings. In most instances of school-based discipline, students leave with a sense of shame that permeates among their peers.[33] Brother Karega instead starts by having students who made a mistake share their perceptions and recognize the error, and then quickly moves from a narrative of situation recognition to an explicit definition of the type of manhood worthy of a "king" label. By redirecting the discussion from a fight involving three boys to a narrative about the responsibilities of men, he reframes possibilities for the students themselves. In a traditional approach, these young people might be labeled as "troubled" or "violent." Instead, they are given the responsibility of leadership under the assumption that, as "Kings," they can and must set a good example for younger students and protect their school community.

Given that research has indicated that restorative justice approaches are rendered ineffective outside the scope of broader schoolwide implementation,[34] it is important that this process of provoking students to reflect on and talk about community leadership reflected a schoolwide ethos that education is about engaging constructively with and helping the community. This is a school ecosystem that continues to benefit from sustained and overarching commitment to an approach that provides students opportunities to recognize their errors, work on understanding and restoring their role in the community, and adopt specific practices to support and add value to the community.

CONCLUSION

While theories of school justice and cultural relevancy are important, pragmatic application of those ideas is essential for the modern-day educator. In a season where time is precious and individuals struggle to work effectively in urban schools, communities that adopt restorative justice approaches have the potential to create positive impacts on how young people see themselves and others. The vignette we highlighted models an expert approach to empathy, identity development, and support. While the passion Brother Karega used when he spoke with these young people could not be captured on the page, the students' willingness to accept a new standard for who they should be reflects their understanding that respect, love, and a challenge were being placed in their lives.

While not always successful and rarely easy, restorative justice approaches are rooted in thinking differently about who students are and who they can be. As opposed to default assumptions that students' mistakes reflect their limitations, the approach highlighted here assumes that young people make many mistakes in their pathway toward adolescence and adulthood. The students involved in this incident were labeled, but not in ways commonly encountered in urban schools. By moving away from pejorative labels such as "troublemaker," "violent," and "aggressive," Brother Karega offered opportunities for students to see themselves as "leaders," "protectors, "and "role models." Those involved bought into this approach because the school community consistently views and enacts education as a tool for social change. As research on restorative justice continues to provide educators with evidence of what is possible, the powerful potential of restorative justice will undoubtedly serve all, as more young people are given a chance to identify their humanity, take accountability, and redirect their identities in empowering ways.

9 "They Were Just Living Their Lives": *Reconceptualizing Civic Identity, Membership, and Agency in Second-Grade Social Studies*

Noreen Naseem Rodríguez

THE PURPOSE OF CIVIC EDUCATION is purportedly to prepare US citizens to participate in a democracy.[1] However, the civic project of public schooling has historically focused on assimilation; creating "good citizens" who fit neatly into Anglo-Saxon, Protestant conceptualizations of what it means to be American: white, English-speaking, Christian, and middle class.[2] Joseph Kahne and Ellen Middaugh argue that "students' broad commitment to civic participation will be enhanced when they develop the sense that they have the *capacity* to be effective as civic actors, when they are *connected* to groups and other individuals who share their commitments and/or can facilitate their involvement and effectiveness as civic actors, and when they have formed particular and strong commitments with respect to specific social issues."[3]

With young children, civic education begins with obedience, patriotism, and personal responsibility.[4] These concepts are also normed to the white middle class and are enforced by the predominantly white, female, middle-class elementary teaching workforce.[5] Decades of research demonstrate that Black and Brown youth are disproportionately subjected to discipline and punishment in school spaces as early as preschool, often for actions and behaviors that are rarely addressed in the same way for their white peers, demonstrating that only *some* children are allowed to exhibit civic agency without consequence.[6]

Youth who are Black, Indigenous, Latinx, Asian American, undocumented, LGBTQ, and/or practice non-Christian religions often exist beyond the bounds of "good citizens" and subsequently experience second-class citizenship in schools and society, leading some to refuse to identify themselves as US citizens altogether, due to their marginalized status in society.[7] Youth who exist on the margins have fewer civic opportunities in school and see scant reflections of self in school curricula. When such reflection does occur, they often see those with whom they identify (or are identified) relegated to specific moments in the past or portrayed in a negative light, as occurs when Black leadership is solely connected to enslavement or the civil rights movement, or Muslims are only mentioned in the contemporary period in relation to the September 11, 2001, terrorist attacks.[8] A transformative justice vision of civic education thus requires ontological and epistemological reorientations in the teaching of civic identity, agency, and resistance to center Black, Indigenous, and People of Color (BIPOC) as communities who have continually struggled to exercise their rights in recognition of their full humanity in a nation built upon white supremacy and oppression.

While many scholars have engaged in such civic reorientations with BIPOC and other marginalized youth in and outside of formal spaces of schooling, this work is largely concentrated at the secondary level with adolescents and young adults.[9] In addition, recent scholarship on civic agency and engagement with young learners evades explicit attention to race, the impacts of ethnoracial difference on the ways BIPOC youth experience civic membership, and how the ethnoracial identity of adults in power might impact responses to the civic agency of BIPOC youth.[10] This chapter highlights the ways in which Virginia Ye, an experienced Asian American teacher at a large public elementary school in an urban Texas school district, engaged her second-grade students in broader conceptualizations of civic education. In particular, Virginia added nuance and complexity to the superficial civic narratives traditionally offered to young children by examining the long civil rights movement and Japanese American incarceration, ending the school year with a unit centered on social change.[11]

RECONCEPTUALIZING CIVIC AGENCY WITH *SYLVIA AND AKI*

Virginia, the only Asian American teacher at her school, had taught there for eight years. During the 2015–16 academic year, she taught a second-grade class composed entirely of Black, Latinx, and mixed-race students; schoolwide, student demographics at the time were 90 percent Latinx and 8 percent Black. I met Virginia in the fall of 2015, when she agreed to take part in a larger study of Asian American elementary educators who taught Asian American histories during the spring of 2016. Virginia dedicated far more instructional time to this work than any other study participant, and I was in her classroom dozens of times during the spring semester as a participant observer during social studies and related literacy lessons. In addition to classroom observations, which were audio- and video-recorded and later transcribed, I collected classroom artifacts (photographs of classroom charts and teacher notes, student journals) and conducted three lengthy off-site semistructured interviews with Virginia, in addition to informal post-lesson debriefs and lesson planning discussions at school.

Virginia dedicated the beginning of the spring semester to what Jacquelyn Dowd Hall describes as the long civil rights movement. In contrast to the dominant narrative, which takes place from the *Brown v. Board of Education* decision in 1954 through the Civil Rights Act of 1964 and Voting Rights Act of 1965, Hall argues that the Black freedom movement actually began in the 1930s and lasted through the 1970s.[12] As the contemporary conditions experienced by Black people are a result of enslavement, Jim Crow, and a range of subsequent policies and practices dedicated to their disenfranchisement, some situate the Black freedom movement even earlier in time, and because voter suppression and police brutality against Black communities (among other struggles) continue in the present, many argue that the Black freedom movement is ongoing.[13] Virginia read aloud picturebooks to her class about enslaved resistance, the traditional civil rights movement, and contemporary individuals such as Coretta Scott King and Toni Morrison.

As this unit concluded, Virginia reflected, "We've been learning a lot about African Americans and how they, during the civil rights movement, they overcame a lot and they were discriminated against." She also realized that she had presented civil rights struggles as "a Black-and-white issue," and that this binary might "open doors for understanding that there's a lot of other kinds of discrimination happening." Therefore, in the final week of February, she introduced the topic of Japanese American incarceration to her second-grade students. "I wanted them to realize that, hey, there's a lot of different kinds of discrimination, here's another example." After this week of instruction, centered on the picturebook *The Bracelet*, Virginia's student teacher took over primary teaching duties for the next two months.[14] However, once her student teacher's required hours were completed, Virginia ended the semester with a social change unit that returned to the topic of Japanese American incarceration.

The last four weeks of the school year were spent reading aloud Winifred Conkling's *Sylvia and Aki*, a middle-grade novel based on the real story of two young girls during World War II.[15] The book's protagonists are Mexican American Sylvia Mendez and Japanese American Aki Munemitsu, who narrate their experiences in alternating chapters. After the bombing of Pearl Harbor and Roosevelt's Executive Order 9066, the Munemitsu family was forced to leave their thriving asparagus farm and move into barracks at a War Relocation Authority prison camp in Poston, Arizona. Meanwhile, the Mendez family leased the Munemitsu farm and attempted to enroll their children at the nearby Westminster School. However, the family was told that their children must attend the Mexican school, which was farther away, had fewer resources, and focused on vocational education. The Mendez family sued the school district and eventually won their case, ending school segregation in California and setting precedent for the *Brown v. Board of Education* decision.

As Virginia read the opening scenes of the book, in which Sylvia and her aunt and cousins were denied enrollment at Westminster School, designated only for white children, her second-grade students reacted audibly. "That's messed up!" one child marveled. Virginia offered students ample time to discuss their responses to the text, first with a partner and then with the whole class. Confirming their comprehension, she asked, "Why were [the Mendez children] being told to go to the other school?" One child responded, "Because [the school staff] think that they're Mexican." Later, another child protested, "She's still American!" As they neared the end of the first chapter, Virginia returned to the students' comments. "[Noemi] was talking about how this reminded her of Rosa Parks and what happened [when she was arrested on the bus]. How does this remind you of some of the other books we've read?"

Students were quick to reply with examples related to segregation in busing and schools, including Rosa Parks and Ruby Bridges, and articulated skin color as the reason for this physical separation. When Virginia probed as to *why* this happened, Ariana explained, "[white people] don't like the Black people going to the white school." Students connected these events to what they had learned during their introduction to Japanese American incarceration through *The Bracelet*, as well as to stories from earlier in the school year. During the read-aloud of the third chapter of *Sylvia and Aki*, a student named Noemi shared, "I think that they're treating the people that are Mexican almost like the Black people and Martin Luther King, Jr." In response, Virginia wrote the word *inferior* on the dry erase board beside her at the carpet, where all students could see it.

"Can you say that? When you treat someone like they are inferior to you, that means that you think you're better than them. . . . In these books that we're reading, in a lot of the people that we've read [about] like Martin Luther King, the people are treated like they are—" Her students, unprompted yet in unison, declared, "inferior!" "As if they're inferior," Virginia reiterated. "Now how does that make you feel to know that people are being treated as if they're inferior just based on their skin color?" After students responded, Virginia posed a question to them. "What do you think our classroom would have looked like then?" Students replied "Dirty." "Messy." "Why do you think that our school would be dirty and separated?" Virginia inquired. Noemi, herself Mexican American, offered, "It would have been like a Mexican or Brown place." While Noemi was only speculating, the part of the city where the school was located was indeed historically Latinx, though development likely didn't begin until the 1960s and 1970s. Virginia urged her students to consider how this scenario might have played out for students if they had been in school during the time in which *Sylvia and Aki* was set. "How does that make you feel to think that somebody might treat us like we were inferior?"

After several students replied, Virginia shifted the conversation about inequity to the present. "Can I tell you something? There are still some situations in America today, where there are some schools where there's a lot of students who might be Mexican American, might be African American, whose schools are very run-down, they don't have clean drinking water, they have cracks in their ceiling so water gets through. Their schools are in very bad condition. And you know what? Nobody has done anything about it! Do you think that's fair today?" Students answered with resounding nos, and one student described seeing such a school described on *The Ellen Show*. The show's host, comedian Ellen DeGeneres, donated money to the school to provide technological devices and pay for repairs. Virginia continued, "So that means that some people saw that it wasn't fair, it wasn't just, and they decided to do something about it, right? So, if we see something like that or if we see those things are happening, what do you think we could do?" This was one of many conversations Virginia had with her students that positioned them as change agents, whose voices and opinions mattered, particularly when they observed something unjust or unfair.

While the chapters about the Mendez family helped students understand notions of race and racism, chapters focused on the Munemitsu family's experience at the War Relocation Authority camp in Poston sparked student conversation around what it meant to be American. Students summarized that Aki's father was taken away from the rest of the Munemitsu family because the US government "thought he was a threat." In particular, students articulated that the father was apprehended not because he was guilty of a crime but "because he's Japanese." Noemi, who was shy most of the school year but became increasingly vocal during these class discussions, objected, "He hasn't done anything to no one!" To further contextualize the events in *Sylvia and Aki*, Virginia screened an excerpt from a documentary about Fred Korematsu, a Japanese American man who sued the government for unconstitutional imprisonment during World War II.

During the documentary excerpt, a student named Adán gasped audibly. After the video clip ended, Virginia asked, "Adán, what were you thinking about just now? You heard [President Clinton] say Fred [Korematsu]. Did you hear who else?" Adán and several other students responded, "Rosa Parks!" The students were struck by the fact that a president of the United States would hold Japanese American Fred Korematsu in the same regard as famed civil rights leaders Rosa Parks and Martin Luther King, Jr. Virginia asked students what these people had in common. Noemi offered, "Fred and Rosa Parks didn't really have to go to jail for no reason. Because Rosa Parks back then didn't even need to move from the seat because she was where all the [Black] people are supposed to be ... and for no reason they take her to jail." As Virginia's second-grade class progressed through *Sylvia and Aki,* they continued to make connections and comparisons to other examples of injustice and activism across time and place.

As they read the book aloud each day, Virginia was intentional about asking students to summarize prior events before beginning a new chapter. These conversations allowed Virginia to support student comprehension and also allowed multiple students opportunities to articulate their developing understandings around race, racism, and injustice. During one such conversation, Virginia asked what Japanese Americans were doing before they were forced to leave their homes and live in prison camps. "Nothing," Adán replied. "They were just in their house!" "Nothing," Virginia repeated. "They were just living their lives," she paraphrased. Yet, despite having committed no crime or posing a valid threat to the state, Japanese Americans were, as Noemi phrased it, "separated from the white and Mexican people" and imprisoned, nonetheless. As this discussion shifted to comparisons between Japanese Americans and Mexican Americans in the text, a student named Dominique asked, "Why do they have to separate? Because we're different colors and we don't have to separate." Virginia wrote the word *inferior* on the board again and revisited the earlier conversation about contemporary school inequality.

In a final example, the class had a lengthy conversation during a scene in which Sylvia Mendez sees a sign posted in a diner window stating, "NO DOGS OR MEXICANS." Several students gasped audibly as

Virginia read this phrase aloud. Virginia asked them to share what made them uncomfortable with the sign's language. "They're calling them dogs because they don't like them," said Adán. Olga recounted, "A long time ago, there used to be signs that only white people could go and they used to be in a lot of places." Noemi shared, "They think Mexicans are now bad and they think that only white people can stay there . . . like, go away from me." Daisy, normally quiet during whole-group conversations, spoke up: "Whenever she had saw the sign it had kind of hurt her feelings . . . and me, Olga, and Ariana were talking, and me and Olga had said how it hurt our feelings, too, because we're both Mexican American." For Virginia's majority-Latinx students, this particular example of racial injustice was deeply personal. Yet, it was the first time they had encountered such an explicit example of anti-Mexican racism and discrimination in school, despite living in a state with a population that is 40 percent Latinx.

The personal nature of this example of discrimination was resounding, and it came up in later conversations many times, as did the mention of Fred Korematsu, demonstrating that young BIPOC children can both make sense of these issues and profoundly relate to them. When educators of early childhood and elementary children avoid conversations of race, racism, and discrimination, such evasion is often due to the adult's own discomfort. Moreover, white children are overwhelmingly those whose innocence is purportedly in need of protection, while Black and Brown children are often situated outside the public imagination of what childhood means, and thereby are viewed as less than human.[16] If civic education truly aims to prepare all citizens, our youngest learners must be treated *as* citizens and need opportunities to engage with BIPOC civic agency across the entirety of US history in meaningful and consistent ways.

THE POSSIBILITIES OF TRANSFORMATIVE JUSTICE IN CIVICS EDUCATION

Virginia's social change unit, as exemplified by her use of, and students' interactions with, *Sylvia and Aki,* illustrates the possibilities of transformative justice in civics education. In elementary classrooms, conversations around school segregation are often limited to the story of Ruby

Bridges, reducing the concept of racial injustice along a Black/white binary further reinforced by superficial historical narratives of Rosa Parks and Martin Luther King, Jr. While these examples are important, they provide students with a narrow understanding of race and racism that is relegated to the American South and presented as resolved.[17] By expanding the scope of the civil rights narrative in US history long before and after the traditional 1954–65 time period and dedicating prolonged periods of time and discussion to examples such as Mexican American Sylvia Mendez and Japanese Americans Aki Munemitsu and Fred Korematsu, Virginia's second graders were able to understand racism and discrimination as historical and contemporary issues against which many ethnoracial groups have struggled and continue to resist.

The highlighting of Mexican American and Japanese American resistance in Virginia's classroom was particularly important, as dominant historical narratives of BIPOC tend to very briefly mention and quickly resolve issues of oppression, especially with young learners. For example, Black/white segregation in public spaces is overwhelmingly centered in lessons about Martin Luther King, Jr., with the end of segregation typically tidily presented as an outcome of King's March on Washington speech (and a very decontextualized snippet of that speech, at that). Nearly always omitted are the multiple attempts on King's life, federal surveillance of King and many other civil rights activists, and public dislike for King at the time of his murder.[18] This insistence on happy endings and the whitewashing of BIPOC histories is an unfortunate norm in elementary social studies and a disservice to all children, who miss opportunities to learn about and from historical and contemporary figures who have resisted white supremacy in the alleged land of the free and home of the brave.[19]

The cases featured in *Sylvia and Aki* resulted in famous court decisions: *Mendez v. Westminster*, the case initiated and led by Sylvia Mendez's father, ended school segregation in the state of California and is widely cited as precedent for the landmark *Brown v. Board of Education* case that outlawed school segregation nationwide. *Korematsu v. United States* was ruled in 1944, in favor of Japanese American detention as a military necessity; the case was reopened in 1983 with new evidence revealing that Japanese Americans posed no military threat to the United

States. Korematsu's case, voided in 1983 (although the Supreme Court decision still stands), influenced the effort toward redress that culminated in the Civil Liberties Act of 1988.[20] Presentation of the individuals in these cases as "ordinary people," rather than messianic figures like Martin Luther King, Jr., is significant for BIPOC youth, yet rarely occurs in social studies curricula, particularly regarding BIPOC historical figures.[21]

All children need diverse examples of civic members, civic agency, and civic resistance, yet the examples offered time and again to our youngest learners rely on the same white, male pantheon of American heroes, with a negligible number of BIPOC figures included in support of the overarching narrative of American progress and exceptionalism.[22] James Banks has argued that civic education must evolve to prepare students "to participate in the construction of a national civic culture that is a moral and just community that embodies democratic ideals and values."[23] Such a national civic culture must be deliberate in recognizing voices that have been described by author Arundhati Roy as deliberately silenced or preferably unheard.[24] A transformative justice approach in civics education requires disruption of the exclusionary master narrative through the intentional centering of BIPOC stories throughout the curriculum, rather than in isolation.[25] As Virginia and her second-grade students illustrate, such work is powerful, personal, and possible.

SECTION IV

WHY LANGUAGE MATTERS

Carla Shalaby

In second grade, I wrote a story about a leaf that refused to fall when autumn came. It was autobiographical in spirit; a stubborn leaf brought to life by a stubborn child. Proudly, I read the story aloud to my classmates during an Author's Chair session. I knew I was an author because my teacher told me so. She called all of us *writers,* consistently. She labeled the chair *For Authors Only,* and we interacted with one another's use of language from that extraordinary, ordinary chair.

When I got to the end, anticipating the usual applause, constructive feedback, and questions that followed our readings, I instead found that one of my classmates was crying. I remember this as if it happened yesterday. She felt sorry for the leaf, she explained. It made her sad to think about that lone leaf hanging there, even after all its friends and family had moved on. I defended myself by explaining that those leaves just fly off, dry up, and turn into dirt.

"I'd rather turn into dirt than be alive and all alone!" she argued, sobbing.

I looked to my teacher for rescue. "Hmmm," she said. "Look at what an important conversation we've begun." She elevated the discourse beyond an ensuing conflict and instead toward a genuine exchange of ideas. And then she facilitated a discussion on what it really means to be alive, with a group of six- and seven-year-olds, based on a text I had produced.

I remember nothing about the discussion itself because, self-absorbed as I was, I was distracted by the fact that I had scribbled some symbols out of the silver lead of my pencil and those symbols came together to form words and sentences—and, ultimately, a use of language that somehow made another human being cry. It felt like something strange and magical had happened. I didn't know if the magic was good or bad, but I knew it was powerful. I knew that words mattered. I knew that stories could make us wonder what it means to be alive. I knew that the use of language had something to do with being human, and with being in relation to other humans.

That understanding was, of course, not the result of any single event, though this event did do something to cement my understandings of the power of language. I had very progressive, politically conscious, Black teachers for three consecutive years in kindergarten, first grade, and second grade, and they collaborated closely to make their practices and values intentionally consistent across three of the most formative learning years of my life. These educators did not just teach us to read, write, and speak; they taught us the *power* of reading, writing, and speaking, and made sure we understood our responsibility to use that power wisely, strategically, and lovingly. They knew that the use of language was political, cultural work. Through the books, poems, and songs they shared with us, the way they spoke to my mother—who was still practicing her use of English as a native speaker of Arabic—and, most of all, through the everyday model of how *they* used language, I learned that language matters and that the ways we exchange language have everything to do with how we *be human* with one another.

These educators rejected the notion that *sticks and stones may break our bones, but words will never hurt us.* They taught us that words do hurt. Words hurt, and they also heal; they harm and they repair; they shape and assert identities; they open and close possibilities; they assign blame and offer apology; they are both weapons and shields; they frame problems in ways that narrow or broaden solutions. Language matters, and the ways educators treat and use language matters, particularly with respect to how young people come to treat and use language themselves. More than that, the ways educators use language matter to how young people think of themselves and others. The way we talk is a series of lessons to children; they learn from each and every thing we say or don't say, and each and every thing we allow *them* to say or not say.

Let's consider an example. "Line up, boys and girls," is a simple directive I hear ubiquitously in early childhood classrooms. Every time I hear a use of language that is taken for granted because of its frequency and normalcy, I feel compelled to wonder what possibilities it opens up or closes off. Here, the use of language is a command that can range from gentle to threatening, depending on tone and volume. It is a use of language that offers a world in which only two possible gender identities are normalized. It is not meant to be an opportunity for learning or discussion, but a clear and easy directive to simply move potentially unruly young bodies from one place to another.

One alternative to this directive is: "Let's organize ourselves to move through the halls in a way that considers others." This use of language opens up and closes off a different range of possibilities. It closes the possibility of speed and efficiency. But what possibilities does it open? It is an invitation to solve a problem rather than a command to comply with an already-solved problem. So the possibility of learning and discussion is now open. It presents the goal as being considerate to others, which offers up new possibilities for how we might move; are there alternatives to a silent line that is still considerate of others? Because it draws focus away from compliance with a rule-based command and instead toward consideration for other people as our primary purpose, it is a use of language that becomes part of restorative practice. Instead of children making decisions based on the desire to avoid punishment, they instead make decisions based on the desire to care about other people. This phrasing also eliminates one everyday example of exclusion and othering produced by phrases such as "boys and girls."

Language creates futures because the way we talk impacts the way children think, what they believe to be normal, and how they understand the purpose(s) of our time together in school. "Let's organize ourselves" is a different use of power than "line up." These differences are not semantic. The language signals something about how educators position themselves in relation to young people, how they understand their purpose and role, their power and authority.

Language matters beyond simply avoiding the egregiously harmful labels often assigned: good kids and troublemakers, low and high readers, above or below grade level students, remedial or gifted learners. It matters beyond eliminating the kinds of frames that have us calling Black and Brown schools "disadvantaged" instead of calling wealthy white schools "intentionally overadvantaged." Like the movement to abolish prisons and police, our use of language is as much about what we want to build as it is about what we want to dismantle. What futures can educators and young people create, together, through language? What restorative possibilities might we open up? What educational purposes can we shift through language? What models of power can we offer through our words?

Rather than be afraid to use the wrong language—intimidated by how easy it is to cause harm through language—educators can feel empowered to make really exciting, intentional decisions about how to use language in support of love, to center the struggle for justice in how we use power, and to offer young people models of language that open up the possibility of relating to each other in humane ways that give rise to collective care. If we know that language matters, let's not just stop using it to cause harm. Let's use language—with intention, clarity, and purpose—to heal.

10 Restoring What Matters:
Reflections on Classroom Language Practices and Ideologies

Hannah Graham,[1] *National Louis University*
Adam Musser,[1] *University of California–Davis*

WE ARE CONCERNED with an unoriginal but persistent challenge: how to prepare teachers to teach in ways that humanize all students. Much has been written on the teacher mindsets necessary to provoke change and challenge systems of oppression in schools.[2] As former middle and high school classroom teachers and current university teacher educators, we have spent ample time considering and presenting curricula that push our students to reflect critically on the ideologies and biases that have resulted in opportunity gaps and an education debt,[3] harmful zero-tolerance policies, and pejorative adultist attitudes toward young people.[4]

Recent scholarship has enjoined educators to (re)consider connections between theory, mindset, and practice by (re)emphasizing the role of practice in creating equitable learning spaces. Enhancing this call, Maisha T. Winn has urged practitioners to reflect on *in situ* positions and tools that evoke meaningful change in classrooms.[5] In this chapter, we reflect on the core of Winn's four-part framework and the mediational role of facilitative language in our own classrooms as a means to explore the complex meta and consequential aspects of endeavors to transform teacher education.

THEORY AND PRACTICE:
MOVING TOWARD RESTORATIVE LANGUAGE PRAXIS

Recent scholarship in K–12 classrooms reflects revitalized efforts to catalogue the precise practices necessary to spark learning. While the work of teacher education spirals perennially between theory and practice, critical interpretations of classroom communities and facilitation efforts that promote or quash equity have renewed interest in bridging the perceived divide between these two domains. Recent findings suggest that teachers must be taught to engage in practices that exemplify specific theories and epistemologies to be able to actualize them. Deborah Loewenberg Ball argues that preparing teachers to engage in "high leverage practices" is not only vital across grades, areas, and domains but also necessary to ensure educational parity:

> If teachers fail to help significant numbers of their students learn, it may be because they do not receive sufficiently explicit professional training that would help them to do so. To blame the environment, the children, or their parents denies the efficacy of skilled professional practice and violates the fundamental ethical commitment of the teaching profession: to help every student succeed.[6]

Moreover, scholars argue that the identification of practices is integral to the manifestation of social justice in education.[7] Without them, teachers and student teachers may revert to "business as usual" modes of teaching and learning, some of which may even be couched and justified using the language of asset pedagogies. In presenting a paradigm-to-stance theory of restorative justice work, Winn proposes a framework with four concentric stances: History Matters, Race Matters, Justice Matters, and Language Matters. At the center of this framework is language, which provides tools for educators to "build or dismantle potential futures" and build socio-critical literacies in which lived experiences are valued, nurtured, and centered.[8]

We recognize that teacher practices cannot be our only concern. Every practice is informed by ideology. All teachers, including teacher educators, have deeply held, nuanced, and often unexamined ideologies about schooling, teaching, and learning. Writing of students "anxious to learn the latest teaching methods—methods that they hope will somehow magically work on minorit[ized] students," Lilia Bartolomé warns teacher educators against inflated dependence on teaching methods:

> Although it is important to identify useful and promising instructional programs and strategies, it is erroneous to assume that blind replication of instructional programs or teacher mastery of particular teaching methods, in and of themselves, will guarantee successful student learning, especially when we are discussing populations that historically have been mistreated and miseducated by the schools.[9]

Teacher education, the collective undertaking of teacher educators and the student teachers they "educate," requires a paradigm shift. With others in this book, we argue for a shift toward restorative transformative justice in education that restores students' humanity and transforms teaching and learning in all schools. To advance dialogue and scholarship around actualizing this task, we turn to the closest source of evidence we have: our own practice. This chapter highlights teaching narratives that showcase how we have struggled to make our own shifts toward justice, equity, and freedom through language use in our classrooms, particularly noting how our identities have played key roles in determining what to designate as ideal language practices, and how.

HANNAH'S NARRATIVE:
IDEOLOGY AND PRACTICE IN AN ELEMENTARY READING COURSE FOR TEACHER CANDIDATES

When undergraduate elementary school teacher candidates who are required to take my content area reading course enter my classroom on the first day, we always begin in a circle. I ask, *"Why are you here?"* and *"What positive reading experiences do you recall from your childhood?"* The group dependably reflects the teaching force in the United States, which is overwhelmingly white and female. As these new students share thoughts and memories, a pattern begins to emerge: most report having experiences in school that they would like to learn how to replicate. In fact, candidates regularly report affirming experiences in school that "proved" they are good readers. I am still surprised at the number of times candidates report standardized test score receipt as an encouraging and memorable experience.

These stories are indicative of the post–No Child Left Behind, heavily standardized, and unrelentingly standards-aligned educational milieu my candidates were raised in. In such contexts, reading is mercilessly metricized into predetermined components. Achieving proficiency is contingent upon finding what the text "says" and rewarded with concrete accolades (e.g., moving to a "higher" group of readers or being allowed to read from the next level of book choices). To many of my students, the process of finding the "correct answer" is *how* a person learns to read, whereas time spent reading with family members is pleasant but extraneous to development. These teacher candidates articulate an expectation that our class will prepare them to engage in practices they experienced: how to level books, sort students, and fill "gaps" in knowledge. While I would like to spend every class critiquing these very ideologies, scholarship suggests that offering solutions and problematizing systems must be central components of the teaching and learning process, or my students will likely revert to whatever new method or "phantom" policies are in use in their prospective schools.[10] My candidates take another course in early reading methods further into their program, so we focus on reading contexts and processes, which I recognize as a unique opportunity to connect epistemologies, practices, and possibilities.

It is (still) essential to establish that there is a problem with how reading is conceptualized in schools, particularly given my students' self-reported "positive" experiences with learning to read in settings that rely on denigration of some for others to succeed. The crux of the syllabus lies in its focus on language: how the words used to designate textual interpretations on the spectrum of "bad" to "good" send messages to children about who they are as readers, students, and people, and the racialized impact of these categories. To begin, we read James Paul Gee's *Discourse Systems and Aspirin Bottles* alongside sections of Arlette Ingram Willis's *Reading Comprehension Research and Testing in the U.S.*, a comprehensive history of the white-hegemonic reading comprehension testing system and its reliance on seemingly benign terms (e.g., "best" answer) to instantiate dominant lenses.[11] These readings create opportunities to discuss how common metaphors (e.g., climbing the reading ladder); monologic language; and white, hetero-centric lenses broadly mediate reading experiences and expectations, revealing the myopic epistemologies that dominate our schools and create false hierarchies among readers.

To imagine how teachers might use language to disrupt patterns of instruction that focus on getting the "right" answer, we read Maren S. Aukerman's *When Reading It Wrong Is Getting It Right* and segments of Mary Margaret Juzwik and colleagues' *Inspiring Dialogue: Talking to Learn in the Secondary English Classroom*. We examine texts as a starting point for dialogic conversation and the engagement of all students (rather than conversations to "find"); watch videos of classrooms in action; and imagine the kinds of questions, dialogic stances, and spaces that might quell or propel discussion when students bring varied interpretations to bear.[12] In their midterm and final papers, many of my students write about how the course altered their understandings of reading and sparked within them a newfound commitment to engaging in processes that value multiple interpretations as a means of moving classroom spaces toward equity.

It is never as simple as that, though. As we discuss the texts, I become deeply aware of the meta and racialized undercurrents at play in our space. I point out to candidates that I am a white woman commanding and receiving authority regarding the very material I present precisely because of my identity, introducing a core understanding: white interpretation of educational material is the norm and any other interpretation is situated as an incorrect diversion. Moreover, I explain, designations of "good" and "bad" interpretation are inherently racialized and stymie hopes of equity.

These currents, and my identification of what teachers "should" do, often play out in pronounced and complicated ways. Last year, a white student stopped our class with an urgent question related to her recent visit to a charter school in a nearby city wherein the student population and administrators were nearly all Black. This school was clearly and proudly steeped in the hegemonic practices we read about and disparaged in class. Worried about choosing the "right" way to teach, and noting that the language practices we discussed in class seemed like long-term solutions and more complicated than the program this charter school had purchased, she wondered aloud which practices would best prepare students to achieve in an already unfair system? I was immediately reminded of Lisa Delpit's *Other People's Children* and the great number of people who desperately want children to succeed in an unfair system.[13]

As this student spoke, my own insistence on a single ideology and corresponding practice (equity through dialogism) as unquestionably "right" seemed precarious and patronizing. I had not considered or created an opportunity for students to explore the (necessary) navigation between practices that I had presented as incommensurate in a zero-sum game. In reality, nearly all my students will end up teaching in diverse schools where they must make numerous and often layered decisions about how to navigate school curricula in ways that advance all students' sense of worth. If pedagogic practices and the ideologies that undergird them are polarized as "good" or "bad," what use are efforts to navigate?

Discovering with each course I teach the importance of practicing what I preach about looking beyond good/bad practice binaries, I have become very intentional about providing examples of teachers who are pursuing equity under various constraints and for various reasons.

As a white woman, I am also reminded that my own understandings of practice, ideology, and urgency will always be tempered by the opportunities afforded by my whiteness. Rather than presenting practices with a matching ideology, which further reifies the deeply problematic concept of one-fits-all "best" practice, I seek instead to forefront the radical act of navigation toward transformational equity. The mantra that language matters needs to be couched: our focus is on stance, goal, *and* practice. Language mediates my own preservice teacher understandings of the role of language. I become more cognizant with each semester that what and how I present sets up the next generation of teachers to embrace a critical journey that sees language as the journey, not the goal.

ADAM'S NARRATIVE:
NAMES, LANGUAGE, AND RESTORATIVE JUSTICE
IN UNDERGRADUATE EDUCATION COURSES

The start of every new quarter or semester is exciting. I get excited to redesign the syllabus and meet new students, and for the energy teaching provides across my other professional responsibilities. There are often sixty or seventy undergraduate students in my education courses, and not all of them want to be teachers. Although my syllabus makes clear that our course will introduce a paradigm shift from education focused on classroom compliance and social control to an educational commitment that cultivates relationships, this is not a teacher education course. I organize my syllabus around the aforementioned four pedagogical stances—History Matters, Race Matters, Justice Matters, and Language Matters—and introduce restorative justice ethics throughout the course.[14] Always, I ask myself, *"What am I trying to restore when I advance restorative justice stances in my pedagogy?"*

There is a lot about education and schooling that I want no part in restoring. The dehumanizing treatment of students and their families who are seen as not valuing education, erasure of Black and Indigenous epistemologies that offer interconnected understandings of our relationships to each other and the earth, punitive disciplinary approaches that parents would never tolerate for their own children—none of these norms are worth restoring. In his reflections twenty-five years after publishing *Changing Lenses: Restorative Justice for Our Times*, Howard Zehr writes that "re- words are problematic because many stakeholders and others interested in this field are not seeking to go back to a previous state of being but forward to new or better conditions."[15]

What, then, do practitioners seek to restore when we bring restorative justice into our classrooms? The answer I return to, until another emerges, is full humanity. While there are positive implications for my own and others' humanity as restorative justice educators, as well, it is the humanity of students, too often stripped away by years and years of mainstream methods of schooling, that I particularly try to restore in my classes. To paint a picture of this process, I share two examples of my efforts and the role of language in these efforts.

I am a cisgender, heterosexual, white male, continuously learning and unlearning ideologies that inform my pedagogies. Particularly in schools and classrooms, spaces designed to elevate white language practices and ideologies, I try to show, on the very first day, that I am aware of the historical causes that have put me in a position to become and be the teacher at the front of the room.[16] One way I have done this is by showing Kimberlé Crenshaw's TEDWomen Talk, "The Urgency of Intersectionality."[17] Crenshaw draws attention to the disparity between our knowledge of the names of Black boys and men killed by police (e.g., Freddie Gray, Eric Garner, Tamir Rice, Michael Brown) and our knowledge of the names of Black girls and women killed by police (e.g. Tanisha Anderson, Meagan Hockaday, Aura Rosser, Michelle Cusseaux). After articulating her theory of intersectionality, Crenshaw closes her talk with a moving tribute to the lives of Black girls and women killed by police. As Abby Dobson joins Crenshaw on stage to sing "Say Her Name," the audience watches video images of police violence against Black women and girls and still images of girls and women who have died by the hands of the police.

I thought a lot about showing Crenshaw's TEDWomen Talk in class. I did not want to use the deaths and trauma of Black women and girls to show my students I was "woke," and I was aware of ongoing debate about showing images of Black death, often captured on bystanders' cell phone cameras, on social media platforms. Some argue, "We have to show this," while others plead, "We don't need to see more Black death online." I finally decided this TEDWomen Talk was a way to say to my class that this is what our education together will be like. We will center Black women. We will center endarkened epistemologies. We will name state-sanctioned oppression, violence, and murder. And we will do all that as we ask, "How do we teach in ways that stop the killing?"[18]

As often happens on the first day, my pacing was off. We watched Crenshaw's talk up to the very last minute of class. There was no time to say or share anything. While several students formed a line to speak to me, one waited patiently in the back of the room, until everyone left. She then told me how uncomfortable she had been watching Crenshaw's talk. Not because of the message, which she agreed with, but because the sounds and images of police violence had triggered memories of abuse and violence she had experienced/suffered/survived in her own life at the hands of powerful men. She had found herself at the back of a small classroom, in the dark, on the first day of class, having a panic attack with no real way out of the space. And my intention had been to restore her humanity.

I did not know this student. I did not know her story. I hardly even knew her name. And as she told me what it felt like to be stuck in the back of the classroom among unfamiliar peers as I projected images and sounds of male-perpetrated violence against women into the room, I was in shock. She left soon after she told me and I took the bus home, thinking about what to say in the email I would write to her. In it, I thanked her for being brave enough to share what she told me, acknowledged the pain I caused her, and promised to do better. What I did not do, in my email, was ask her how I could make it right. Though she returned to class the following week, she eventually dropped the course.

When we say that language matters, what do we mean? What does it mean for a teacher to tell eighty undergraduate students in a mid-level education course that language matters? How does a teacher show that language matters? I no longer show Crenshaw's TEDWomen Talk on the first day of class. Instead, I ask students, *"Who are you?"* and *"Why are you here?"* I personally answer those questions first, setting an example with a type of response not often shared in undergraduate lecture courses on day one—or any day.

> My name is Adam, and the most important thing you can know about me is that I am a father. Being a dad is the best thing in the world, and I love my daughter more than I knew I could love anybody. I am also a partner to a woman who does amazing things, a son, a brother, an uncle, a friend, a student, a teacher. I love to cook, and eat, and drink wine with my family and friends. I used to be a runner. I love to read. I have always been good at school because schools were made for me to be good at. I am here because I think education can be a transformative, humanizing project toward freedom, and that it's often not. I am here to learn with you and from you because I know that you possess knowledge and wisdom and creativity and genius that I don't know about and that most of your schooling has never asked you to share. I am here because I love teaching and learning this way.

From there commences a breathtaking and inspirational collective sharing of stories among strangers. With one class, this took almost two days. After this process is over, when we have just begun the work of using language to build community that will sustain us while we read and view texts that are true and terrifying, I ask students to design name tags. With colored pencils or markers or crayons or plain, blue Bic pens, students sketch their names and pronouns large enough for all to see. I ask students to think about what they know about their names as they create their name tag, and then, in small groups, we share the stories of our names.

The first assigned course reading, which students complete after designing their name tags, is "Teachers, Please Learn Our Names! Racial Microaggressions and the K–12 Classroom." In it, Rita Kohli and Daniel G. Solórzano write that for many "Students of Color, a mispronunciation of their name is one of the many ways in which their cultural heritage is devalued."[19] They continue, pointing out that:

> When a child goes to school and reads textbooks that do not reference her culture, sees no teachers or administrators that looks like her, and perhaps does not hear her home language, the mispronunciation of her name is an additional example for that student that who they are and where they come from is not important.[20]

One student wrote in her response piece that she resented her parents for her nonwhite name and remembered asking her mother if she could have an English name so that students and teachers would not make fun of her and make her feel small. Her name had been given to her by a Buddhist monk, respected by her parents, yet her schooling experiences in the United States made her want a white, English name, like Caroline. After our first week of class, after she had designed her name tag, shared her name story, and read Kohli and Solórzano's piece, this student also wrote:

> After today I no longer will put (Caroline) after my name just in case someone would have a preference towards the anglicized, meaningless name that does not represent who I am: a proud Korean-American being the first one in her family to attend and graduate from a university.

Our names are often our first experience with language. If we believe that language matters, we must honor and value our students' names. And we must show them that we do, truly, honor and value them as learners and as individuals. As a monolingual, English-only speaker who cannot roll his *r*'s or make the sounds required to say many Chinese, Vietnamese, and Hmong names properly, I recognize that failure to pronounce my students' names correctly is my failure, not theirs. I tell them this, and I invite them to help me learn how to say their names. They are the teachers. I am the student.

CONCLUSION

As scholars dedicated to the craft of teaching and growth in our practice, we see the work of reflecting on our experiences as vital to instantiating discussions surrounding the everyday responsiveness of our practice. How do we put language practices into use while teaching the next generation of teacher learners? How do we teach for and about practices that transform while creating the space for students to experience these practices—and still attend to the urgency that is an inevitable part of teaching and learning in dire sociopolitical contexts? *What* are we trying to restore when we use language restoratively? The fact we are both white educators is not ancillary to this work. Our whiteness confers unwarranted authority while shielding us from rebuke. We make our mistakes with regret, but without fear.

To be clear, our mistakes can be quite harmful, as Adam's was for the student forced to confront panic in the back of his classroom on her first day in a new learning community. A restorative justice paradigm suggests that we should not end our apologies with the statement *"I'm sorry,"* but with the question *"How can I make this right?"* That is, after all, the question all critical, justice-oriented teachers are asking themselves—and *this* can represent any and every harmful thing our students experience, both in and outside of school settings.

For some decades, teacher education has appropriately been concerned with mindset. The examined and unexamined ideologies teachers hold shape how they will enact every new method and pedagogical practice. The good intentions of well-meaning teachers are not enough to overcome the ideologies of competition and racialized difference that continue to dominate schooling today. It is most important, then, that we use and practice language in ways that clarify which teaching ideologies we advance and which we resist. When Hannah helps students understand there is no such thing as "good" and "bad" readers, and Adam asks students to listen to stories of their peers' names, we seek to manifest ideologies of humanity and interrelatedness that are at the heart of restorative justice frameworks.[21]

In education, where manifestation has too often been understood as replicable practice, language practices are vital in communicating intention to teacher candidates and their future students. A meditation on the complexities of walking this line, our reflections highlight how our identities will always mediate the practices we choose to present and advocate. What follows is the not-so-simple truth: we will always need to revisit, audit, and rethink *why* we consider practices and presentations optimal, and related understandings must be informed by emergent revelations about ourselves, our students, and our context.

11 Transforming Social Studies Education:
Lessons from Youth on Why Language Matters

Elizabeth Montaño

AS A TWENTY-YEAR OLD junior in college, I became a paraeducator (educational assistant) at a large and diverse public middle school in Los Angeles. I was responsible for supporting teachers with students identified as English language learners. One of my assignments was a sixth-grade humanities (language arts and social studies) class with over thirty students. On my first day, when I walked into the classroom, the teacher immediately pointed to the back of the room, where three Latina Spanish-speaking students sat at a round table with index cards, pencils, and a Dr. Seuss book. Each student looked up at me, wondering who I was. I spoke to them in Spanish, asking their names and what they had learned in this class. They spoke very little, yet I was shocked to learn that the back of the classroom had been their designated space the entire semester. I wondered who would have helped them if I had not taken the position. We opened the Dr. Seuss book and I began reading it aloud while they created flashcards for vocabulary words such as *cat, mat,* and *hat*. Meanwhile the rest of their classmates read novels and poetry and learned about ancient Egypt.

LANGUAGE MATTERS

The work we did for the rest of the semester provided me with experiential underpinnings that aligned my future practice to the Language Matters stance of Maisha T. Winn's restorative justice framework.[1] The three youth in this class were labeled and misplaced as students who could not learn with the rest of their classmates. I, a Chicana, daughter of Mexican immigrants and a Spanish-speaking college student, was hired to not only help the students but ultimately take charge of them and their learning. The adults in the school were not taking responsibility for the education of students labeled as "English language learners." Winn states that "being mindful about how one uses language to speak to and about children—especially children from historically marginalized communities—is foundational to healthy relationships and should never be undermined."[2] The students in this classroom were being spoken to in a language they were not familiar with and spoken about in the most harmful ways. Setting out to change that, I worked with this group for the rest of the semester, twice a week, for one class period.

We started a project exploring terms related to their new schooling experiences, including *teacher, cafeteria, nutrition,* and *books*. We walked around campus taking pictures of different people and places using a disposable camera. Then, students created a bilingual book about their school for future "newcomer" students. As they were learning the English language, they were also learning about schools and communities in personally relevant ways. With our growing relationship, the three students asked me many questions, such as why Black and Brown youth were always in detention and why the ESL (English as a Second Language) classrooms were located in the furthest bungalows. While they expressed gratitude and excitement about being in school, I knew they were experiencing and dealing with trauma as newcomers to the school, community, and country. There were teachers in the school who did not answer their questions, and there were cafeteria workers who refused to serve them if they did not speak English. Students knew that they were labeled and treated differently, yet they showed up everyday to learn.

I had no teacher training, yet in many ways I understood the students better than most of their teachers. My family was working class and immigrated from Mexico in the early 1970s. I, too, was bussed to a magnet school away from my neighborhood school. Yet, my experiences differed in that I was labeled "gifted" and went to predominantly white schools where none of my teachers looked like me. It became important for me to provide these students with rich and culturally relevant English language arts and social studies instruction.[3] We finished the semester by reading *The House on Mango Street*, by Sandra Cisneros, and writing our own stories. Students wrote of injustices faced by family members who were exploited as laborers and experienced police harassment. I planned lessons and activities they could do when I was not in class with them. Most impactful that year were the lessons I learned from their stories and experiences as newcomers; learnings that led me to seek a teaching credential in Secondary English.

LEARNING FROM YOUTH

My time working with these students impacted me greatly, and I went on to teach middle school for eleven years. This chapter serves as a reflection of how my middle school students pushed my teaching to center the importance of language and taught me to be a justice-centered educator. My goal as a teacher was to create learning experiences for students that encouraged them to be critical thinkers and allowed them to see themselves in the curriculum. In this chapter, I share how my students utilized curricula to question historical events, historical injustices, and various legacies of those injustices evident in their own lived experiences. Each example shows how language mattered for students' processes of questioning and centering justice in the curriculum. It has been twenty years since my first teaching experience, and as I reflect on those experiences, I see alignment with scholars today who seek to transform education through the lens and work of restorative justice. In this chapter I reflect on how student experiences pushed me to enact a Language Matters pedagogical stance throughout my language arts and social studies instruction.

WHY LANGUAGE MATTERS IN THE SOCIAL STUDIES CLASSROOM

When I started my K–12 teaching career, I did not use the language of restorative justice when referring to my teaching. Throughout the years, I have encountered paradigms that speak to the ways that I have approached teaching and learning. In 2018, Maisha T. Winn proposed a pathway to transforming education through restorative justice, asking educators to develop discourses that "allow participants to capitalize on their individual and shared histories in order to construct more accurate portrayals of who they are and their positionality in the world."[4] Winn outlines a set of complementary pedagogical stances that allow educators and administrators to shift mindsets in ways that prepare them to successfully initiate and continue the ongoing work of restorative justice.

Winn's framework situates History Matters, Race Matters, Justice Matters, and Language Matters as pedagogical stances that allow an individual or learning community to begin the work of "disrupting inequities and dismantling racial and other injustices," in addition to replacing the "boundaries and barriers associated with hurtful histories, policies, practices, and labels."[5] The fourth stance, Language Matters, calls educators to challenge labels and notions of citizenship, provide critical language, and readjust discourses. In essence, Language Matters asks educators to dismantle language that harms students and their families and communities. In this chapter, I reflect on instances where my students taught me how Language Matters in the teaching of social studies, and share suggestions regarding how teachers can utilize language, narratives, and discourses around students' histories and experiences to center justice at the heart of teaching and improve educational experiences for minoritized children and youth.

SOCIAL STUDIES AS A TRANSFORMATIVE SPACE

I began teaching in 2001, fresh out of a teacher education program in northern California. I was hired by a small charter school in Oakland to teach eighth-grade humanities, eighth-grade physical education, seventh-grade physical education, and Spanish for Spanish speakers. I was twenty-three years old with a credential in teaching secondary English as I prepared to teach these four content areas while completing my master's thesis. Students of various linguistic backgrounds with wildly diverse school experiences shared one classroom. The eighth-grade American history curriculum was my saving grace. I worked with a more experienced teacher who adapted the *History Alive* curriculum and made it relevant and accessible to our student population.[6] We had very few resources but a clear sense that our students could and should engage in a social studies curriculum relevant to their lives and experiences as youth of color growing up in Oakland.

Ten days into my first year of teaching, I woke up to the news of airplanes striking the Twin Towers in New York City. It was an ominous feeling, but I got ready for work and was unsurprised to find a full classroom of students. We spent all morning discussing students' feelings, fears, and questions. What stood out was the confusion felt by Muslim, Black, undocumented, and other youth as to how a "war" would impact them and their families. Students wrote poems that week reflecting their fears and challenges in this post-9/11 world. There were so many uncertainties, and it became even more important to weave rich justice-centered social studies learning into our daily curriculum.

While I had received training that I believed would help me support language and literacy development among students in grades 6–12, I struggled with adapting these pedagogical practices in my own classroom contexts. What was missing from my teaching were the student voices that would eventually enrich my pedagogical and instructional practices. As a first-year teacher I made many mistakes, but something that stayed with me was the value of listening to students, adapting the curriculum to their interests and needs, and centering justice in the social studies curriculum. The following reflections relate to some of the many instances where my middle school students' experiences and perspectives helped me center justice and language in my instruction.

Perspectives of Conquest

After teaching four years of sixth grade, I was asked to loop with my students and teach seventh grade. I had always heard, "If you can teach seventh grade, you can teach anything," and was frankly terrified. There was one bright light of switching to seventh grade: teaching the Americas! Despite the fact that Latina/o/x students represent over 50 percent of the student population in California public schools,[7] this is the only point at which the California History-Social Science (CA HSS) Standards include content related to Pre-Columbian Mesoamerican and Andean civilizations.[8] Grade 7 standards require that students know and are able to describe geographic locations, farming techniques, societal roles, artistic and oral traditions, and achievements associated with the Aztec, Mayan, and Incan civilizations, respectively. One standard asks students to explain how Aztec and Incan civilizations were defeated by the Spanish. Despite the opportunity to create rich content around these themes, scholars have shown that the (one) unit on Mesoamerican civilizations is often poorly taught and riddled with stereotypes and misrepresentations, often with overwhelming emphasis on ritual sacrifice.[9] While the *History Alive* curriculum attempts to provide students with historical thinking and perspective taking, it remains limited in scope and frames history from the traditional American narrative removed from students' roots and lived experiences.

Given that 90 percent of the students in my classroom traced their roots to Mexico and Central America, it became imperative that I create a robust unit of study that went beyond state standards. I wanted to connect phenomena and patterns in history to current Latina/o/x experiences in Los Angeles. As we began the unit, we looked at images collected from museums and online forums in order to form a KWL (What I Know, What I Want to Know, What I Learned) on the unit. Students typically knew the Aztec civilization was in Mexico, but beyond that there were few things they felt they knew (at least initially). When students mentioned the Spaniards, some students appeared confused by the terms *conquistador* and *colonizer*. To break down some of the confusing language, I wrote up and organized terms such as *civilization, civil, civilized* by their roots and word parts (table 11.1). This activity supported language and content development for everyone in the room and allowed us to start subsequent conversations by tracing epistemological definitions and labels. Students created a vocabulary chart in their notebooks, where they also drew pictures and brainstormed additional terms that fit with the vocabulary we focused on.

The language lesson was not part of the curriculum and emerged from student exploration. Students wondered why the term *colonist* was applied to the British who settled in what is now the United States, yet the Spaniards were labeled *conquistador* (conqueror). Allowing students to explore the power of language and think through the decision to refer to a Spaniard as a *conquistador*, rather than a *colonizer*, in a particular

TABLE 11.1 Conquest terminology

Conquest	Colonize	Civilization
Conquer	Colony	Civilized
Conquistador	Colonizer	Civil
	Colonist	
Mission		Spain
Missionary	Christianity	Spanish
	Christian	Spaniard
	Christ	

text gave us all opportunities to agree on the importance of terminology when contextualizing a significant event in history. It became a necessary practice to explore how our history books describe and name colonization in different contexts. Students wondered if it was a "good thing" to be a colony, noting that it sounded like Americans did not like to be colonized, though American colonists were "the good guys."

We then made connections to how Mexico and other Latin American countries had to fight for their independence from Spain, much like the US had to fight for independence from England. We questioned the term *revolution* and why in the US it is labeled as positive only when Americans are leading the cause but often labeled as negative when discussing other nations' efforts to seek independence. Year to year, students wondered how Spain and England described these *conquests* and subsequent *revolutions* in their own textbooks. The connections between the language used in textbooks and the perspectives of each country in describing their story led to critical questions about how power influences whose history gets told.

Translating the Conquest

One activity adapted from the *History Alive* curriculum gave students opportunities to act out skits regarding life in the great city of Tenochtitlan, incorporating farming techniques, religious practices, and initial contact between Aztecs and Spaniards. The curriculum included images of the *mercados* and descriptive information from the textbook. I added primary documents written in both Spanish and English that allowed students to delve deeper into the perspectives of various groups in Tenochtitlan. Students had four class periods to read the material; organize their skits; create their dialogue, sets, and props; and perform their skits. The group acting out a meeting between Aztecs and Spaniards went last. When they began, students in Spaniard roles spoke Spanish, students in Aztec roles spoke very little, mostly using gestures, and one student, who identified as Filipina (I will call her Isabel), took on the role of Malintzin, the famous interpreter of the Aztecs. While there are many perspectives regarding whether Malintzin was an asset or a traitor to the Aztecs, students gave her a central role in their skit. During moments of interpretation between Aztecs and Spaniards, Isabel spoke in Tagalog to the Aztecs and an approximated form of Spanish when speaking to the Spaniards. Part of the act was that the students who were interpreting Aztecs would nod and rely on Isabel as their main source of communication. The students interpreting Spaniards utilized this trusting relationship to take advantage and eventually conquer the Aztec empire. The rest of the class listened intently and created a roar of applause when the skit was completed.

Not only had Isabel's group propelled her to a vital role as a needed interpreter, but they had cleverly utilized language to include their peers in the difficult exchange between groups of people who knew nothing about each other's cultures, norms, or intentions. What was truly remarkable was that this exchange sparked an important discussion about Spain's colonization of the Philippines. The conversation emerged organically, as students mentioned terms they had heard in Tagalog that sounded to them like Spanish, and so forth. Though Isabel had been in our school for two years, her peers had never connected with her culture or her history. One student admitted that he assumed she was "Mexican" all these years. The opportunity to engage in such deep ways with the intricacies and intersections of language, legacies of colonization, and the omission of valuable knowledge in history grounded many powerful relational and learning moments in our classroom.

CA HSS standards ask students to explain how the Aztecs were defeated by the Spaniards but do little to foster a justice-oriented inquiry into colonization and the societal impacts of colonization. Students' abilities to utilize language, ask questions, and make such connections allowed our class to explore beyond state standards and embark on parallel journeys of self-discovery. Students learned about the Spanish colonization of the Philippines, which is never referenced in the K–8 curriculum. Students began to conduct their own research on Spanish terms derived from Nahuatl and Mayan, as well as other terms they use that have Indigenous roots. Student inquiry led to an emphasis on acquiring empowering language and knowledge to define one's place in history. My partner teacher, whose focus was math and science content (she held a master of arts degree in Latin American studies), taught students to use Mayan math. Having empowered language led students to speak up, to ask us for more, and to insert their interests in the curriculum.

Translating Our Rights

After two years of teaching seventh grade, I was able to loop with my seventh graders and went back to teaching eighth grade. My students, who had been a critical impetus for my growth as a social studies teacher, would be my teachers once again. Grade 8 CA HSS Standards begin with the American Revolution, yet it is common for students to need a refresher on how we became colonies that sought independence. In addition, even though students had heard of the Constitution and Bill of Rights, very few students had contextualized how and why these events came to be, or how history continues to impact our daily experiences. Studying the Preamble of the Constitution brought all these questions to the forefront.

To start, the term *preamble* is not commonly used today, and this Preamble is a very long sentence featuring clauses and complex syntax, in addition to several words and phrases that are unfamiliar to students. However, the Preamble is an important focus in the curriculum because it gives students access to the perceived intentions behind the Constitution and the many interpretations of the Constitution across the years. Typical curricular pathways require students to memorize and recite the Preamble, but I knew that for my students, reciting it would not allow them to truly understand it and question it. I began teaching the Preamble by breaking up the clauses and creating a comic strip of each section:

We, the people of the United States, in order to form a more perfect Union, **establish justice**, INSURE DOMESTIC TRANQUILITY, `provide for the common defense,` promote the general welfare, and **secure the blessings of liberty to ourselves and our posterity**, *do ordain and establish this Constitution for the United States of America.*

During classroom discussions, students questioned the language of the Preamble as a document establishing the rights of citizens, and also the limitations of those rights, given that the Preamble applied to "highly-educated, rich, white men." Students questioned how the terms *union, welfare, posterity,* and *justice* were meant back then and how these terms have evolved into our current understandings. One student wondered why it was okay to promote welfare in our Preamble, yet *welfare* had come to be a negative term applied to poor people in need of government support.

One year, I assigned students a project to "translate" the Preamble and apply it to different communities that they felt needed to establish their rights. We brainstormed in class before they went home to create colorful posters. When they returned to class with their projects, I was amazed. Students wrote preambles giving voice to many marginalized communities: *We the girls, We the Mexicans, We the soccer players, We the inmigrantes, We the taggers,* etc. Through this assignment, students exercised their understandings of rights and the language different communities use to define their rights. For example, the preamble for "girls" used terms such as *equality, leader,* and *strong,* yet when students wrote as "inmigrantes," they used terms such as *papeles, citizenship, green card,* and *derechos.*

Students worked to turn negative labels into positive ones. Students really understood that the language they used to represent various communities was crucial to creating meaning in this project. Some students challenged each other during their presentations. One would say, "I don't think taggers would say that" or "Can you use a term in Spanish to make your message stronger?" Through this work, our class was not only able to understand the language of the Preamble but also apply and question it. Students shared their understandings of how language can represent a marginalized community but how it can also stigmatize the community.

Labels and Perceptions

The month of May always signaled the beginning of the dreaded state exams in California. My eighth-grade students had nine days of testing that included English, math, social studies, and science content. The eighth-grade social studies test covered material from CA HSS Grade 6–8 Standards. During those first two weeks of May, when it felt impossible to engage students in new material, I planned enriching, short activities. One fifth of May, I asked students to engage with the following questions: *What is Cinco de Mayo? Why do we celebrate Cinco de Mayo? How is it celebrated in Mexico versus the US?*

Cinco de Mayo commemorates the historical defeat of the French by a small Mexican army in the state of Puebla. This event was not in the CA HSS Standards (nor in the textbook), yet every year students shared stories of how they had to learn a Mexican dance in elementary school and how they grew up thinking Cinco de Mayo was Mexico's Independence Day (which is actually September 16). For class, I asked students to search for historical information and find images depicting the holiday in both the US and Mexico. Students found advertisements from alcohol companies showing no "Mexicans" celebrating the holiday. They found many images of women in bathing suits advertising restaurant celebrations and alcohol specials. Students brought up issues regarding the commercialization of the holiday and what it means when people are anxious to celebrate a holiday but not celebrate the people. One student said, "They want to drink the margaritas, but they don't want Margarita to have papers." Students moved beyond the historical significance of holidays to analyze the placement of Mexican and other Latina/o/x communities in US society.

While doing online research related to Cinco de Mayo, one student uncovered information nobody in the class had ever been taught. According to several historical sources, the Mexican army, after defeating the French at the battle of Puebla, supported the US Union army by preventing the French from joining the Confederacy during the Civil War. Students in this class were in awe that such an important Mexican contribution had been kept from them in all their studies of the Civil War. This discovery led to further investigations on the role of Black leaders such as

Frederick Douglass and the pressure he put on Lincoln to "end the war," as well as the heroic acts of Black soldiers who fought for a country that did not view them as fully human. We analyzed an image of the rapper Kanye West wearing a confederate flag as a sign of defiance. Through this inquiry, we worked together as a classroom community to shift prevalent narratives that leave incomplete or completely erase the contributions of marginalized groups and individuals.

Most importantly, middle school students showed deepening consciousness when applying historical events to their daily realities being Latina/o/x and living in Los Angeles. They shared stories of flying to Guatemala and seeing poverty amidst the richness of their parents' homelands. They reflected on the ironies and injustices of their parents being respected professionals in their home countries but now cleaning homes and maintaining gardens due to their citizenship status in the United States. Students felt conflicted about their feelings toward "generous bosses" who treated their parents with kindness while at the same time exploiting their labor. Using the lens of social studies, many students shared their experiences of looking "too Brown" or speaking "too white." Most importantly, discussions of historical events led students to problematize their existence in a social structure that causes them to both seek and resist acceptance as youth of color.

TRANSFORMING SOCIAL STUDIES

The reflections I have outlined all come from student discussions sparked by going beyond the traditional curriculum. The students were engaging with mostly teacher-created activities, yet the discussions that led to many teachable moments were student directed. Students in these classrooms were over 90 percent Latina/o/x; many were first-generation US-born and most were bilingual or multilingual. The emphasis on language was intentional, as students were expected to improve their academic and content knowledge and demonstrate mastery of English on mandated assessments. Yet, these instances where language mattered to centering a wider and more balanced array of historical perspectives, to demanding rights, to questioning injustice, and to challenging labels marked our transformation of the social studies curriculum.

These instances shaped me, my teaching, and my outlook on teaching social studies. Most importantly, these reflections serve as a way for me to imagine how teachers, teacher educators, and student advocates can reclaim a commitment to social studies not just as a discipline but a means to transform students' experiences in schools. Social studies curricula have the potential to humanize and validate the experiences of children and youth, while at the same time providing inquiry-driven high-level instruction that allows students to learn from history how to transform and question ongoing and emerging injustices in their own communities.

I was not trained as a social studies teacher, nor am I a social studies pedagogue, yet for nine years I immersed myself in the world of middle school social studies. For the last eight years I have been teaching in schools of education in different cities and contexts, and I know that what I have learned from youth about the power of language, the values of justice, and the critical questioning of our historical past is unrivaled. I have found that preservice teachers preparing to teach social studies have thought it difficult to imagine transforming social studies instruction when they themselves experienced traditional social studies instruction that emphasized rote memorization, furthered a procolonial stance, and failed to question the many injustices faced by minoritized populations in the past and present. Even as student teachers, they had rarely encountered or experienced justice-oriented social studies instruction centered on youths' lived experiences.

Despite these tensions, several scholars and teacher educators have helped me prepare preservice teachers to teach social studies; their work pushes teacher educators to reexamine how they train teachers of minoritized populations:

- Ruchi Agarwal-Rangnath looks at how K–8 teachers can approach social studies and ethnic studies through a social justice and equity lens.[10]
- LaGarrett King's work examines how Black history is taught and interpreted in the K–12 setting.[11]
- Timothy Monreal focuses on transforming middle school social studies and examines the experiences of Latinx students and teachers in the new South.[12]

- Noreen Naseem Rodríguez studies critical uses of diverse children's literature to understand Asian American and Latinx experiences in the US.[13]
- Maribel Santiago's work examines how Latinx history is produced and consumed in K–12 classrooms.[14]

When the curriculum asks students to question historical injustices and understand how those injustices have impacted their own experiences and the experiences of marginalized and oppressed groups, we as educators can help students define restorative practices. Educators who learn, honor, and historicize restorative justice are able to engage restorative justice as a foundation for how they view and approach history, the curriculum, and justice, rather than seeing restorative justice as another tool for classroom management.[15] The social studies curriculum should incorporate students' experiences, affirm their cultures, and provide supported opportunities for them to question society and transform how they approach justice in their everyday lives.

12

When the Game Is Rigged from the Start:
Teaching for Epistemic Justice in Troubled Times

Melissa Braaten

WALKING INTO THE eighth-grade classroom at Hickory Middle School (HMS), where Ms. J, Ms. F, and Mrs. C worked together as a teaching team, blew my mind. I also team-taught eighth grade, but unlike this team, I did not teach all subjects, nor did I teach fifty-five students in one double-sized classroom. Ms. J and Ms. F got it right when they welcomed me into their steamy space early in September: "Whew, it gets smelly in here since we don't have air conditioning! So, we just let it all hang out. Time to get real about middle school."

Teachers at HMS work together in teams to design and support students' learning experiences across all subject areas. On Team Jazzy-Flashy-Cool, when one teacher takes a leading role, the other two teachers automatically shift into support roles. Teammates serve as extensions of the lead teacher, walking around, listening, and talking with students; watching carefully; and noticing details about their shared student community that would likely escape the attention of a solo teacher. I was captivated watching them coordinate their work.

The two years I spent with Team Jazzy-Flashy-Cool and their colleagues across Glacier City School District (GCSD) were fraught with policy initiatives and new administrative practices. GCSD's long history of racial and social disparity had become a public accountability issue at the focus of state- and districtwide policy initiatives. At first, teachers such as those on Team Jazzy-Flashy-Cool were excited by the new initiatives. "Finally," they said, "racial disparities and social injustices that have been part of our city for so long will get some attention and not be swept once again under the rug." But, within the first year, Team Jazzy-Flashy-Cool started to question whether the goal was really a justice-oriented change for their students. So, when new policy initiatives threatened their team's ideas about justice and what it would cost to play the accountability game in the ways defined by GCSD and HMS leadership, this team concluded that the game was rigged from the start. Quietly, they resisted.

The work of this teacher team brings three questions into focus. What meanings of *justice* are used by educators and embodied in tools and language? What theories and practices are employed by educators striving for justice in education? How do theories, practices, and meanings of justice shape teaching, learning, and identities?

In this chapter, I explore epistemic (in)justice as a critical dimension of justice-centered pedagogy, highlighting how language matters for creating humanizing learning experiences with youth. Epistemic justice refers to having one's knowledge and ways of knowing recognized as valid and having those contributions heard and understood. Two stories of quiet resistance highlight how one team of teachers worked together against the grain in their school to embody their pedagogical stance. The chapter concludes by revisiting questions about teaching for epistemic justice in troubled times.

JUSTICE AND LANGUAGE MATTER FOR HUMANIZING SCIENCE TEACHING

Maisha T. Winn offers a four-part framework for transformative educational practice outlining how history, race, justice, and language matter when creating spaces for young people to learn and grow in schools. Winn's justice and language stances are central to the stories of Team Jazzy-Flashy-Cool because the teaching team "dare[s] to imagine a world where everyone—irrespective of race, ethnicity, socioeconomic status, gender, sexuality, or ability—is able to live with dignity and is recognized as belonging."[1] Fundamentally, Team Jazzy-Flashy-Cool strives to "cultivate a generation of children who are free: free from labels that do not reflect their full humanity, free from categories that disrupt teachers' ability to engage with some of them, free from the threat of punishment in places of learning, and free to be confident learners."[2]

When education is humanizing, school can confer dignity and engage youth in belonging, flourishing, and being fully human.[3] Humanizing classrooms are free from limiting labels and categories, resolve conflicts through restorative rather than punitive responses, and treat identity building as central to adolescent development.[4] Academic subject areas matter when considering how schools and schooling can dehumanize people. In academic subjects such as science, knowledge is imbued with power, and gatekeeping is tightly controlled to manufacture and maintain status and prestige.[5] Historically, success in science at school has come at a high cost for young people who describe having to check dimensions of their identities, languages, and cultures at the door in exchange for academic success.[6] In this way, science in school is centrally about justice.

Teaching for Epistemic Justice

Epistemic justice entails questions about who counts as knowledgeable, whose knowledge and inquiries count as legitimate, and who defines whose and which knowledge counts. Miranda Fricker points out that while we may aspire to a world where epistemic justice is the norm, the opposite is more likely to be true.[7] Epistemic *injustice* is, in fact, the default experience for many people because power and status disparities, structural inequalities, and other factors make the proverbial playing field—which Alison Bailey instead refers to as *the knowing field*—inequitable.[8]

In schools, epistemic injustices are perpetuated in small (but impactful) ways related to how curricular tools and assessments forward epistemic messages about whose knowledge counts and what counts as high-status knowledge. Epistemic injustices are also maintained through persistent pedagogical patterns that resist centering and responding to students' interests and identities, despite decades of efforts to change things. As Ben Kotzee explains, epistemic injustices become further infused into schooling when authoritative knowledge hierarchies and organizational structures tend not to give young people's contributions much epistemic credit.⁹

Epistemic injustices thrive in the ways people interact with each other. When a person speaks their mind, but listeners fail to really hear and understand their ideas, the lack of reciprocity, being genuinely heard and understood, can contribute to epistemic injustice.¹⁰ Sometimes, listeners actively smother another person's contributions, further exacerbating a growing sense of epistemic injustice. Epistemic justice, then, comes down to being able to speak one's mind, share ideas, be heard and understood, and have one's contributions counted as legitimate forms of knowledge building.

GETTING TO KNOW GLACIER CITY, HICKORY MIDDLE SCHOOL, AND TEAM JAZZY-FLASHY-COOL

Glacier City School District is a mid-sized district serving a Midwestern city with a long history of disparities in every arena of life, spanning health care, housing, policing, and education. At the time of this study, all GCSD schools were being publicly scrutinized for longstanding educational disparities that had motivated GCSD to launch a new strategic plan called The Great Teaching Initiative. This initiative entailed (1) increased investment in assessment tools anchoring data-driven improvement of academic performance in mathematics and literacy; and (2) increased attention to evaluating teachers' pedagogical practice with specific focus on "structured teaching."¹¹

One of twelve middle schools in Glacier City School District, Hickory Middle School serves northeast Glacier City. Students in the HMS community self-identify according to the following racial and ethnic breakdown: 25 percent identify as African American, 30 percent identify as Latinx, 30 percent identify as white, just under 10 percent identify as Asian American, and just under 10 percent identify as multiracial. Nearly 40 percent of HMS students are emerging bilingual students.

Teams at HMS generate fun names to refer to themselves. Team Jazzy-Flashy-Cool is a fitting name for the teacher-leaders responsible for the students in this group. Teaming up enables teachers to develop interdisciplinary projects and specialize in specific disciplines as needed. Ms. J specialized in literacy and special education. Ms. F specialized in social studies. Mrs. C specialized in math and science. Team Jazzy-Flashy-Cool described the school's integrated approach to subject-area expertise and ability to design learning experiences focused on intersections between subjects as a key feature that made HMS special. Most often, however, this teaching team remarked that team teaching made HMS special because every middle school student could be known and seen for who they were and who they were becoming.

Team Jazzy-Flashy-Cool spoke often about racial, linguistic, and cultural identities, as well as their own and their students' gender identities and sexualities. All three teachers on this team identify as white women; two identify as lesbians and the third identifies as straight. All three are married and two have young children. Their classroom space prominently displayed rainbow flags, pink triangles, icons, and role models from LGBTQ+ communities alongside posters and artwork depicting Black and Latinx icons. Audre Lorde standing in front of a chalkboard, Frida Kahlo's intense gaze into the camera, and Bayard Rustin at the shoulder of Dr. Martin Luther King, Jr., were among the posters on the walls of their large classroom.

Like many classrooms, this one featured a Word Wall filled with handwritten vocabulary words displaying new terms with a definition and perhaps a picture or diagram to support student learning. The terms on the wall in this classroom were not the typical fare of academic English vocabulary, instead featuring terms such as *clapback*, *salty*, and *ratchet* with definitions for this descriptive language cogenerated by students and teachers. This team of teachers was, indeed, jazzy, flashy, and cool, and this was apparent in their close relationships with each other, with their students, and with their students' families.

During the two years that I spent immersed in realities at GCSD, I shadowed teachers through their day-to-day work. I took detailed descriptive field notes and collected artifacts such as photos of wall displays and documents distributed in schools to build a rich description of how teachers and teaching shifted during the Great Teaching Initiative. I conducted interviews with teachers focused on key events from each week, each semester, and each academic year. I also expanded outwards from teachers' experiences to identify other stakeholders important to teachers and teaching. I interviewed school- and district-level leaders whose work intersected with teachers' experiences through meetings, panels, working groups, or professional development. Through these connections, I was invited to join districtwide subgroups, including a book group focused on data-driven improvement and a science education leadership team.

HOW TEAM JAZZY-FLASHY-COOL WORKED AGAINST THE GRAIN

Two case studies illustrate how this teacher team worked against the grain to resist and transform what they perceived as harmful, dehumanizing, and unjust language and practices valued as part of GCSD's Great Teaching Initiative. In the first case, teachers refused to smother a student's emerging identity in exchange for test scores and simultaneously worked to push HMS leadership to recognize this student's academic capabilities using other forms of evidence. In the second case, teachers refused to engage in pedagogies rooted in deficit perspectives toward students, choosing instead to trust students' interests and pursue their questions as valid forms of disciplinary inquiry. Both cases point to different, often paradoxical, meanings of justice used by educators and embodied in the tools, language, and practices employed at HMS.

Refusing to Smother a Student's Passion in Exchange for Test Scores

Early in my first year at HMS, I joined Team Jazzy-Flashy-Cool and another eighth-grade team for a "data day." On data days, teachers gathered in their teams to review spreadsheets of testing data compiled by the member of the school's leadership team designated "data point person." On this particular data day, teachers reviewed a large spreadsheet of students' most recent scores on a mathematics test the GCSD superintendent called "an early warning system" because it occurred before the high-stakes statewide testing window later in the school year.

The Jazzy-Flashy-Cool teacher-team and three additional eighth-grade teachers were tasked with scanning through spreadsheets to identify students whose most recent math test score was above, near, or below a "cut-off" score. The data point person described cut-off scores as early signals about whether students would successfully pass the statewide mathematics test. Once students were identified as below the cut-off score, teacher-teams were supposed to fill out paperwork to initiate a mid-term change to the student's daily activities. If a student's test score was above or at the cut-off score, no change would be made to the student's schedule. If, on the other hand, a student's test score was below the cut-off score, the student would be pulled from normal daily activities for the last hour of the school day and routed into a remedial test preparation session. At HMS, the last hour of the school day is typically used for elective classes such as engineering/robotics, leadership team, and visual and performing arts programming that includes a range of dance and music groups.

Initially, the Team Jazzy-Flashy-Cool teachers agreed to embark on the task set forth for that data day, albeit with plenty of skepticism about the merits of hand-coding and sorting students based on data from one math test. They remarked: "OK, we'll play along; this isn't really decision-making. We're just sorting, kind of by hand, when the spreadsheet could do all of this for us, but whatever." Ms. J, Ms. F., and Mrs. C. removed the staple from their packet of spreadsheet documents and shared three different colored highlighters to color-code students as above, at, or below the math test cut-off score. After a few minutes, Ms. J turned to Mrs. C and said:

> Wait, but this score isn't accurate. I mean, I watched him take that test. He basically just stood behind his chair and hit the button over and over until the test was done. He was in a hurry to get to dance team; you know how he is in seventh hour. Plus, hasn't his work in math been getting better and better this term?

Mrs. C replied, "Yeah, he's doing great. Let's ask [Principal] Dave. Hey, Dave!" At the center of the data day initiative was a strong statement from school and district leaders about the importance of making educational decisions based on evidence so students would be provided with the educational opportunities they needed and not denied opportunities based on whims or biases. The dilemma identified by Ms. J and Mrs. C was an important moment for HMS teachers now confronting two different and disparate pieces of evidence. Decisions now in the hands of the teacher-teams were highly consequential for students' schedules. In this case, the student in question was passionate about dance team participation and would be pulled out of dance team and rerouted into a test-preparation/remediation class on the basis of one instance of math testing. Mrs. C described the situation to Principal Bandera:

> So, we're looking at [a student's] score—it's not really representative of how he's doing in math. His work in class is getting better every day. Is this a case where, since we have evidence that contradicts this score, we can make a decision to keep his schedule "as-is," even though this score is below the cut-off?

Principal Bandera responded, "Well, that's not really evidence, what you are saying. It's more like personal knowledge, which is great, but the data—the evidence—is what's on this chart. We have to make data-driven, evidence-based decisions. No matter what." Without further discussion, Principal Bandera walked away from the table to attend to other groups of teachers. Teachers in Team Jazzy-Flashy-Cool looked stunned. They sat silently with unblinking eyes and mouths wide open. Finally, Ms. F broke the silence:

> That's crap! We know this score is bogus. If we change his schedule, it means he's in this math recovery class—scripts, worksheets, timed drills—he'll have a meltdown. He'd stop coming to school if he had to miss dance team. It's the whole reason he comes to school. It's what makes him human and alive.

The teachers of Team Jazzy-Flashy-Cool turned to their colleagues and to me to explain more about the student in question. They described the student as a vibrant, gay, Black boy full of verve and music who prided himself in creating extravagant fashion choices and never stopped dancing. They described the joy and recognition of reliving the identity development that takes place during early adolescence for LGBTQ+ youth and, for Team Jazzy-Flashy-Cool, stripping this student of the activity that makes him fully human was too high a price to pay for a data-driven policy initiative that clearly did not have this student's interests at heart.

Officially, African American students in GCSD were designated as a high-priority "focus group," meaning the data-driven instructional improvement initiatives were meant to concentrate on improving educational outcomes for Black students. However, "focus group" language was not used among teachers and school leaders. Instead, teachers and leaders informally referred to this demographic as "hot list" or "watch list," and often identified individual Black students as "target kids." Such shifts in language carry specific connotations that can negatively impact the educational experiences of children, even amidst and in relation to initiatives ostensibly aimed at improving educational outcomes. Placing African American children on a "hot list" or a "watch list" and thinking of the boy in Team Jazzy-Flashy-Cool as a "target kid" suggests danger and situates such students as suspect and problematic. Language born from routines of identifying children as above, at, or below benchmarks, along with language of hot lists, watch lists, and targets, creates an atmosphere ripe for continued epistemic injustice for youth in schools.

Team Jazzy-Flashy-Cool teachers critiqued this language in year-end interviews, noting that such language is dehumanizing and connected to ideologies that doom African American youth to a lifetime of injustices. These educators recognized epistemic injustice when a student's capability in mathematics was rendered invisible and not valuable in a system organized around a particular form of data use, and also when this student's passion for dance was not valued as a legitimate pursuit worthy of cultivation in school. Furthermore, the teachers on Team Jazzy-Flashy-Cool were starting to recognize another type of epistemic injustice: their own expertise and knowledge of educational justice for the students in their care were not valued by their school or district leaders. Epistemic injustice became even more visible as a norm the following year.

Choosing to Teach What Kids Want to Know

In my second year at HMS, the Team Jazzy-Flashy-Cool teachers became more vocal in their resistance of epistemic injustices inherent in GCSD's Great Teaching Initiative. Ms. J, Ms. F, and Mrs. C investigated and interrogated the racist and marginalizing histories of using standardized testing to sort and categorize people and gatekeeping to limit access to educational opportunities.[12] They also questioned the continued emphasis of district- and school-level leaders on targeting children for remediation by focusing on racial categories. In faculty meetings, Team

Jazzy-Flashy-Cool teachers spoke out about the problems of framing educational injustices solely as an "achievement gap" without attending to social, economic, and political injustice. In addition, they objected to how language used in discussions about academic achievement reinforced white students' achievements as the norm and positioned all other students' performance in relation to that ideal. Finally, they objected to a key instructional feature of the Great Teaching Initiative, pulling students from elective coursework to work on remedial skill-building drills, a practice they considered dehumanizing.

All but the last objection raised by these educators was dismissed by HMS school leaders, who, after experimenting with a variety of remediation and test preparation activities, ultimately decided that pulling students from their electives was not improving test scores quickly enough to meet gap-closing goals set forth by the district. A new plan was born—but it also did not address the objections that had been raised by Team Jazzy-Flashy-Cool teachers. Under the new plan, HMS teachers were required to continue identifying "focus groups" of students falling below the benchmark on literacy and math tests. Instead of sending students out to special remediation and test preparation sessions, though, teachers were tasked with coming up with literacy and math learning experiences to "reteach" specific literacy and math skills with the clear aim of ensuring "target kids" would meet or exceed the benchmark on the next round of testing. Team Jazzy-Flashy-Cool teachers refused. Ms. F said, "Screw this. We're teaching about what the kids want to know. I don't care what they think."

Instead of reteaching math and literacy goals using packaged skill-based drills recommended by HMS leaders, Team Jazzy-Flashy-Cool turned to the kids and asked what they wanted to work on. Kids responded that they wanted to learn about the brain, head injuries, concussions, and whether it was true that teenage brains were a mess. Ms. J spoke for the team when she said regarding the principal, "What's he gonna do? Fire us? No way. We've been here longer than him and we wrote the dang rubrics. He doesn't recognize our expertise or listen to us, but he won't get in the way."

Team Jazzy-Flashy-Cool pressed onwards, capitalizing on students' interests to build science learning experiences that took students' questions seriously. Mrs. C capitalized on student interest in questions about human brain development to create student-driven research experiences. Some student teams became experts on recent incidences of long-term brain damage reported by professional athletes who had experienced numerous concussions and head injuries. Some teams became experts in dementia and Alzheimer's disease, sparked by an interest in learning more about conditions experienced by elders in their families and community. Other teams worked from a myth-busting stance motivated by a goal of finding out the truth about their own adolescent brains. Surely, students argued, teenage brains operated like adult brains with full impulse-control and decision-making capabilities. Students worked in small groups pursuing their questions with interest.

Team Jazzy-Flashy-Cool teachers circulated, and when they noticed patterns in students' questions about brain anatomy and physiology, they paused the student-driven research process to engage in more traditional science teaching. This approach allowed the teaching team to provide relevant science content information just in time to build on students' questions. During these instances of traditional science teaching, school and district leaders might have recognized the "structured teaching" pedagogical model valued by the Great Teaching Initiative, but this direct instruction was only provided in response to student questions, in the context of student-driven inquiries. As such, it was quite different in spirit to the status quo "I do, we do, you do" teacher-delivered lessons familiar to and desired by school and district leaders.

Using rubrics that they had developed and were used schoolwide to monitor and document students' progress in writing, Team Jazzy-Flashy-Cool teachers leaned heavily on existing curricular and pedagogical tools such as science kits, interactive science notebook practices, and district-adopted math and social studies instructional materials. There was nothing terribly radical about their curriculum and instruction, other than the fact that they listened to kids and situated their learners within a larger social, cultural, and political context for academic work. What was radical about Team Jazzy-Flashy-Cool's work was unwavering recognition that test-based accountability measures focused on "target" students are rooted in oppressive language and ideologies—that this was a game that was rigged from the start and would never lead to epistemic justice for their students. The radical enactment, then, was their practice of teaching against the grain of schooling by putting kids' questions and ideas first.

RIGGED FROM THE START

Looking back on my time with Team Jazzy-Flashy-Cool, I am struck by how the teachers' disillusionment with most features of GCSD's Great Teaching Initiative fueled their efforts to teach against the grain and work toward epistemic justice for their students. At the center of this relationship between disillusionment and teaching against the grain are different meanings of justice held by educators and embodied in various tools, language, and practices.

How Language Matters for Epistemic Justice

Different meanings of justice held by teachers and school and district leaders were embodied in the tools and language in use in HMS. For school and district leaders, justice was a matter of accounting for access to the next grade level of coursework and, ultimately, high school graduation, followed by post–high school options such as college or employment. The view of justice as a matter of tallying progress toward academic achievements was visible in these leaders' use of accounting practices and trust in testing tools and spreadsheets of testing data.

Wrapped up in these accounting practices was a particular type of language that troubled Team Jazzy-Flashy-Cool teachers, who worried that it could perpetuate epistemic injustices in schooling. Accounting practices of academic achievement often employ a language of comparing student groups to a benchmark that is often derived from the academic achievement of another group of students, who are situated and treated as the norm or ideal. It was in this vein that GCSD and HMS leaders' talk about educational equity and justice efforts used language about "high" and "low" students who were "above" or "below" a desired level of achievement.

This comparative language invariably includes language connected, either tacitly or explicitly, to language of categorization by race and ethnicity, (dis)ability, and gender. As a result, educators frequently encapsulated students into fixed categories (e.g., "Black boys") defined through comparative language (e.g., "below"), framing this group of youth as "target" kids. HMS and GCSD leaders tended to treat comparisons and categories as concepts with settled meanings that were no longer up for questioning; this language was simply part of an accepted game of data-driven educational improvement. Leaders and plenty of HMS teachers accepted these parameters of the game and worked from this pedagogical stance without argument, trusting that accountability and management logics, reliance on particular achievement data, and use of the described language norms around race, (dis)ability, and gender could unproblematically serve as a proxy for educational equity and justice.

Team Jazzy-Flashy-Cool teachers operated from a different pedagogical stance, rooted in a different definition of justice. For this group of teachers, working for justice meant seeing and hearing students' ideas and experiences as valid ways of knowing that merit attention. This perspective mirrors Cynthia Townley's image of epistemic justice as featuring and relying on trust of people who are often distrusted and validation of knowledge and ways of knowing that are often dismissed out of hand.[13] As an extension of this justice-oriented pedagogical stance, Team Jazzy-Flashy-Cool teachers used pedagogical practices that elicited, worked with, and responded to students' questions, interests, and identities—not as gimmicks, but as valid bids and starting points for further knowledge exploration.

The teaching team's vision for justice echoed Miranda Fricker's stance that epistemic justice can happen only when there is constant vigilance and resistance against epistemic injustices inherent in systems of schooling and society.[14] Rather than viewing schooling and the GCSD Great Teaching Initiative and its data-driven accountability practices as a game to be played by the rules, Team Jazzy-Flashy-Cool viewed it as a game that was rigged from the start, wherein neither they nor their students were ever positioned as possible winners. This is the crux of Alison Bailey's image of the unlevel knowing field, a space that never positions certain people—or their questions, ideas, experiences, and knowledge contributions—as "level," precluding fair play.[15] Rather than play this type of game, these educators chose to change the game, at least inside their own classroom, in the interest of providing more humane and just educational experiences for their students.

Why Epistemic Justice Matters in Troubled Times

Shadowing teachers for two years as they confronted, grappled with, and resisted policy initiatives aimed, at least in principle, at reducing educational disparities highlighted profound paradoxes about freedom, humanity, and justice in schools. The transformative pedagogies of Team Jazzy-Flashy-Cool teachers, who worked to position youth as people who are trustworthy and sensible, and should be free to pursue the questions and ideas that matter to them, provided a tangible example of what epistemic justice could look like in middle school science and math learning contexts. These educators had a profound impact on me because I saw how relentlessly they had to work against what Kristie Dotson calls the epistemic violence and silencing experienced in everyday life in power-laden spaces such as schools.[16] To work for freedom, humanity, and justice as a teacher is to resist oppression, inhumanity, and injustice in nearly every aspect of how school works. This feels paradoxical. Teaching for epistemic justice in troubled times means working to sustain and expand transformative pedagogies, even while immersed in school settings and teaching communities that operate from truly perplexing paradoxical stances.

Conclusion
Why Futures Matter: Toward a Fifth Pedagogical Stance

Maisha T. Winn

I RECENTLY WALKED in to observe a high school class and found students seated at desks that had been organized into an inner and an outer circle for a Socratic seminar. Even before receiving the handout, I knew which text was being discussed because a student in the inner circle stated, "I agree, the plant was a symbol because Mama had the plant in the apartment, and in the new house it could become a garden." Lorraine Hansberry's *A Raisin in the Sun*.

"If your pilot hasn't spoken," the teacher said, "you can use a sticky note and say 'What about this?'" The "pilots" in this context were students in the inner circle engaging in knowledge building and thoughtful literary analysis of the play. Their "co-pilots" were listening intently so they could support their pilots and prepare to switch roles. While Socratic seminars are not new, and on any given day one might find classroom communities engaged in this activity, many students do not have these robust learning opportunities. Two decades ago, Garrett Duncan raised the alarm that schools serving primarily marginalized children and communities often use "urban pedagogies," approaches focused on managing and even policing Native American, African American, Latinx, and other marginalized cohorts of children.[1] Urban pedagogies rob children of their right to an education that prepares them for positive and valuable futures that they have yet to imagine, and racism or racist ideas that spur urban pedagogies render generations of Black children in particular of an "education" and "imagination" that gives them access to futures.[2]

The purpose of this discussion is to inspire further thinking on how transformative justice education—approaches that seek to animate restorative justice theory and praxis so communities can make the changes their stakeholders identify as necessary—can be leveraged to center children's futures in ways that reflect hope and expansive thinking. This edited volume has engaged very seriously with the future of restorative and transformative justice in education through core subjects such mathematics, social studies, English language arts, and science. It is important to note that this work is also critical in and through digital media[3] and Ethnic Studies (see López, Dueñas, and López, this volume). If schools want to seriously invest in the futures of their students, administrators and educators alike must identify and embrace ways to maximize the learning and affirmation that can potentially be nurtured through (not despite) the wide spectrum of intellectual and relational encounters that occur in the school environment.

A FOCUS ON FUTURES

As I continue to engage in and build on conceptual mapping for the pedagogical stances that I argue are essential components of paradigm shifting toward justice in US schools—*History Matters, Race Matters, Justice Matters,* and *Language Matters*—I have come to understand the need for a fifth stance, *Futures Matter*. I see *Futures Matter* as a stance that grows from an ongoing commitment to developing portals or opportunities through which multiply-marginalized youth can begin to plan for and enact agentive futures and lives characterized by thriving. *Futures Matter* is defined throughout my research and practice as an invitation to stakeholders in a community of practice to excavate spaces wherein all members of our global community are actively encouraged to imagine and have optimism about multiple pathways forward. Communities of practice that engage a *Futures Matter* stance are keenly interested in leveraging community building and restorative responses to spark transformative learning experiences.[4]

A *Futures Matters* pedagogical foundation requires reorienting one's self to the disciplines. A haunting passage in Ta-Nehisi Coates's *Between the World and Me* brings this relationship between academic content areas and the purposes of education and schooling to bear for Black bodies (and, in my experience, also bodies that have experienced "Blackening"[5] and anti-Blackness). Arguing that the world "had no time" for Black childhood, Coates asks how one could expect schools to make an investment in Black children:

> Algebra, Biology, and English were not subjects so much as opportunities to better discipline the body, to practice writing between the lines, copying the directions legibly, memorizing theorems extracted from the world they were created to represent. All of it felt so distant to me.... Why precisely, was I sitting in this classroom? The question was never answered. I was a curious boy but the schools were not concerned with curiosity. They were concerned with compliance.[6]

In later writing, Coates returns to the site of his "indelible failures," the classroom, but this time for a class required for those seeking financial support during unemployment, describing this site as a space in which he was "a forever conduct problem" and "forever in need of improvement."[7] He noted that the classroom brought immediately to mind experiences of being viewed as "forever failing to work up to potential." The identity of failure becomes all too easily fixed when young learners are made to feel they can never climb out of an inevitable abyss, a reality about which Coates muses:

> And I know that there are black boys and black girls out there lost in a Berumuda Triangle of the mind or stranded in the doldrums of America, some of them treading and some of them drowning, never feeling and never forgetting. The most precious thing I had then and the most precious thing I have now—my own curiosity.[8]

Coates's teachers could never have projected that he would become a National Book Award Winner, or that Nobel Prize–winning author and icon Toni Morrison would refer to one of his books as "required reading."

In fact, Coates's experience—which he recognizes as a series of experiences incredibly familiar to Black boys and Black girls throughout the country today—is a "forever" cycle of being situated and directed as a being without hope for a future of any intellectual impact or social value. Futures, in the context of education, continue to be reserved for a select few. It is for this reason that the *Futures Matter* stance is so essential and so perpetually timely.

Arguing that "envisioning and making the future must be a massively public endeavor," Marina Gorbis troubles the futurist landscape in its narrow conception of who gets to determine and imagine futures.[9] Noting that foresight tools tend to be distributed within corporate contexts, to those already in possession of resources, Gorbis revisits futurist Alvin Toffler's famous essay "The Future as a Way of Life," making the observation that "tools for futures thinking and futures making" need wider distribution:

> [W]e can distribute these signals of the future more widely to engage more people, instill curiosity, and engagement in our collective futures. What would they want to do if they had access to these technologies? How would they use them in their own lives? What would they want to avoid? How would they want to shape their evolution?[10]

It is in this vein that the purpose of the *Futures Matter* pedagogical stance is to prepare Indigenous, Black, Latinx, and other marginalized young people and their families with foresight and futures tools, and to support within and among classroom and school communities the cultivation of a keen eye and robust dialogue regarding the valuable futures of all youth. To do this, anti-Blackness must be addressed. People would not be chanting "Black Lives Matter" if there were not substantial evidence demonstrating the contrary, including the vulnerability and disposability of Black bodies. The question is, can schools engage in futures work—especially schools that primarily serve Black children?

During a foresight tool training session coordinated by Institute for the Future that I recently had the opportunity to participate in, my colleague Arya Lau, who does not work in the field of education, offered this comment when I attempted to describe the *Futures Matter* pedagogical stance and my desire to engage educators in a serious way around investing in the futures of multiply-marginalized children and youth, "schools cannot extricate themselves from the present day to day." Schools are indeed inundated with the "nows" of attendance, truancy, and discipline, all of which reflect lenses and priorities that are reactionary rather than visionary. I have entered school spaces and been inundated with digital bulletins, posters, and handouts dedicated to daily attendance messages. Arya took very seriously what I was attempting to do and tempered it with the observation that schools are not in the business of futures or foresight. This is one reason the work in this volume is so essential. How can educators engage themselves in a pedagogy of the future? How can an algebra teacher, biology teacher, and English teacher reorient themselves to the futures of their students and the very disciplines they teach? What would it mean to leverage disciplines to foster intellectual curiosity rather than body management, policing, control, and "acceptable" high-stakes test performance? A transformative justice approach to education makes futures possible across the disciplines; here the disciplines are not weapons used against children but worthy of reexamination to provide deeper engagement.

It is no coincidence that the opening chapter of this edited volume examines the new three Rs for education: resistance, resilience, and reimagination. In February 2019, I was able to visit Roosevelt High School in Los Angeles, California, where Eduardo López, Roxana Dueñas, and Jorge López teach and learn from and with students participating in a class called "My Boyle Heights," a course that examines the legacy of activism in the Boyle Heights community in Los Angeles. I experienced first-hand what it means to teach resistance, resilience, and reimagination as Roosevelt High School students shared stories of feeling shame when their parents communicated in Spanish in public spaces or their lack of self-esteem when a cousin with lighter skin or a head of red hair was exalted as good looking over their many kin with black or brown hair. In that classroom space, students are taught to understand such experiences as moments of mis-education that are part of an insidious process of "spirit murder" and the steady erosion and erasure of one's culture, heritage, self-pride, and self-confidence.[11] An Ethnic Studies context and the guidance of educators who maintain a keen eye toward and firm commitment to restorative justice allowed members of this learning community to begin to articulate and heal these harms, providing the young learners therein with a supported opportunity to be in right relationship with themselves and their communities.

López, Dueñas, and López's work can also be contextualized within the notion of historiography for the future, grounding a project I am engaged in that examines the histories of Independent Black Institutions established in the late 1960s and early 1970s. This is about creating an education of knowledge of self and self-reliance and learning as early and often as possible, embodying for children that their lives and their families' lives matter. Because this work is not new, the Historiography for the Future project seeks to engage documentary source materials from Independent Black Institutions to learn about how educators in previous generations sought to create teaching and learning spaces that bolstered student agency.

HISTORIOGRAPHY FOR THE FUTURE

Futures Matter is informed by historiographies of Independent Black Institutions,[12] which I have argued are the original sites of futures work within Black communities. I borrow from Robin D. G. Kelley when I state that my future-oriented historiography is an effort to "keep [freedom] dreams alive" and draw from pedagogical possibilities Black parents and teachers had to imagine when public schools failed them in the past.[13] A mapping of how the Transformative Justice Education framework emerged would show the extent to which this work was preceded by freedom struggles for a meaningful and robust education, for Black children in particular.

In the opening vignette, the classroom teacher leveraged the Socratic seminar method to engage themes in *A Raisin in the Sun*. The classroom teacher, white and female, created space in which her students, largely Black and Brown, could grapple with themes in Hansberry's classic text that still have relevance in the twenty-first century. She guided and got out of the way. She leveraged a play that troubled the so-called American dream for Black families and brought the English language arts curriculum alive. Historiography for the future begins in a similar place. Elsewhere, I detail the life and work of Jitu Weusi, formerly Les Campbell, a cofounder of the Uhuru Sasa Shule Black community school established in Brooklyn, New York, in 1968 following the Ocean Hill–Brownsville struggle for community control of public schools. He shared with me a story of his classroom teaching before parting ways with the New York Department of Education. A trained high school teacher, Weusi was "punished" after taking his students to a celebration of the life of Malcolm X, despite getting permission from parents and guardians. According to Weusi, the school leadership did not approve of this experience and punitively placed him in an elementary school classroom setting for which he had not been trained. Drawing from his wealth of literary knowledge and experience, as well as his desperation to cultivate purpose and belonging among his African American students, Weusi selected a poem written in 1963 by Margaret Burroughs entitled "What Shall I Tell My Children Who Are Black (Reflections of an African-American Mother)?" Burroughs goes through a number of scenarios in which Black children face anti-Blackness and racist ideas; however, the last stanza shifts toward focusing her energy on providing Black children the opportunity to learn about the many contributions people of African descent have made to civilizations: "And his heritage shall be his weapon," writes Burroughs, "And his armor; will make him strong enough to win/Any battle he may face." I recounted Weusi's experience in my book *Black Literate Lives: Historical and Contemporary Perspectives*:[14]

> Weusi's "punishment" was being "demoted" to teaching even though his teaching license was specifically for "junior and senior high school social studies only." Weusi believed he was being used to control students at the elementary school who the administration and staff feared. Admittedly, Weusi "stuck pretty close to the script" during his first year of teaching in New York City schools in 1962. However, by February 1963, he saw that the curriculum was not working. "It was a white curriculum and the kids were bored," Weusi explained and he knew he had to do something else for his students. Weusi explained the day he came across a poem entitled "What shall I tell my children who are Black?" by Margaret Burroughs, a close colleague of Gwendolyn Brooks, and how he was overwhelmed with its relevance to Black lives in the 1960s. Weusi decided to take Burroughs' poem and divide

it into stanzas so that students could analyze the poem and create presentations in small groups. Weusi shook his head in disbelief as if he was reliving the moment: "These kids just took it and ran. It made all the difference." (Weusi, personal communication)

The labor of Weusi and the other Black teachers who formed the African American Teachers Alliance resulted in a visionary and future-oriented cultural center, the EAST, which housed a school, newspaper, and performance space called "The Black Experience in Sound," signaling an expansive understanding of Black creativity. Most performers donated their performances to raise money for the school. Weusi and fellow Black teachers could then teach freedom, collective freedom, without the restrictions imposed by the New York Department of Education. Some Black educators referred to this as "Correct Black Education" or "Afric/kan-centered." Haki Madhubuti's 1973 book, *From Plan to Planet: Life Studies: The Need for Afrikan Minds and Institutions*, asserted this education grounded in Identity, Purpose, and Direction.[15] I have come to think of these three pillars as Past, Present, and Future, when considering a *Futures Matter* stance. "From there to here"—one of the enduring memories of my time interviewing Jitu Weusi about the EAST, Uhuru Sasa, and *Black News*—reflected his sense that the current education climate needed the work of Independent Black Institutions to build capacity for what is referred to as cultural relevance, and now mandatory Ethnic Studies classes in states such as California. I agree wholeheartedly, and assert that these historiographies move us from there, to here, and beyond.

Notes

INTRODUCTION

1. Lena Howland, "Elk Grove Schools Moving to Online Teaching to Finish School Year, District Says," *ABC10.com*, March 23, 2020, https://www.abc10.com/article/news/health/coronavirus/elk-grove-schools-moving-to-online-to-finish-school-year/103-5ec9b5a2-33e9-414d-95fd-962af2772770.
2. Andover Public Schools, "Family and Caregiver Playbook for Continuous Learning," 2020, https://s3.amazonaws.com/scschoolfiles/685/family_and_caregiver_playbook.pdf.
3. Nidia Bautista, "Distance Learning During Coronavirus Worsens Race, Class Inequity in Education," *Teen Vogue*, May 1, 2020, https://www.teenvogue.com/story/distance-learning-low-income-students.
4. Arundhati Roy, "The Pandemic Is a Portal," *Financial Times*, April 3, 2020, www.ft.com/content/06647198-77b9-11ea-9840-1b8019d9a987.
5. Maisha T. Winn, *Justice on Both Sides: Toward a Restorative Justice Discourse in Schools* (Cambridge, MA: Harvard Education Press, 2018); US Department of Education Office for Civil Rights, *Civil Rights Data Collection: Data Snapshot School Discipline*, March 2014, http://www2.ed.gov/about/offices/list/ocr/docs/crdc-discipline-snapshot.pdf; Wisconsin Council on Children and Families, *Race to Equity: A Baseline Report on Racial Disparities in Dane County*, October 2013, http://racetoequity.net/dev/wp-content/uploads/WCCF-R2E-Report.pdf.
6. Grace Toohey, "Body Camera Video Shows 6-Year-Old Orlando Girl Arrested at School," *Tampa Bay Times*, February 25, 2020, https://www.tampabay.com/news/florida/2020/02/25/body-camera-video-shows-6-year-old-orlando-girl-arrested-at-school/.
7. Winn, *Justice on Both Sides*; Maisha T. Winn, Rita Alfred, and Hannah Graham, *Restorative and Transformative English in the Classroom* (Washington, DC: National Council of Teachers of English Principles in Practice Series, 2019).
8. Winn, *Justice on Both Sides*; Maisha T. Winn, "Toward a Restorative English Education," *Research in the Teaching of English* 48, no. 1 (2013): 126–36.
9. Winn, *Justice on Both Sides*.
10. Winn, *Justice on Both Sides*.

11. Erika C. Bullock and Erica R. Meiners, "Abolition by the Numbers: Mathematics as a Tool to Dismantle the Carceral State (and Build Alternatives)," *Theory into Practice* 58, no. 4 (2019): 338–46.
12. Darnel Degand, "Stereotypes vs. Strategies for Digital Media Artists: The Case for Culturally Relevant Media Production," *Theory into Practice* 58, no. 4 (2019): 368–76.
13. Cati V. de los Rios, Danny C. Martinez, Adam D. Musser, Asha Canady, Patrick Camangian, and Patricia D. Quijada, "Upending Colonial Practices: Toward Repairing Harm in English Education," *Theory into Practice* 58, no. 4 (2019): 359–67.
14. Alexis Patterson and Salina Gray, "Teaching to Transform: (W)holistic Science Pedagogy," *Theory into Practice* 58, no. 4 (2019): 328–37.
15. Winn, *Justice on Both Sides*.

SECTION I

1. Elizabeth G. McRae, *Mothers of Massive Resistance: White Women and the Politics of White Supremacy* (New York: Oxford University Press, 2018).
2. McRae, *Mothers of Massive Resistance*, 144.
3. Lawton B. Evans, *First Lessons in Georgia History* (Woodstock, GA: American Book Company, 1922), 232.
4. McRae, *Mothers of Massive Resistance*, 144.
5. Eve Watling, "'Gone with the Wind' 80th Anniversary: 15 Things You Did Not Know About the Classic Movie," *Newsweek*, February 1, 2019, www.newsweek.com/gone-wind-80th-anniversary-15-things-you-didnt-know-about-classic-movie-1314659.
6. McRae, *Mothers of Massive Resistance*.
7. Jason Williams, "Now That Your Kids Are Home, Teach Them Black History They Won't Learn in the American Educational System," May 24, 2020, https://trudreadz.com/2020/05/24/now-that-your-kids-are-home-teach-them-black-history-they-wont-learn-in-the-american-educational-system/.
8. Nicol Turner Lee, "One Year After the Charlottesville Riots and Still No New Kerner Commission," Brookings Institute, August 9, 2018, www.brookings.edu/blog/fixgov/2018/08/09/one-year-after-the-charlottesville-riots-and-still-no-new-kerner-commission/.
9. David Montanaro, "Joey Jones: 'Shame on' the NYT for 'Cheap' Op-ed on US Military and White Supremacy," May 25, 2020, www.foxnews.com/media/joey-jones-shame-new-york-times-military-white-supremacy.
10. McRae, *Mothers of Massive Resistance*.
11. Jarvis Givens, *Fugitive Pedagogy: Carter G. Woodson and the Art of Black Teaching* (Cambridge, MA: Harvard University Press, in press); Vanessa Siddle Walker, *The Lost Education of Horace Tate* (New York: The New Press, 2018).
12. Walker, *Lost Education of Horace Tate*, 4.
13. S. Miller and Nicholas Davis, "The Effect of White Social Prejudice on Support for American Democracy," *Journal of Race, Ethnicity, and Politics*, in press.
14. This quote comes from page 24 of a 1923 *Fort Valley Catalogue* available in the Fort Valley Historical Archives in Georgia.

CHAPTER 1

1. Paolo Freire, *Pedagogy of the Oppressed*, trans. Myra Bergman Ramos (New York: Continuum, 1970); Lilia Bartolome, "Beyond the Methods Fetish: Toward a

Humanizing Pedagogy," *Harvard Educational Review* 64, no. 2 (1994): 173–95; Django Paris and H. Samy Alim, ed., *Culturally Sustaining Pedagogies: Teaching and Learning for Justice in a Changing World* (New York: Teachers College Press, 2017).
2. ACLU, "California Enacts First-in-the-Nation Law to Eliminate Student Suspensions for Minor Misbehavior," September 27, 2014, www.aclunc.org/news/california-enacts-first-nation-law-eliminate-student-suspensions-minor-misbehavior.
3. Los Angeles Unified School District, "School Climate Bill of Rights," 2013, https://achieve.lausd.net/cms/lib/CA01000043/Centricity/Domain/416/School%20Climate%20Bill%20of%20Rights%20-%20Elementary.pdf.
4. Shawn Ginwright, *Hope and Healing in Urban Education: How Urban Activists and Teachers Are Reclaiming Matters of the Heart* (Abingdon, UK: Routledge, 2015), 30.
5. Howard Zehr, *The Little Book of Restorative Justice* (Intercourse, PA: Goodbooks, 2002), 68.
6. Carolyn Boyes-Watson and Kay Pranis, *Heart of Hope Resource Guide: Using Peacemaking Circles to Develop Emotional Literacy, Promote Healing and Build Healthy Relationships* (St. Paul, MN: Living Justice Press, 2010).
7. Jennifer A. O'Day and Marshall S. Smith, "Quality and Equality in American Education: Systemic Problems, Systemic Solutions," in *The Dynamics of Opportunity in America*, ed. Irwin Kirsch and Henry Braun (Berlin: Springer, 2016), 297–358.
8. Maisha T. Winn, *Justice on Both Sides: Transforming Education Through Restorative Justice* (Cambridge, MA: Harvard Education Press, 2018).
9. Winn, *Justice on Both Sides*, 34.
10. Winn, *Justice on Both Sides*, 31.
11. Freire, *Pedagogy*; Antonia Darder, *Freire and Education* (New York: Routledge, 2015).
12. Elexia Reyes McGovern and Tracy Lachica Buenavista, *Ethnic Studies with K–12 Students, Families, and Communities: The Role of Teacher Education in Preparing Educators to Serve the People* (Los Angeles, CA: UCLA Center Xchange, 2016).
13. Derrick Bell, "An Epistolary Exploration for a Thurgood Marshall Biography," *Harvard Blackletter Journal* 6 (1989); Richard Delgado and Jean Stefancic, ed., *Critical White Studies: Looking Behind the Mirror* (Philadelphia, PA: Temple University Press, 1997), 51–67.
14. Tara J. Yosso, "Whose Culture Has Capital? A Critical Race Theory Discussion of Community Cultural Wealth," *Race, Ethnicity and Education* 8, no. 1 (2005): 69–91; Daniel G. Solorzano and Dolores Delgado Bernal, "Examining Transformational Resistance Through a Critical Race and LatCrit Theory Framework: Chicana and Chicano Students in an Urban Context," *Urban Education* 36, no. 3 (2001): 308–42.
15. Paris and Alim, *Culturally Sustaining Pedagogies*.
16. Mere Berryman and Sonja Bateman, "Effective Bicultural Leadership: A Way to Restore Harmony at School and Avoid Suspension," *Set: Research Information for Teachers* 1 (2008): 25–29; Winn, *Justice on Both Sides*.
17. Paris and Alim, *Culturally Sustaining Pedagogies*.
18. Iris HeavyRunner and Joann Sebastian Morris, *Traditional Native Culture and Resilience* (St. Paul, MN: Center for Applied Research and Educational Improvement, 1997).

19. Bill Bigelow and Bob Peterson, ed., *Rethinking Columbus: The Next 500 Years*, 2nd ed. (Milwaukee, WI: Rethinking Schools Ltd., 1998).
20. Susan Gage, *Colonialism in the Americas: A Critical Look* (British Columbia, Canada: Victoria International Development Education Association, 1991).
21. Winn, *Justice on Both Sides*, 38.
22. Staci Haines, *The Politics of Trauma: Somatics, Healing, and Social Justice* (Berkeley, CA: North Atlantic Books, 2019), 195.
23. Haines, *The Politics of Trauma*.
24. Winn, *Justice on Both Sides*, 7.
25. Melanie Bertrand, E. Sybil Durand, and Taucia Gonzalez, "We're Trying to Take Action: Transformative Agency, Role Re-mediation, and the Complexities of Youth Participatory Action Research," *Equity & Excellence in Education* 50, no. 2 (2017): 142.
26. Nicole Mirra, Antero Garcia, and Ernest Morrell, *Doing Youth Participatory Action Research: Transforming Inquiry with Researchers, Educators, and Students* (New York: Routledge, 2016).
27. Winn, *Justice on Both Sides*, 34.
28. Winn, *Justice on Both Sides*, 7.
29. Eduardo López, Jorge López, and Roxana Dueñas, *Reimagining Internal Transformational Resistance in High School Ethnic Studies* (manuscript submitted for publication, 2020).
30. Solorzano and Delgado Bernal, "Examining Transformational Resistance."
31. Tara J. Yosso, *Critical Race Counterstories Along the Chicana/Chicano Educational Pipeline* (New York: Routledge, 2006).
32. Winn, *Justice on Both Sides*, 145.
33. Zehr, *Little Book*.
34. Winn, *Justice on Both Sides*.

CHAPTER 2

1. Ruth Morris, *A Practical Path to Transformative Justice* (Toronto: Rittenhouse Press, 1994).
2. Ruth Morris, *Stories of Transformative Justice* (Toronto: Canadian Scholars' Press, 2000), 5.
3. Maisha T. Winn, *Justice on Both Sides: Transforming Education Through Restorative Justice* (Cambridge, MA: Harvard Education Press, 2018), 34.
4. Kimberlé Crenshaw, "Demarginalizing the Intersection of Race and Sex: A Black Feminist Critique of Antidiscrimination Doctrine, Feminist Theory and Antiracist Politics," *University of Chicago Legal Forum* (1989): Article 8.
5. Subini A. Annamma and Deb Morrison, "DisCrit Classroom Ecology: Using Praxis to Dismantle Dysfunctional Education Ecologies," *Teaching and Teacher Education* 73 (2018): 70–80.
6. Drawing from Crenshaw, I capitalize *Black, Asian, Latinx*, and other multiply-marginalized groups because they "constitute a specific cultural group and, as such, require denotation as a proper noun.... By the same token, I do not capitalize 'white,' which is not a proper noun, since whites do not constitute a specific cultural group." See Kimberlé Crenshaw, "Mapping the Margins: Intersectionality, Identity Politics, and Violence Against Women of Color," *Stanford Law Review* (1991): 1244.
7. Tadashi Dozono, "The Passive Voice of White Supremacy: Tracing Epistemic and Discursive Violence in World History Curriculum," *Review of Education,*

Pedagogy, and Cultural Studies (2020): 4.
8. As starting points to explore these three examples, see, respectively, Roxanne Dunbar-Ortiz, *An Indigenous Peoples' History of the United States*, vol. 3 (Boston, MA: Beacon Press, 2014); Dyan Watson, Jesse Hagopian, and Wayne Au, *Teaching for Black Lives* (Milwaukee, WI: Rethinking Schools, 2018); Bill Bigelow, *A People's History for the Classroom* (Milwaukee, WI: Rethinking Schools, 2008).
9. See, respectively, Nolan L. Cabrera et al., "Missing the (Student Achievement) Forest for All the (Political) Trees: Empiricism and the Mexican American Studies Controversy in Tucson," *American Educational Research Journal* 51, no. 6 (2014): 1084–1118; Cati V. de los Ríos, Jorge López, and Ernest Morrell, "Toward a Critical Pedagogy of Race: Ethnic Studies and Literacies of Power in High School Classrooms," *Race and Social Problems* 7, no. 1 (2015): 84–96; Jerry Flores, "A Race Conscious Pedagogy: Correctional Educators and Creative Resistance Inside California Juvenile Detention Facilities," *Association of Mexican American Educators Journal* 9, no. 2 (2015): 18–30.
10. Zeus Leonardo, "The Color of Supremacy: Beyond the Discourse of 'White Privilege,'" *Educational Philosophy and Theory* 36, no. 2 (2004): 137–52.
11. Cheryl E. Matias and Janiece Mackey, "Breakin' Down Whiteness in Antiracist Teaching: Introducing Critical Whiteness Pedagogy," *Urban Review* 48, no. 1 (2016): 12.
12. Subini A. Annamma, *The Pedagogy of Pathologization: Dis/abled Girls of Color in the School-Prison Nexus* (New York: Routledge, 2018).
13. Angela Valenzuela, *Subtractive Schooling: US-Mexican Youth and the Politics of Caring*, 3rd ed. (Albany, NY: SUNY Press, 2010).
14. bell hooks, *All About Love: New Visions* (New York: Harper Perennial, 2001), 19.
15. hooks, *All About Love*, 6.
16. Daniel Solórzano, Miguel Ceja, and Tara Yosso, "Critical Race Theory, Racial Microaggressions, and Campus Racial Climate: The Experiences of African American College Students," *Journal of Negro Education* 69, no. 1/2 (2000): 60.
17. Beth Richie, *Arrested Justice: Black Women, Violence, and America's Prison Nation* (New York: New York University Press, 2012).
18. Rebecca Epstein, Jamilia J. Blake, and Thalia González, *Girlhood Interrupted: The Erasure of Black Girls' Childhood* (Washington, DC: Center on Poverty and Inequality, Georgetown Law, 2017).
19. Anne Gregory and Michael B. Ripski, "Adolescent Trust in Teachers: Implications for Behavior in the High School Classroom," *School Psychology Review* 37, no. 3 (2008): 337–53.
20. See, respectively, Jeffrey Duncan-Andrade, "Note to Educators: Hope Required When Growing Roses in Concrete," *Harvard Educational Review* 79, no. 2 (2009): 181–94; Valenzuela, *Subtractive Schooling*; Valentina Migliarini and Subini Annamma, "Applying Disability Critical Race Theory (DisCrit) in the Practice of Teacher Education in the United States," in *Oxford Research Encyclopedia of Education*, ed. J. Lampert (New York: Oxford University Press, 2019), 1–20.
21. Maxine McKinney de Royston et al., "'He's More Like a "Brother" than a Teacher': Politicized Caring in a Program for African American Males," *Teachers College Record* 119, no. 4 (2017): 32.
22. Annamma, *Pedagogy of Pathologization*.
23. Douglas C. Baynton, "Disability and the Justification for Inequality in American History," in *The New Disability History: American Perspectives*, ed. Paul K. Longmore and Lauri Umansky (New York: New York University Press, 2001), 33–57.

24. See, respectively, David Connor and Susan L. Gabel, "'Cripping' the Curriculum Through Academic Activism: Working Toward Increasing Global Exchanges to Reframe (Dis)ability and Education," *Equity & Excellence in Education* 46, no. 1 (2013): 100–18; Nirmala Erevelles, "Educating Unruly Bodies: Critical Pedagogy, Disability Studies and the Politics of Schooling." *Educational Theory* 50, no. 1 (2000): 25–47; Jane Dunhamn et al., "Developing and Reflecting on a Black Disability Studies Pedagogy: Work from the National Black Disability Coalition," *Disability Studies Quarterly* 35, no. 2 (2015), https://dsq-sds.org/article/view/4637/3933.
25. Crenshaw, "Demarginalizing the Intersection."
26. Subini A. Annamma, David Connor, and Beth A. Ferri, "Dis/ability Critical Race Studies (DisCrit): Theorizing at the Intersections of Race and Dis/ability," *Race, Ethnicity and Education* 16, no. 1 (2013): 1–31.
27. Nirmala Everelles and Andrea Minear, "Unspeakable Offences: Untangling Race and Disability in Discourses of Intersectionality," *Journal of Literary & Cultural Disability Studies* 4, no. 2 (2010): 127–45.
28. Annamma et al., "Dis/ability Critical Race Studies."
29. Fiona Kumari Campbell, "Ableism as Transformative Practice," in *Rethinking Anti-Discriminatory and Anti-Oppressive Theories for Social Work Practice*, ed. Christine Cocker and Trish Hafford-Letchfield (London: Red Globe Press, 2014), 81.
30. Gloria Ladson-Billings, "Just What Is Critical Race Theory and What's It Doing in a Nice Field Like Education?," *International Journal of Qualitative Studies in Education* 11, no. 1 (1998): 17.
31. Subini A. Annamma et al., "Challenging the Ideology of Normal in Schools," *International Journal of Inclusive Education* 17, no. 12 (2013): 1278–94.
32. Cheryl Harris, "Whiteness as Property," *Harvard Law Review* 106 (1993): 1707–93.
33. Donna Y. Ford, "Ensuring Equity in Gifted Education: Suggestions for Change (Again)," *Gifted Child Today* 35, no. 1 (2012): 74–75.
34. Todd Grindal et al., "Racial Differences in Special Education Identification and Placement: Evidence Across Three States," *Harvard Educational Review* 89, no. 4 (2019): 525–53.
35. Juliet E. Hart Barnett, Elizabeth D. Cramer, Beth Harry, Janette K. Klingner, and Keith M. Sturges, "The Continuum of 'Troubling' to 'Troubled' Behavior: Exploratory Case Studies of African American Students in Programs for Emotional Disturbance," *Remedial and Special Education* 31, no. 3 (2010): 148–62.
36. David Osher, Darren Woodruff, and Anthony E. Sims, "School Makes a Difference: The Overrepresentation of African American Youth in Special Education and the Juvenile Justice System," in *Racial Inequity in Special Education*, ed. Daniel J. Losen and Gary Orfield (Cambridge, MA: Harvard Education Press, 2002), 93–116.
37. Barbara Ransby, *Ella Baker and the Black Freedom Movement: A Radical Democratic Vision* (Chapel Hill: University of North Carolina Press, 2003).
38. Oral History Interview with Ella Baker, April 19, 1977, Interview G-0008, Southern Oral History Program Collection (#4007) (Southern Oral History Program Collection, Southern Historical Collection, Wilson Library, University of North Carolina at Chapel Hill).
39. Werner Troesken, "The Limits of Jim Crow: Race and the Provision of Water and Sewerage Services in American Cities, 1880–1925," *Journal of Economic History* 62, no. 3 (2002): 735.

40. Ransby, *Ella Baker*.
41. Oral History Interview with Ella Baker.
42. Ransby, *Ella Baker*, 152.
43. Ella J. Baker, "Memoranda," 1959, https://www.crmvet.org/docs/5910_sclc_baker.pdf and https://www.crmvet.org/docs/5910_sclc_baker-crusade.pdf.
44. Ransby, *Ella Baker*, 187.
45. Stephen Tuck, *We Ain't What We Ought to Be: The Black Freedom Struggle from Emancipation to Obama* (Cambridge, MA: Harvard University Press, 2010).
46. Ransby, *Ella Baker*, 254.
47. Baker, "Memoranda."
48. Charles Payne, "Ella Baker and Models of Social Change," *Signs: Journal of Women in Culture and Society* 14, no. 4 (1989): 885–99.
49. Payne, "Ella Baker and Models," 897–898.
50. Ella J. Baker, "Developing Community Leadership," 1970, https://www.crmvet.org/info/70_baker_community_ldsp.pdf.
51. Jenée Desmond-Harris, "Check Out This Incredible Collection of Rosa Parks' Personal Writings and Photos," 2015, https://www.vox.com/2015/2/4/7977373/rosa-parks-collection-documents.
52. Peter Dreier, "The Amazing Rosa Parks Story Too Few People Still Know," *Salon*, December 6, 2015, https://www.salon.com/2015/12/06/the_amazing_rosa_parks_story_too_few_people_still_know/.
53. Jeanne Theoharis, *The Rebellious Life of Mrs. Rosa Parks* (Boston, MA: Beacon Press, 2015).
54. Mary Hull, *Rosa Parks* (New York: Infobase Publishing, 2009).
55. Dorothy E. Roberts, *Killing the Black Body: Race, Reproduction, and the Meaning of Liberty* (New York: Pantheon, 1997).
56. Jeanna Theoharris, "What You Might Not Know About Rosa Parks," *HistoryNet*, 2014, https://www.historynet.com/what-you-might-not-know-about-rosa-parks.htm.
57. Theoharis, *The Rebellious Life*, xv.
58. Rosa Parks, "Rosa Parks Papers: Writings, Notes, and Statements, 1956–1998; Drafts of Early Writings; Autobiographical," Manuscript/Mixed Material Retrieved from the Library of Congress, Circa 1956, Undated, https://www.loc.gov/item/mss859430227/.
59. Tyler Tynes, "Rosa Parks' Life After the Bus Was No Easy Ride," *History*, February 4, 2019, para 11, https://www.history.com/news/rosa-parks-later-years-aftermath.
60. Parks, "Rosa Parks Papers."
61. Theoharis, *The Rebellious Life*, xvii.
62. Theoharis, *The Rebellious Life*,, xiii.
63. Annamma, *Pedagogy of Pathologization*.
64. Sheila McCauley Keys, *Our Auntie Rosa: The Family of Rosa Parks Remembers Her Life and Lessons* (New York: Random House, 2015), 171–72.
65. Stephanie Y. Evans, "Black Women's Historical Wellness: History as a Tool in Culturally Competent Mental Health Services," Association of Black Women Historians, 2019, para 4, http://abwh.org/2019/06/21/black-womens-historical-wellness-history-as-a-tool-in-culturally-competent-mental-health-services/.
66. Annamma, *Pedagogy of Pathologization*, 150.
67. Kris D. Gutiérrez, P. Zitlali Morales, and Danny C. Martinez, "Re-mediating Literacy: Culture, Difference, and Learning for Students from Nondominant Communities," *Review of Research in Education* 33, no. 1 (2009): 212–45.

68. Annamma, *Pedagogy of Pathologization*, 152.
69. Annamma, *Pedagogy of Pathologization*, 155.
70. Paolo Freire, *Pedagogy of the Oppressed* (New York: Continuum, 1970).

CHAPTER 3
1. Ta-Nehisi Coates, "The Case for Reparations," *The Atlantic*, June 2014, www.theatlantic.com/magazine/archive/2014/06/the-case-for-reparations/361631/?gclid=EAIaIQobChMIgdf1hvaa6wIVFY3ICh1AyAa6EAAYASAAEgLM2vD_BwE.
2. Ta-Nehisi Coates, *Between the World and Me* (Melbourne: Text Publishing, 2015).
3. Angelina Castagno, "'I Don't Want to Hear That!': Legitimating Whiteness Through Silence in Schools," *Anthropology & Education Quarterly* 39, no. 3 (2008): 314–33; H. Richard Milner, "Constructing Societal Curriculum Sites and Instructional Practices That Elicit Student Thinking About Race and Education" (working paper, University of Michigan TeachingWorks, 2016).
4. Bianca J. Baldridge, "Relocating the Deficit: Reimagining Black Youth in Neoliberal Times," *American Educational Research Journal* 51, no. 3 (2014): 440–72.
5. Brian D. Christens, Lawrence T. Winn, and Adrienne M. Duke, "Empowerment and Critical Consciousness: A Conceptual Cross-Fertilization," *Adolescent Research Review* 1, no. 1 (2016): 15–27.
6. Maisha T. Winn, *Transforming Justice: Transforming Teacher Education* (Ann Arbor: University of Michigan, TeachingWorks, 2016); Django Paris and Maisha T. Winn, *Humanizing Research: Decolonizing Qualitative Inquiry with Youth and Communities* (Thousand Oaks, CA: Sage Press, 2013).
7. Pierre Bourdieu, "Cultural Reproduction and Social Reproduction," in *Power and Ideology in Education*, ed. J. Karabel and A. H. Halsey (New York: Oxford University Press, 1977), 487–511; Pierre Bourdieu, "The Forms of Capital," in *Handbook of Theory Research for the Sociology of Education*, ed. J. G. Richardson (Westport, CT: Greenwood Press, 1986): 241–258.
8. W. E. B. Du Bois, *The Philadelphia Negro: A Social Study* (Philadelphia: University of Pennsylvania Press, 1899).
9. Du Bois, *The Philadelphia Negro*, xvii.
10. Steve Mills, "Madison—The New Promised Land," *Chicago Tribune*, March 28, 1995, http://articles.chicagotribune.com/1995-03-28/news/9503280167_1_mayor-paul-soglin-generouswelfare-benefits-wisconsin.
11. Lawrence T. Winn and Maisha T. Winn, "Expectations and Realities: Education, the Discipline Gap, and the Experiences of Black Families Migrating to Small Cities," *Race and Social Problems* 7, no. 1 (2014): 73–83.
12. Tara J. Yosso, "Whose Culture Has Capital? A Critical Race Theory Discussion of Community Cultural Wealth," *Race Ethnicity and Education* 8, no. 1 (2005): 69–91.
13. Wisconsin Council on Children and Families, *Race to Equity: A Baseline Report on the State of Racial Disparities in Dane County*, 2013, http://racetoequity.net/baseline-report-state-racial-disparities-dane-county/.
14. S. Steinholf, *Geography of Opportunity Capital Region, Wisconsin: Alternatives to Incarceration: MOSES* (presentation to the First Unitarian Society, Madison, Wisconsin, 2014).
15. Steinholf, *Geography of Opportunity*.
16. Catherine R. Squires, "Rethinking the Black Public Sphere: An Alternative Vocabulary for Multiple Public Spheres," *Communication Theory* 12, no. 4 (2002): 446–68.

17. Bryant Keith Alexander, "Fading, Twisting, and Weaving: An Interpretive Ethnography of the Black Barbershop as Cultural Space," *Qualitative Inquiry* 9, no. 1 (2003): 105–28.
18. US Department of Education Office for Civil Rights, *Civil Rights Data Collection: Data Snapshot School Discipline*, March 2014, http://www2.ed.gov/about/offices/list/ocr/docs/crdc-discipline-snapshot.pdf; Sandra Black, Laura Giuliano, and Ayushi Narayan, "Civil Rights Data Show More Work Is Needed to Reduce Inequities in K–12 Schools," December 9, 2016, https://obamawhitehouse.archives.gov/blog/2016/12/08/civil-rights-data-show-more-work-needed-reduce-inequities-k-12-schools#:~:text=Home-,Civil%20Rights%20Data%20Show%20More%20Work%20is%20Needed,Inequities%20in%20K%2D12%20Schools&text=Data%20show%20persistent%20disparities%20in,inequities%20in%20K%2D12%20outcomes.
19. Jeffrey Michael Reyes Duncan-Andrade and Ernest Morrell, *The Art of Critical Pedagogy: Possibilities for Moving from Theory to Practice in Urban Schools* (New York: Peter Lang, Inc., 2008).
20. Winn, *Transforming Justice*.
21. Gloria Ladson-Billings, "Toward a Theory of Culturally Relevant Pedagogy," *American Educational Research Journal* 32, no. 3 (1995): 465–91.
22. Milner, "Constructing Societal Curriculum Sites."
23. Michelle Alexander, *The New Jim Crow: Mass Incarceration in the Age of Colorblindness* (New York: The New Press, 2012).
24. Shawn A. Ginwright, "Black Youth Activism and the Role of Critical Social Capital in Black Community Organizations," *American Behavioral Scientist* 51, no. 3 (2007): 87.
25. Garrett Albert Duncan, "Beyond Love: Critical Race Ethnography of the Schooling of Adolescent Black Males," *Equity & Excellence in Education* 35, no. 2 (2002): 131–43.
26. Maisha T. Winn, *Justice on Both Sides: Transforming Education Through Restorative Justice* (Cambridge, MA: Harvard Education Press, 2018).

SECTION II

1. Shaun R. Harper, Edward J. Smith, and Charles H. F. Davis, III, "A Critical Race Case Analysis of Black Undergraduate Student Success at An Urban University," *Urban Education* 53, no. 1 (2016): 3–25; Jessica C. Harris, "Whiteness as Structuring Property: Multiracial Women Students' Social Interactions at a Historically White Institution," *Review of Higher Education* 42, no. 3 (2019): 1023–50; Tyrone C. Howard, *Why Race and Culture Matter in Schools*, 2nd ed. (New York: Teachers College Press, 2020); H. Richard Milner and Tyrone C. Howard, *Rac(e)ing to Class: Confronting Poverty and Race in Schools and Classrooms* (Cambridge, MA: Harvard University Press, 2015); Howard C. Stevenson, *Promoting Racial Literacy in Schools: Differences That Make a Difference* (New York: Teachers College Press, 2014); Maisha T. Winn, *Justice on Both Sides: Transforming Education Through Restorative Justice* (Cambridge, MA: Harvard Education Press, 2018); Carter G. Woodson, *The Mis-Education of the Negro* (Washington, DC: The Associated Publishers, 1933).

CHAPTER 4

1. Toni Morrison, *Playing in the Dark: Whiteness and the Literary Imagination* (Cambridge, MA: Harvard University Press, 1992), 47.

2. Ibram X. Kendi, *Stamped from the Beginning: The Definitive History of Racist Ideas in America* (New York: Nation Books, 2016).
3. Frances Lee Ansley, "Stirring the Ashes: Race, Class and the Future of Civil Rights Scholarship," *Cornell Law Review* 74, no. 6 (1989): 1024.
4. Cheryl I. Harris, "Whiteness as Property," *Harvard Law Review* 106, no. 8 (1993): 1746.
5. Mariana Souto-Manning and Ayesha Rabadi-Raol, "(Re)Centering Quality in Early Childhood Education: Toward Intersectional Justice for Minoritized Children," *Review of Research in Education* 42 (2018): 203–25.
6. Sharon Ryan and Susan Grieshaber, "It's More Than Child Development: Critical Theories, Research, and Teaching Young Children," *Young Children* 59, no. 6 (2004): 49; see also Nora E. Hyland, "Social Justice in Early Childhood Classrooms: What the Research Tells Us," *Young Children* 65, no. 1 (2010): 83.
7. Eduardo Bonilla-Silva, "More Than Prejudice: Restatement, Reflections, and New Directions in Critical Race Theory," *Sociology of Race and Ethnicity* 1, no. 1 (2015): 75.
8. Ryan and Grieshaber, "More Than Child Development."
9. Harris, "Whiteness," 1709.
10. Elizabeth A. Harris, "Racial Segregation in New York Schools Starts with Pre-K, Report Finds," *New York Times*, September 20, 2016, www.nytimes.com/2016/09/21/nyregion/racial-segregation-in-new-york-schools-begins-in-pre-k-report-finds.html.
11. Maisha T. Winn, *Justice on Both Sides: Transforming Education Through Restorative Justice* (Cambridge, MA: Harvard Education Press, 2018), 19.
12. Subini Ancy Annamma, Darrell D. Jackson, and Deb Morrison, "Conceptualizing Color-Evasiveness: Using Dis/ability Critical Race Theory to Expand a Color-Blind Racial Ideology in Education and Society," *Race Ethnicity and Education* 20, no. 2 (2017): 147–62.
13. Rachel Berman et al., "Nothing, or Almost Nothing, to Report: Early Childhood Educators and Discursive Constructions of Colorblindness," *International Critical Childhood Policy Studies* 6, no. 1 (2017): 52–65.
14. Terry Husband, Jr., "'I Don't See Color': Challenging Assumptions About Discussing Race with Young Children," *Early Childhood Education Journal* 39, no. 6 (2012): 365.
15. Gloria Swindler Boutte, Julia Lopez-Robertson, and Elizabeth Powers-Costello, "Moving Beyond Colorblindness in Early Childhood Classrooms," *Early Childhood Education Journal* 39, no. 5 (2011): 335–42.
16. Harris, "Whiteness," 1750.
17. Louise Derman-Sparks, Carol Tanaka Higa, and Bill Sparks, "Children, Race and Racism: How Race Awareness Develops," *Interracial Books for Children Bulletin* 11, no. 3/4 (1980), https://www.teachingforchange.org/wp-content/uploads/2012/08/ec_childrenraceracism_english.pdf; Mary Ellen Goodman, *Race Awareness in Young Children* (Boston, MA: Addison-Wesley, 1952); Mariana Souto-Manning, *Multicultural Teaching in the Early Childhood Classroom: Strategies, Tools, and Approaches, Preschool–2nd Grade* (New York: Teachers College Press, 2013).
18. Boutte, Lopez-Robertson, and Powers-Costello, "Moving Beyond Colorblindness."
19. Mariana Souto-Manning, "Transforming University-Based Teacher Education: Preparing Asset, Equity, and Justice Oriented Teachers Within the Contemporary Political Context," *Teachers College Record* 121, no. 6 (2019): 1–26.

20. Boutte, Lopez-Robertson, and Powers-Costello, "Moving Beyond Colorblindness"; Derman-Sparks, Higa, and Sparks, *Children, Race and Racism*; Terry Husband, Jr., "He's Too Young to Learn About That Stuff: Antiracist Pedagogy and Early Childhood Social Studies," *Social Studies Research and Practice* 5, no. 2 (2010): 61–75; Souto-Manning, *Multicultural Teaching*.
21. Flora Farago, *Early Childhood Educators' Beliefs, Attitudes, and Classroom Practices Regarding Race and Gender* (doctoral dissertation, Arizona State University, 2016), 11.
22. Phyllis A. Katz and Jennifer A. Kofkin, "Race, Gender, and Young Children," in *Developmental Psychopathology: Perspectives on Adjustment, Risk, and Disorder*, ed. S. Luthar et al. (UK: Cambridge University Press, 1997), 51–74.
23. Lawrence A. Hirschfeld, "Children's Developing Conceptions of Race," in *Handbook of Race, Racism, and the Developing Child*, ed. S. Quintana and C. McKown (Hoboken, NJ: Wiley & Sons, 2008), 37–54.
24. Boutte, Lopez-Robertson, and Powers-Costello, "Moving Beyond Colorblindness."
25. Howard Zehr, *The Little Book of Restorative Justice* (New York: Good Books, 2015).
26. Winn, *Justice on Both Sides*, 26.
27. Winn, *Justice on Both Sides*, 20.
28. Margaret R. Beneke and Gregory A. Cheatham, "Race Talk in Preschool: Academic Readiness and Participation During Shared-Book Reading," *Journal of Early Childhood Literacy* 19 (2019): 107–33.
29. Harris, "Whiteness," 1714.
30. Marta D. Collier, "Changing the Face of Teaching: Preparing Educators for Diverse Settings," *Teacher Education Quarterly* 29, no. 1 (2002), 49–59; Mildred J. Hudson and Barbara J. Holmes, "Missing Teachers, Impaired Communities: The Unanticipated Consequences of *Brown v. Board of Education* on the African American Teaching Force at the Pre-Collegiate Level," *Journal of Negro Education* 63, no. 10 (1994): 388–93; Gloria Ladson-Billings, "Landing on the Wrong Note: The Price We Paid for *Brown*," *Educational Researcher* 33, no. 7 (2004): 3–13; Madeline Will, "65 Years After 'Brown v. Board,' Where Are All the Black Educators?," *Education Week*, May 24, 2019, www.edweek.org/ew/articles/2019/05/14/65-years-after-brown-v-board-where.html.
31. Harris, "Whiteness," 1714.
32. Harris, "Whiteness," 1751.
33. Wanda J. Blanchett, "Disproportionate Representation of African American Students in Special Education: Acknowledging the Role of White Privilege and Racism," *Educational Researcher* 35, no. 6 (2006): 24–28; Bryan McKinley Jones Brayboy, Angelina E. Castagno, and Emma Maughan, "Equality and Justice for All? Examining Race in Education Scholarship," *Review of Research in Education* 31, no. 1 (2007): 159–94; Keffrelyn D. Brown, "Teaching in Color: A Critical Race Theory in Education Analysis of the Literature on Preservice Teachers of Color and Teacher Education in the US," *Race Ethnicity and Education* 17, no. 3 (2014): 326–45; Prudence L. Carter and Kevin G. Welner, *Closing the Opportunity Gap: What America Must Do to Give Every Child an Even Chance* (UK: Oxford University Press, 2013); Tahari Apirom Jackson, "Which Interests Are Served by the Principle of Interest Convergence? Whiteness, Collective Trauma, and the Case for Anti-Racism," *Race Ethnicity and Education* 14, no. 4 (2011): 453–59; Rita Kohli, Marcos Pizarro, and Arturo Nevárez, "The 'New Racism' of K–12 Schools: Centering Critical Research on Racism," *Review of Research in

Education 41, no. 1 (2017): 182–202; Marguerite Anne Fillion Wilson, Denise Gray Yull, and Sean G. Massey, "Race and the Politics of Educational Exclusion: Explaining the Persistence of Disproportionate Disciplinary Practices in an Urban School District," *Race Ethnicity and Education* 23, no. 1 (2020): 134–57.
34. National Center for Education Statistics, "Racial/Ethnic Enrollment in Public Schools," 2017, https://nces.ed.gov/programs/coe/indicator_cge.asp.
35. Seth Gershenson et al., *The Long-Run Impacts of Same-Race Teachers* (Bonn, Germany: Institute of Labor Economics, 2017); Ana Maria Villegas and Jacqueline Jordan Irvine, "Diversifying the Teaching Force: An Examination of Major Arguments," *Urban Review* 42, no. 3 (2010): 175–92.
36. See, for example, US Department of Education, *The State of Racial Diversity in the Educator Workforce*, 2016, https://www2.ed.gov/rschstat/eval/highered/racial-diversity/state-racial-diversity-workforce.pdf.
37. Hudson and Holmes, "Missing Teachers."
38. Iesha Jackson and Michelle Knight-Manuel, "'Color Does Not Equal Consciousness': Educators of Color Learning to Enact a Sociopolitical Consciousness," *Journal of Teacher Education* 70, no. 1 (2019): 65–78; Mariana Souto-Manning and Ranita Cheruvu, "Challenging and Appropriating Discourses of Power: Listening to and Learning from Successful Early-Career Early Childhood Teachers of Color," *Equity and Excellence in Education* 49, no. 1 (2016): 9–26; Brigitte Vittrup, "Color Blind or Color Conscious? White American Mothers' Approaches to Racial Socialization," *Journal of Family Issues* 39, no. 3 (2018): 668–92.
39. Mariana Souto-Manning and Jessica Martell, "Toward Critically Transformative Possibilities: Considering Tensions and Undoing Inequities in the Spatialization of Teacher Education," *Teachers College Record* 121, no. 6 (2019): 1–42.
40. Richard Milner, Francis Pearman, and Ebony McGee, "Critical Race Theory, Interest Convergence, and Teacher Education," in *Handbook of Critical Race Theory in Education*, ed. M. Lynn and A. D. Dixson (Abingdon, UK: Routledge, 2013), 339–54; Souto-Manning, "Transforming University-Based Teacher Education"; Souto-Manning and Rabadi-Raol, "(Re)Centering Quality."
41. Winn, *Justice on Both Sides*.
42. Mariel Padilla, "Officer Under Investigation After Arresting 6-Year-Olds, Chief Says," *New York Times*, September 23, 2019, www.nytimes.com/2019/09/22/us/6-year-old-arrested-orlando-florida.html.
43. Berman et al., "Nothing, or Almost Nothing."
44. Na'ilah Suad Nasir and Victoria M. Hand, "Exploring Sociocultural Perspectives on Race, Culture, and Learning," *Review of Research in Education* 76, no. 4 (2006): 457.
45. Winn, *Justice on Both Sides*, 145.
46. Daniel G. Solórzano and Tara J. Yosso, "Critical Race Methodology: Counter-Storytelling as an Analytical Framework for Education Research," *Qualitative Inquiry* 8, no. 1 (2002): 23–44.
47. Solórzano and Yosso, "Critical Race Methodology," 31.
48. Solórzano and Yosso, "Critical Race Methodology."
49. Solórzano and Yosso, "Critical Race Methodology," 36.
50. US Government Accountability Office, *Discipline Disparities for Black Students, Boys, and Students with Disabilities*, 2018, www.gao.gov/assets/700/690828.pdf.
51. Nicky Zizaza, "'A Literal Mug Shot of a 6-Year-Old Girl:' Grandmother Outraged Over Child's Arrest," *ClickOrlando.com*, September 23, 2019, www

.clickorlando.com/2019/09/23/a-literal-mug-shot-of-a-6-year-old-girl-grandmother-outraged-over-childs-arrest/.
52. bell hooks, *We Real Cool: Black Men and Masculinity* (Abingdon, UK: Routledge, 2004).
53. Winn, *Justice on Both Sides,* 8.
54. Winn, *Justice on Both Sides,* 26.
55. Zehr, *Little Book,* 86.
56. Kay Pranis, *The Little Book of Circle Processes: A New/Old Approach to Peacemaking* (New York: Good Books, 2005); Zehr, *Little Book.*
57. Winn, *Justice on Both Sides,* 8.

CHAPTER 5

1. Ruth Wilson Gilmore, "Abolition Geographies and the Problem of Innocence," in *Futures of Black Radicalism,* ed. Gaye Theresa Johnson and Alex Lubin (New York: Verso Books, 2017), 225–40.
2. Erika C. Bullock, "Mathematics Curriculum Reform as Racial Remediation: A Historical Counterstory," in *Critical Race Theory in Mathematics Education,* ed. Julius Davis and Christopher C. Jett (New York: Routledge, 2019), 75–97; Erika C. Bullock and Erica R. Meiners, "Abolition by the Numbers: Mathematics as a Tool to Dismantle the Carceral State (and Build Alternatives)," *Theory into Practice* 58, no. 4 (2019): 338–46.; Danny B. Martin, "Equity, Inclusion, and Antiblackness in Mathematics Education," *Race Ethnicity and Education* 22 (2019): 459–78.
3. Bullock and Meiners, "Abolition"; Erica Meiners, *Right to Be Hostile: Schools, Prisons, and the Making of Public Enemies* (New York: Routledge, 2007).
4. Bullock and Meiners, "Abolition,".
5. Micol Seigel, *Violence Work: State Power and the Limits of Police* (Durham, NC: Duke University Press, 2018), 10.
6. Seigel, *Violence Work,* 127.
7. Robert Q. Berry III, Mark W. Ellis, and Sherrick Hughes, "Examining a History of Failed Reforms and Recent Stories of Success: Mathematics Education and Black Learners of Mathematics in the United States," *Race Ethnicity and Education* 17 (2014): 540–68; Bullock, "Mathematics Curriculum Reform"; Bullock and Meiners, "Abolition."
8. National Research Council, *Adding It Up: Helping Children Learn Mathematics* (Washington, DC: National Academies Press, 2001).
9. Berry, Ellis, and Hughes, "Examining a History"; Bullock, "Mathematics Curriculum Reform"; Martin, "Equity, Inclusion, and Antiblackness."
10. André Gorz, *Strategy for Labor: A Radical Proposal* (Boston: Beacon, 1967). Ruth Wilson Gilmore has expanded and popularized this idea more recently, particularly in relation to prison–industrial complex abolition.
11. Rochelle Gutiérrez, "A 'Gap-Gazing' Fetish in Mathematics Education? Problematizing Research on the Achievement Gap," *Journal for Research in Mathematics Education* (2008): 357–64.
12. Bullock, "Mathematics Curriculum Reform"; Robert T. Carter and A. Lin Goodwin, "Racial Identity and Education," *Review of Research in Education* 20, no. 1 (1994): 291–336; William F. Tate IV, "Critical Race Theory and Education: History, Theory, and Implications," *Review of Research in Education* 22, no. 1 (1997): 195–247.
13. Stefano Harney and Fred Moten, *The Undercommons: Fugitive Planning & Black Study* (Brooklyn, NY: Autonomedia, 2013), 114.

14. Elizabeth de Freitas, "Plotting Intersections Along the Political Axis: The Interior Voice of Dissenting Mathematics Teachers," *Educational Studies in Mathematics* 55, no. 1/3 (2004): 263.
15. Gloria Anzaldúa, *Borderlands/La Frontera: The New Mestiza*, 4th ed. (San Francisco: Aunt Lute Books, 2012).
16. Robin D. G. Kelley, *Freedom Dreams: The Black Radical Imagination* (Boston: Beacon Press, 2002); Bettina L. Love, *We Want to Do More Than Survive: Abolitionist Teaching and the Pursuit of Educational Freedom* (Boston: Beacon Press, 2019).
17. Laurie H. Rubel, Maren Hall-Wieckert, and Vivian Y. Lim, "Teaching Mathematics for Spatial Justice: Beyond a Victory Narrative," *Harvard Educational Review* 86, no. 4 (2016): 556–79; Laurie H. Rubel et al., "Teaching Mathematics for Spatial Justice: An Investigation of the Lottery," *Cognition and Instruction* 34, no. 1 (2016): 1–26.
18. The focus on state-level changes in mathematics graduation requirements is inspired by the dissertation research of Cassidy Kist, a doctoral candidate in the Department of Educational Leadership and Policy Analysis at the University of Wisconsin, Madison.
19. *Coins, Cops, & Communities: A Toolkit* is available at www.afsc.org/resource/coins-cops-and-communitiestoolkit.
20. This is an adaptation of an exercise developed two years prior to teach about the military budget and illustrate that nearly 60 percent of the federal discretionary budget in the US is allocated toward war and militarism every year.
21. American Friends Service Committee, *What Do You Know About Chicago Spending on Police?*, video, November 17, 2016, www.afsc.org/video/what-do-you-know-about-chicago-spending-police.

CHAPTER 6

1. Danny B. Martin, "Learning Mathematics While Black," *Educational Foundations* 26 (2012): 47–66. With permission from Dr. Ebony O. McGee, the title of this chapter plays off the title of this article by Martin.
2. Maisha T. Winn, *Justice on Both Sides: Transforming Education Through Restorative Justice* (Cambridge, MA: Harvard Education Press, 2018).
3. Danny B. Martin, "Researching Race in Mathematics Education," *Teachers College Record* 111, no. 2 (2009): 295–338.
4. Danny B. Martin, Paula Groves Price, and Roxanne Moore, "Refusing Systematic Violence Against Black Children: Toward a Black Liberatory Mathematics Education," in *Critical Race Theory in Mathematics Education*, ed. Julius Davis and Christopher C. Jett (New York: Routledge, 2019), 32–55.
5. Danny B. Martin, "Equity, Inclusion, and Antiblackness in Mathematics Education," *Race Ethnicity and Education* 22, no. 4 (2019): 459–78.
6. Kara Jackson, "The Social Construction of Youth and Mathematics: The Cases of a Fifth-Grade Classroom," in *Mathematics Teaching, Learning, and Liberation in the Lives of Black Children*, ed. Danny B. Martin (New York: Routledge, 2009), 175–99.
7. Julius Davis and Danny B. Martin, "Racism, Assessment, and Instructional Practices: Implications for Mathematics Teachers of African American Students," *Journal of Urban Mathematics Education* 2, no. 2 (2008): 45–68; Victoria M. Hand, "The Co-Construction of Opposition in a Low-Track Mathematics Classroom," *American Educational Research Journal* 47, no. 1 (2010): 97–132.

8. Heidi B. Carlone and Angela Johnson, "Understanding the Science Experiences of Successful Women of Color: Science Identity as an Analytic Lens," *Journal of Research in Science Teaching* 44, no. 8 (2007): 1187–1218.
9. Maisie L. Gholson and Darrius D. Robinson, "Restoring Mathematics Identities of Black Learners: A Curricular Approach," *Theory into Practice* 58, no. 4 (2019): 347–58.
10. Jackson, "Social Construction"; Martin, Price, and Moore, "Refusing Systematic Violence."
11. Maisie L. Gholson, Erika Bullock, and Nathan Alexander, "On the Brilliance of Black Children: A Response to a Clarion Call," *Journal of Urban Mathematics Education* 5 (2012): 1–7; Jacqueline Leonard and Danny B. Martin, *The Brilliance of Black Children in Mathematics: Beyond the Numbers and Toward New Discourse* (Charlotte, NC: Information Age Publishing, 2013); Martin, "Learning Mathematics."
12. Figure 2 shows the same task as figure 1, despite the comparative discoloration of figure 2.
13. Erna Yackel and Paul Cobb, "Sociomathematical Norms, Argumentation, and Autonomy in Mathematics," *Journal for Research in Mathematics Education* 27, no. 4 (1996): 458–77; Marcy B. Wood, "Mathematical Micro-Identities: Moment-to-Moment Positioning and Learning in a Fourth-Grade Classroom," *Journal for Research in Mathematics Education* 44, no. 5 (2013): 775–808.
14. Elizabeth G. Cohen and Rachel A. Lotan, *Designing Groupwork: Strategies for the Heterogeneous Classroom* (New York: Teachers College Press, 2014).
15. Yackel and Cobb, "Sociomathematical Norms."
16. National Council of Teachers of Mathematics, *Principles and Standards for School Mathematics* (Reston, VA: National Council of Teachers of Mathematics, 2000).
17. Doug Lemov, *Teach Like a Champion 2.0: 62 Techniques That Put Students on the Path to College*, 2nd ed. (San Francisco: Jossey-Bass, 2015).
18. Dorothy Holland Herring and Jean Lave, *History in Person: Enduring Struggles, Contentious Practice, Intimate Identities* (Santa Fe, NM: School of American Research Press, 2001).
19. See, for example, Danny B. Martin, "Beyond Missionaries or Cannibals: Who Should Teach Mathematics to African American Children?," *High School Journal* 91, no. 1 (2007): 6–28.
20. Martin, "Beyond Missionaries or Cannibals," 13.
21. Martin, "Beyond Missionaries or Cannibals," 14.
22. Martin, "Beyond Missionaries or Cannibals," 11.
23. Spyros Spyrou, *Disclosing Childhoods* (London: Palgrave MacMillan, 2018), 128.

SECTION III

1. Henry A. Giroux, "Hard Lessons: Neoliberalism, Education, and the Politics of Disposability," *Policy Futures in Education* 7, no. 5 (2009): 570–73; Chris Herring, *Punitive Containment and Contesting Neoliberalism: The Roots and Implications of Homeless Camps in America* (PhD diss., Central European University, 2010).
2. Michelle Alexander, *The New Jim Crow: Mass Incarceration in the Age of Colorblindness* (New York: The New Press, 2010).
3. Alissa R. Ackerman and Rich Furman, "The Criminalization of Immigration and the Privatization of the Immigration Detention: Implications for Justice," *Contemporary Justice Review* 16, no. 2 (2013): 251–63; Eunice Hyunhye Cho et al.,

Justice-Free Zones: US Immigration Detention Under the Trump Administration (New York: ACLU Research Report, 2020).
4. Emily Holden, "Flooding Will Affect Double the Number of People Worldwide by 2030," *The Guardian*, April 23, 2020.
5. Anna North, "Every Aspect of the Coronavirus Pandemic Exposes America's Devastating Inequalities: Far from an 'Equalizer,' the Virus Is Affecting Already Marginalized Americans the Most," *Vox*, April 10, 2020; Kiley Russell, "Federal Anti-Immigration Policies Exacerbate Covid-19 Impact on People of Color," *Bay City News Foundation*, June 27, 2020; Eugene Scott, "Did Coronavirus Lay Bare Inequalities? Not to Those Who Were Monitoring Them Before," *Washington Post*, May 20, 2021.
6. Kenya Downs, "When Black Death Goes Viral, It Can Trigger PTSD-Like Trauma," *Nation*, PBS News Hour, July 22, 2016; Ashlee Marie Preston, "Sorry, Consuming Trauma Porn Is Not Allyship. Why Aren't Black Victims Afforded the Same Dignity in Death as White Victims?," *Marie Claire*, June 9, 2020.
7. Michelle Fine, *Framing Dropouts: Notes on the Politics of An Urban High School* (Albany, NY: SUNY Press, 1991); Pedro A. Noguera, "The Trouble with Black Boys: The Role and Influence of Environmental and Cultural Factors on the Academic Performance of African American Males," *Urban Education* 38, no. 4 (2003): 431–59; Eve Tuck, "Humiliating Ironies and Dangerous Dignities: A Dialectic of School Pushout," *International Journal of Qualitative Studies in Education* 24, no. 7 (2011):): 817–27.
8. Wayne Au, "Teaching Under the New Taylorism: High-Stakes Testing and the Standardization of the 21st Century Curriculum," *Journal of Curriculum Studies* 43 (2011): 25–45; Wayne Au, "Meritocracy 2.0: High-Stakes, Standardized Testing as a Racial Project of Neoliberal Multiculturalism," *Educational Policy* 30, no. 1 (2016): 39–62.
9. Danfeng Soto-Vigil Koon, "Education Policy Networks: The Co-Optation, Coordination, and Commodification of the School-to-Prison Pipeline Critique," *American Educational Research Journal* 57, no. 1 (2020): 371–410.
10. James Boggs and Grace Lee Boggs, *Revolution and Evolution in the Twentieth Century* (New York: Monthly Review Press, 1974/2008).
11. A. A. Akom, Julio Cammarota, and Shawn Ginwright, "Youthtopias: Towards a New Paradigm of Critical Youth Studies," *Youth Media Reporter* 2, no. 4 (2008): 1–30.
12. Savannah Shange, *Progressive Dystopia: Abolition, Antiblackness, and Schooling in San Francisco* (Durham, NC: Duke University Press, 2019).
13. Paolo Freire, *Pedagogy of the Oppressed* (New York: Continuum, 1970/2000), 34.

CHAPTER 7

1. Cary Funk and Kim Parker, *Women and Men in STEM Often at Odds over Workplace Equity* (Washington, DC: Pew Research Center, 2018).
2. US Department of Education, Institute of Education Sciences, National Center for Education Statistics, "Number and Percentage Distribution of Science, Technology, Engineering, and Mathematics (STEM) Degrees/Certificates Conferred by Postsecondary Institutions, by Race/Ethnicity, Level of Degree/Certificate, and Sex of Student: 2008–09 through 2015–16," 2017.
3. US Department of Education, Institute of Education Sciences, National Center for Education Statistics, "The Nation's Report Card: 2015 Science Assessment," 2015.

4. Shirley M. Malcolm, "400 Years and (Re)counting," *Science* 365, no. 6459 (2019): 1221.
5. Alexis Patterson and Salina Gray, "Teaching to Transform: The (W)holistic Science Pedagogy," *Theory into Practice,* 58, no. 4, (2019): 328–37.
6. Mariana Souto-Manning and Lawrence Torry Winn, "Toward Shared Commitments for Teacher Education: Transformative Justice as an Ethical Imperative," *Theory into Practice* 58, no. 4 (2019): 308–17.
7. Yvonne Gold and Robert A. Roth, *Teachers Managing Stress and Preventing Burnout: The Professional Health Solution* (Washington, DC: The Falmer Press, 1993), 141.
8. Brent G. Richardson and Margery J. Shupe, "The Importance of Teacher Self-Awareness in Working with Students with Emotional and Behavioral Disorders," *Teaching Exceptional Children* 36, no. 2 (2003): 8–13.
9. Henry A. Giroux, *Theory and Resistance in Education: A Pedagogy for the Opposition* (South Hadley, MA: Bergin & Garvey), 154–55.
10. James Paul Gee, "Identity as an Analytic Lens for Research in Education," *Review of Research in Education* 25, no. 1 (2000): 99–125.
11. Edna Tan and Angela Calabrese Barton, "Transforming Science Learning and Student Participation in Sixth Grade Science: A Case Study of a Low-Income, Urban, Racial Minority Classroom," *Equity & Excellence in Education* 43, no. 1 (2010): 38–55; Salina Gray, "Is Science for All? The Relationship Between Middle and High School Science Students' Perceptions of Race and Their Science Affinity-Identities" (doctoral diss., Stanford University, 2014); Alexis Patterson, Deana Scipio, Melissa Braaten, Salina Gray, Rhona Freelon, Bryan Brown, and Maisha T. Winn, "Spotlight on Transformative Justice in Science" (handout, Transformative Justice in Education [TJE] Center, University of California, Davis, Davis, California, 2018).
12. Stephen Brookfield, *Becoming a Critically Reflective Teacher* (San Francisco: Jossey-Bass, 1995).
13. Elliot Eisner, *The Educational Imagination: On the Design and Evaluation of School Programs*, 3rd ed. (New York: Macmillan, 1994).
14. P. David Pearson, Elizabeth Moje, and Cynthia Greenleaf, "Literacy and Science: Each in the Service of the Other," *Science* 328, no. 5977 (2010): 459–63.
15. Matthew C. Nisbet and Robert K. Goidel, "Understanding Citizen Perceptions of Science Controversy: Bridging the Ethnographic-Survey Research Divide," *Public Understanding of Science* 16, no. 4 (2007): 421–40.
16. Stuart Jay Olshansky and Leonard Hayflick, "The Role of the WI-38 Cell Strain in Saving Lives and Reducing Morbidity," *AIMS Public Health* 4, no. 2 (2017): 127–38.
17. Rutledge M. Dennis, "Social Darwinism, Scientific Racism, and the Metaphysics of Race," *Journal of Negro Education* 64, no. 3 (1995): 243–51.
18. Obed Norman, "Marginalized Discourses and Scientific Literacy," *Journal of Research in Science Teaching* 35, no. 4 (1998): 337–474.
19. Alexis Patterson, Deb Morrison, and Alexandra Schindel, "What's Science Got to Do with It? Possibilities for Social Justice in Science Classroom Teaching and Learning," in *Possibilities in Practice: Social Justice Teaching in the Disciplines*, ed. Summer Melody Pennell et al. (New York: Peter Lang Publishing, 2017), 145–58.
20. Robin Millar and Rosalind Driver, "Beyond Processes," *Studies in Science Education* 14, no. 1 (1987): 58.
21. Patterson, Morrison, and Schindel, "What's Science Got to Do with It?"

22. Amy Lindahl, "Facing Cancer: Social Justice in Biology Class," *Rethinking Schools* 26, no. 4 (2012): 14–18.
23. H. Richard Milner, *Start Where You Are, But Don't Stay There* (Cambridge, MA: Harvard, 2010).
24. Richard M. Ryan and Edward L. Deci, "On Happiness and Human Potentials: A Review of Research on Hedonic and Eudaimonic Well-Being," *Annual Review of Psychology* 52, no. 1 (2001): 141–66.
25. Ryan and Deci, "On Happiness," 142.
26. Reuven Bar-On, "The Impact of Emotional Intelligence on Health and Wellbeing," in *Emotional Intelligence: New Perspectives and Applications*, ed. Annamaria Di Fabio (Norderstedt, Germany: Books on Demand, 2012), 39.
27. Isaac Prilleltensky, "Promoting Well-being: Time for a Paradigm Shift in Health and Human Services," *Scandinavian Journal of Public Health* 33, no. 66 (2005): 54.
28. Robert Phillips, foreword in *Changing Places: How Communities Will Improve the Health of Boys of Color*, ed. Christopher Edley and Jorge Ruiz de Velasco (Berkeley: University of California Press, 2010), x.
29. Peter C. Scales et al., "The Role of Developmental Assets in Predicting Academic Achievement: A Longitudinal Study," *Journal of Adolescence* 29, no. 5 (2006): 691–708.
30. Lindahl, "Facing Cancer," 16.
31. Shawn Ginwright, "A Radical Healing Approach for Young Black Men: A Framework for Policy and Practice," in *Changing Places*, ed. Christopher Edley and Jorge Ruiz de Velasco (Berkeley: University of California Press, 2010), 211.
32. Thalia Gonzalez, "Keeping Kids in Schools: Restorative Justice, Punitive Discipline, and the School to Prison Pipeline," *Journal of Law & Education* 2, no. 41 (2012): 281–335.
33. Heather Strang and John Braithwaite, *Restorative Justice and Civil Society* (Cambridge: Cambridge University Press, 2001).
34. Maisha T. Winn, "Toward a Restorative English Education," *Research in the Teaching of English* 48, no. 1 (2013): 126–35.
35. Jacob Clark Blickenstaff, "Women and Science Careers: Leaky Pipeline or Gender Filter?," *Gender and Education* 17, no. 4 (2005): 369–86.
36. Gray, "Science for All?"
37. Paul C. Gorski and Katy Swalwell, "Equity Literacy for All," *Educational Leadership* 72, no. 6 (2015): 32–40.
38. Maxine Greene, Introduction in *Teaching for Social Justice. A Democracy and Education Reader*, ed. William Ayers, Jean Ann Hunt, and Therese Quinn (New York: New Press, 1998), xxx.
39. Sharron M. Chubbuck and Michalinos Zembylas, "The Emotional Ambivalence of Socially Just Teaching: A Case Study of a Novice Urban Schoolteacher," *American Educational Research Journal* 45, no. 2 (2008): 303.
40. Chubbuck and Zembylas, "Emotional Ambivalence," 302.

CHAPTER 8
1. APA Zero Tolerance Task Force, "Are Zero Tolerance Policies Effective in the Schools? An Evidentiary Review and Recommendations," *American Psychologist* 63, no. 9 (2008): 852; Ronnie Casella, "Zero Tolerance Policy in Schools: Rationale, Consequences, and Alternatives," *Teachers College Record* 105, no. 5 (2003): 872–92.

2. Monique Lane, "Reclaiming Our Queendom: Black Feminist Pedagogy and the Identity Formation of African American Girls," *Equity & Excellence in Education* 50, no. 1 (2017): 13–24; Richard R. Verdugo, "Race-Ethnicity, Social Class, and Zero-Tolerance Policies: The Cultural and Structural Wars," *Education and Urban Society* 35, no. 1 (2002): 50–75.
3. Yolanda Anyon et al., "Restorative Interventions and School Discipline Sanctions in a Large Urban School District," *American Educational Research Journal* 53, no. 6 (2016): 1663–97.
4. Anyon et al., "Restorative Interventions"; Trevor Fronius et al., *Restorative Justice in US Schools: A Research Review* (San Francisco, CA: WestEd Justice and Prevention Training Center, 2016).
5. Wayne Au, "Can We Test for Liberation? Moving from Retributive to Restorative and Transformative Assessment in Schools," *Critical Education* 8, no. 13 (2017): ISSN 1920-4175; Fronius et al., *Restorative Justice in US Schools*.
6. John Braithwaite, "Restorative Justice: Theories and Worries," Visiting experts' papers, 123rd International Senior Seminar, Resource material series, no. 63: 47–56 (Tokyo: United Nations Asia and Far East Institute for the Prevention of Crime and Treatment of Offenders, 2004); Fronius et al., *Restorative Justice in US Schools*.
7. Andrew Brown, Patrick Stacey, and Joe Nandhakumar, "Making Sense of Sensemaking Narratives," *Human Relations* 61, no. 8 (2008): 1035–62; Zoe E. Buck Bracey, "Students from Non-Dominant Linguistic Backgrounds Making Sense of Cosmology Visualizations," *Journal of Research in Science Teaching* 54, no. 1 (2017): 29–57; Gary Klein, Brian Moon, and Robert Hoffman, "Making Sense of Sensemaking 1: Alternative Perspectives," *IEEE Intelligent Systems* 21, no. 4 (2006): 70–73.
8. Jessica Ashley and Kimberly Burke, *Implementing Restorative Justice: A Guide for Schools* (Chicago, IL: Illinois Criminal Justice Information Authority, 2010).
9. Belinda Hopkins, *Just Schools: A Whole School Approach to Restorative Justice* (London, UK: Jessica Kingsley Publishers, 2003), 3.
10. APA Zero Tolerance Task Force, "Zero Tolerance Policies"; Casella, "Zero Tolerance Policy."
11. Anyon et al., "Restorative Interventions"; Fronius et al., *Restorative Justice in US Schools*; Maisha T. Winn et al., "The Right to Be Literate: Literacy, Education, and the School-to-Prison Pipeline," *Review of Research in Education* 35, no. 1 (2011): 157–73.
12. Anyon et al., "Restorative Interventions."
13. K. Beckman, B. McMorris, and A. Gower, *Restorative Interventions Implementation Toolkit* (Minneapolis, MN: University of Minnesota, Healthy Youth Development—Prevention Research Center, 2012); Fronius et al., *Restorative Justice in US Schools*.
14. Allison Ann Payne and Kelly Welch, "Restorative Justice in Schools: The Influence of Race on Restorative Discipline," *Youth & Society* 47, no. 4 (2015): 541.
15. Katherine Cumings Mansfield, Stacey Rainbolt, and Elizabeth S. Fowler, "Implementing Restorative Justice as a Step Toward Racial Equity in School Discipline," *Teachers College Record* 120, no. 14 (2018): 1–22; Greg Ogilvie and David Fuller, "Restorative Justice Pedagogy in the ESL Classroom: Creating a Caring Environment to Support Refugee Students," *TESL Canada Journal* 33 (2016): 86–96.
16. Ashley and Burke, *Implementing Restorative Justice*; Braithwaite, "Restorative

Justice: Theories and Worries"; Lisa Cameron and Margaret Thorsborne, "Restorative Justice and School Discipline: Mutually Exclusive," in *Restorative Justice and Civil Society*, ed. Heather Strang and John Braithwaite (Cambridge, UK: Cambridge University Press, 2001), 180–94; Fronius et al., *Restorative Justice in US Schools.*

17. Fronius et al., *Restorative Justice in US Schools*, 19.
18. Au, "Test for Liberation"; Fronius et al., *Restorative Justice in US Schools.*
19. Leon Benade, "Shame: Does It Have a Place in an Education for Democratic Citizenship?," *Educational Philosophy and Theory* 47, no. 7 (2015): 661–74; Fronius et al., *Restorative Justice in US Schools.*
20. Fronius et al., *Restorative Justice in US Schools*, 5.
21. Anyon et al., "Restorative Interventions"; Fronius et al., *Restorative Justice in US Schools.*
22. Lorraine Stutzman Amstutz, *The Little Book of Restorative Discipline for Schools: Teaching Responsibility; Creating Caring Climates* (New York: Simon and Schuster, 2015); Ashley and Burke, *Implementing Restorative Justice.*
23. Au, "Test for Liberation"; Beckman, McMorris, and Gower, *Implementation Toolkit.*
24. Sarah M. Fine, "Teaching in the Restorative Window: Authenticity, Conviction, and Critical-Restorative Pedagogy in the Work of One Teacher-Leader," *Harvard Educational Review* 88, no. 1 (2018): 103–25; Mansfield, Rainbolt, and Fowler, "Implementing Restorative Justice"; Maisha T. Winn, *Girl Time: Literacy, Justice, and the School-to-Prison Pipeline. Teaching for Social Justice* (New York: Teachers College Press, 2011).
25. Maisha T. Winn as cited in Fine, "Teaching in the Restorative Window," 106.
26. Beckman, McMorris, and Gower, *Implementation Toolkit*; Fronius et al., *Restorative Justice in US Schools.*
27. Fronius et al., *Restorative Justice in US Schools*; Adam Voight, Gregory Austin, and Thomas Hanson, *A Climate for Academic Success: How School Climate Distinguishes Schools That Are Beating the Achievement Odds. Full Report* (San Francisco, CA: California Comprehensive Center at WestEd, 2013).
28. Sonia Jain, Henrissa Bassey, Martha A. Brown, and Preety Kalra, *Restorative Justice in Oakland Schools: Implementation and Impacts* (Oakland, CA: Oakland Unified School District. Report, 2014), 22.
29. Fine, "Teaching in the Restorative Window"; Mansfield, Rainbolt, and Fowler, "Implementing Restorative Justice."
30. Ashley and Burke, *Implementing Restorative Justice.*
31. Myriam L. Baker, *DPS Restorative Justice Project Year Three: Year End Report 2008–2009* (Denver: Restorative Justice Colorado, 2009); Myriam L. Baker, Jane Nady Sigmon, and M. Elaine Nugent, *Truancy Reduction: Keeping Students in School* (Washington, DC: US Department of Justice, 2001).
32. Baker, *DPS Restorative Justice Project.*
33. Amstutz, *Little Book*; Benade, "Shame."
34. Baker, Sigmon, and Nugent, *Truancy Reduction*; Fronius et al., *Restorative Justice in US Schools*; Mansfield, Rainbolt, and Fowler, "Implementing Restorative Justice."

CHAPTER 9

1. Kathy Swan et al., *The College, Career, and Civic Life (C3) Framework for Social Studies State Standards: Guidance for Enhancing the Rigor of K–12 Civics,*

Economics, Geography, and History (Washington, DC: National Council for the Social Studies, 2013).
2. James A. Banks, "Citizenship Education and Diversity: Implications for Teacher Education," *Journal of Teacher Education* 52, no. 1 (2001): 5–16.
3. Joseph Kahne and Ellen Middaugh, "High Quality Civic Education: What Is It and Who Gets It?," *Social Education* 72, no. 1 (2008): 35.
4. Katy Swalwell and Katherina A. Payne, "Critical Civic Education for Young Children," *Multicultural Perspectives* 21, no. 2 (2019): 127–32.
5. National Center for Education Statistics, "Number, Highest Degree, and Years of Teaching Experience of Teachers in Public and Private Elementary and Secondary Schools, by Selected Teacher Characteristics: Selected Years, 1999–2000 through 2015–16," Washington, DC, 2017, https://nces.ed.gov/programs/digest/d17/tables/dt17_209.20.asp.
6. Nathaniel Bryan, "White Teachers' Role in Sustaining the School-to-Prison Pipeline: Recommendations for Teacher Education," *Urban Review* 49, no. 2 (2017): 326–45; Bettina L. Love, *We Want to Do More Than Survive: Abolitionist Teaching and the Pursuit of Educational Freedom* (Boston: Beacon Press, 2019); Erica R. Meiners, "The Problem Child: Provocations Toward Dismantling the Carceral State," *Harvard Educational Review* 87, no. 1 (2017): 122–46; Monique Morris, *Pushout: The Criminalization of Black Girls in Schools* (New York: The New Press, 2016).
7. Thea Renda Abu El-Haj, "'I Was Born Here, but My Home, It's Not Here': Educating for Democratic Citizenship in an Era of Transnational Migration and Global Conflict," *Harvard Educational Review* 77, no. 3 (2007): 285–316; Ameena Ghaffar-Kucher, "'Narrow-Minded and Oppressive' or a 'Superior Culture'? Implications of Divergent Representations of Islam for Pakistani-American Youth," *Race Ethnicity and Education* 18, no. 2 (2015): 202–24; Gloria Ladson-Billings, "Culture Versus Citizenship: The Challenge of Racialized Citizenship in the United States," in *Diversity and Citizenship Education: Global Perspectives*, ed. James A. Banks (Hoboken, NJ: Jossey-Bass, 2006); Noreen Naseem Rodríguez, "'Caught Between Two Worlds': Asian American Elementary Teachers' Enactment of Asian American History," *Educational Studies* 55, no. 2 (2019): 214–40; Beth C. Rubin, "'There's Still Not Justice': Youth Civic Identity Development Amid Distinct School and Community Contexts," *Teachers College Record* 109, no. 2 (2007): 449–81; Jesús A. Tirado, "Undocumented, Unafraid, and Precarious: Thinking Through Conceptions of Civics by Undocumented Activists," *Journal of Social Studies Research* 43, no. 2 (2019): 123–31; Amanda E. Vickery, "It Was Never Meant for Us: Towards a Black Feminist Construct of Citizenship in Social Studies," *Journal of Social Studies Research* 39, no. 3 (2015): 163–72.
8. Rudine Sims Bishop, "Mirrors, Windows, and Sliding Glass Doors," *Perspectives* 6, no. 3 (1990): ix–xi; Sally Wesley Bonet, "Educating Muslim American Youth in a Post–9/11 Era: A Critical Review of Policy and Practice," *High School Journal* 95, no. 1 (2011): 46–55; Kahne and Middaugh, "High Quality Civic Education"; Mohammed M. Saleem and Michael K. Thomas, "The Reporting of the September 11th Terrorist Attacks in American Social Studies Textbooks: A Muslim Perspective," *High School Journal* 95, no. 1 (2011): 15–33; Cinthia Salinas, Brooke Blevins, and Caroline C. Sullivan, "Critical Historical Thinking: When Official Narratives Collide with 'Other' Narratives," *Multicultural Perspectives* 14, no. 1 (2012): 18–27; Jeremy Stoddard and Diana Hess, "9/11 and the War on Terror in American Secondary Curriculum Fifteen Years Later," in *Reassessing the Social*

Studies Curriculum: Promoting Critical Civic Engagement in a Politically Polarized, Post–9/11 World, ed. Wayne Journell (Lanham, MD: Rowman & Littlefield, 2016), 15–28; John S. Wills, "Who Needs Multicultural Education? White Students, US History, and the Construction of a Usable Past," *Anthropology & Education Quarterly* 27, no. 3 (1996): 365–89.

9. Dafney Blanca Dabach et al., "Teachers Navigating Civic Education When Students Are Undocumented: Building Case Knowledge," *Theory and Research in Social Education* 46, no. 3 (2018): 331–73; Maria Fránquiz and Cinthia Salinas, "In Search of the Civic Histories, Identities, and Experiences of Latina/o Immigrant Students," in *Learning from Emergent Bilingual Latinx Learners in K–12,* ed. Pablo C. Ramírez, Christian J. Faltis, and Ester J. de Jong (Oxfordshire, UK: Routledge, 2017), 123–36; Shawn Ginwright, Julio Cammarota, and Pedro Noguera, *Beyond Resistance! Youth Activism and Community Change: New Democratic Possibilities for Practice and Policy for America's Youth* (Oxfordshire, UK: Routledge Taylor & Francis Group, 2006); Leona Kwon and Cati V. de los Ríos, "'See, Click, Fix': Civic Interrogation and Digital Tools in a Ninth-Grade Ethnic Studies Course," *Equity & Excellence in Education* 52, no. 2–3 (2019): 154–66; Ariana Mangual Figueroa, "Speech or Silence: Undocumented Students' Decisions to Disclose or Disguise Their Citizenship Status in School," *American Educational Research Journal* 54, no. 3 (2017): 485–523.

10. Dana Mitra and Stephanie C. Serriere, *Civic Education in the Elementary Grades: Promoting Student Engagement in an Era of Accountability* (New York: Teachers College Press, 2015); Katherina Ann Payne, "Young Children's Everyday Civics," *Social Studies* 109, no. 2 (2018): 57–63.

11. Jacquelyn Dowd Hall, "The Long Civil Rights Movement and the Political Uses of the Past," in *The Best American History Essays 2007* (New York: Palgrave Macmillan, 2007), 235–71.

12. Hall, "Long Civil Rights Movement."

13. Angela Y. Davis, *Freedom Is a Constant Struggle: Ferguson, Palestine, and the Foundations of a Movement* (Chicago: Haymarket Books, 2016); Ibram X. Kendi, *Stamped from the Beginning: The Definitive History of Racist Ideas in America* (New York: Random House, 2017).

14. Yoshiko Uchida, *The Bracelet* (New York: Puffin, 1996); see Noreen Naseem Rodríguez, "'But They Didn't Do Nothin' Wrong!' Teaching About Japanese American Incarceration," *Social Studies and the Young Learner* 30, no. 2 (2017): 17–23; Noreen Naseem Rodríguez, "The Challenges of Teaching Japanese American Incarceration with *The Bracelet*." *Bank Street Occasional Papers #42* (in press).

15. Winifred Conkling, *Sylvia & Aki* (Berkeley, CA: Tricycle Press, 2014).

16. Robin Bernstein, *Racial Innocence: Performing American Childhood and Race from Slavery to Civil Rights* (New York: New York University Press, 2011); Michael J. Dumas and Joseph Derrick Nelson, "(Re)Imagining Black Boyhood: Toward a Critical Framework for Educational Research," *Harvard Educational Review* 86, no. 1 (2016): 27–47; Anna C. Falkner, "'Ain't Gonna Let Nobody Turn Me Around': Learning About Race in the Early Grades" (PhD diss., University of Texas at Austin, 2020); Joe R. Feagin and Debra Van Ausdale, *The First R: How Children Learn Race and Racism* (New York: Rowman & Littlefield Publishers, 2001); Erica R. Meiners, "Trouble with the Child in the Carceral State," *Social Justice* 41, no. 3 (2015): 120–44.

17. Hall, "Long Civil Rights Movement"; Noreen Naseem Rodríguez and Amanda E. Vickery, "Much Bigger Than a Hamburger: Problematizing Picturebook

Depictions of Youth Activism in the Civil Rights Movement," *International Journal of Multicultural Education* 22, no. 2 (2020): 109–28; Wills, "Who Needs Multicultural Education?"
18. James C. Cobb, "Even Though He Is Revered Today, MLK Was Widely Disliked by the American Public When He Was Killed," *Smithsonian Magazine*, April 4, 2018, https://www.smithsonianmag.com/history/why-martin-luther-king-had-75-percent-disapproval-rating-year-he-died-180968664/; Peniel Joseph, *The Sword and The Shield: The Revolutionary Lives of Malcolm X and Martin Luther King, Jr.* (New York: Basic Books, 2020); Noreen N. Rodríguez, Michael G. Brown, and Amanda E. Vickery, "Pinning For-Profit? Examining Elementary Preservice Teachers' Critical Analysis of Online Social Studies Resources About Black History," *Contemporary Issues in Technology Education—Social Studies* 20, no. 3 (2020).
19. Susan I. Kent, "Saints or Sinners? The Case for an Honest Portrayal of Historical Figures," *Social Education* 63, no. 1 (1999): 8–12; Herbert Kohl, "The Politics of Children's Literature," in *Rethinking Our Classrooms*, ed. Wayne Au, Bill Bigelow, and Stan Karp (Milwaukee, WI: Rethinking Schools, 2007), 168–71; James W. Loewen, *Lies My Teacher Told Me: Everything Your American History Textbook Got Wrong* (New York: The New Press, 2008); Jeanne Theoharis, *A More Beautiful and Terrible History: The Uses and Misuses of Civil Rights History* (Boston: Beacon Press, 2018).
20. "Facts and Case Summary—Korematsu v. US," *United States Courts*, 2020, https://www.uscourts.gov/educational-resources/educational-activities/facts-and-case-summary-korematsu-v-us.
21. Ashley N. Woodson, "We're Just Ordinary People: Messianic Master Narratives and Black Youths' Civic Agency," *Theory and Research in Social Education* 44, no. 2 (2016): 184–211.
22. Catherine Cornbleth, "Birds of a Feather: People (s), Culture (s), and School History," *Theory and Research in Social Education* 25, no. 3 (1997): 357–62; Bruce VanSledright, "Narratives of Nation-State, Historical Knowledge, and School History Education," *Review of Research in Education* 32, no. 1 (2008): 109–46.
23. Banks, "Citizenship Education and Diversity," 6.
24. Arundhati Roy, "2004 Sydney Peace Prize Lecture," Sydney Peace Foundation, https://sydneypeacefoundation.org.au/wp-content/uploads/2012/02/2004-SPP_-Arundhati-Roy.pdf.
25. Noreen Naseem Rodríguez, "Transformative Justice in Social Studies," *Transformative Justice in Education Working Paper Series* (Davis, CA: Transformative Justice in Education Center, 2020), 1–23.

CHAPTER 10

1. Indicates equal co-authorship and designates each author as co-first author.
2. Lilia Bartolomé, "Beyond the Methods Fetish: Toward a Humanizing Pedagogy," *Harvard Educational Review* 64, no. 2 (1994): 173–94; Kris D. Gutiérrez, "Rupturing White Innocence in Teacher Education: Designing Teacher Education as a Proleptic Activity Through Social Design Experiments," *Teachers College Record* 121, no. 6 (2019): 1–7; Marcelle M. Haddix, "Diversifying Teaching and Teacher Education: Beyond Rhetoric and Toward Real Change," *Journal of Literacy Research* 49, no. 1 (2017): 141–49; Danny C. Martinez, "Imagining a Language of Solidarity for Black and Latinx Youth in English Language Arts Classrooms," *English Education* 49, no. 2 (2017): 179–95; Thomas M. Philip,

"Principled Improvisation to Support Novice Teacher Learning," *Teachers College Record* 121, no. 4 (2019)>; Mariana Souto-Manning, "Toward Praxically-Just Transformations: Interrupting Racism in Teacher Education," *Journal of Education for Teaching* 45, no. 1 (2019): 97–113.
3. Gloria Ladson-Billings, "From the Achievement Gap to the Education Debt: Understanding Achievement in US Schools," *Educational Researcher* 35, no. 7 (2006): 3–12; Gloria Ladson-Billings, "Lack of Achievement or Loss of Opportunity?," in *Closing the Opportunity Gap: What America Must Do to Give Every Child an Even Chance*, ed. Prudence L. Carter and Kevin G. Welner (UK: Oxford University Press, 2013), 11–22.
4. John Bell, *Understanding Adultism: A Major Obstacle to Developing Positive Youth-Adult Relationships* (Somerville, MA: YouthBuild USA, 1995).
5. Maisha T. Winn, *Justice on Both Sides: Transforming Education Through Restorative Justice* (Cambridge, MA: Harvard Education Press, 2018).
6. Deborah Loewenberg Ball and Francesca M. Forzani, "Building a Common Core for Learning to Teach: And Connecting Professional Learning to Practice," *American Educator* 35, no. 2 (2011): 19.
7. Sarah Schneider Kavanagh, "Practicing Social Justice: Toward a Practice-Based Approach to Learning to Teach for Social Justice," in *Reflective Theory and Practice in Teacher Education*, ed. R. Brandenburg et al. (Singapore: Springer, 2017), 161–75.
8. Winn, *Justice on Both Sides*, 39.
9. Bartolomé, "Beyond the Methods Fetish," 174.
10. Judith K. Franzak, "On the Margins in a High-Performing High School: Policy and the Struggling Reader," *Research in the Teaching of English* 42, no. 4 (2008): 466–505.
11. James Paul Gee, "Discourse Systems and Aspirin Bottles: On Literacy," *Journal of Education* 170, no. 1 (1988): 27–40; Arlette Ingram Willis, *Reading Comprehension Research and Testing in the US: Undercurrents of Race, Class, and Power in the Struggle for Meaning* (New York: Routledge, 2012).
12. Maren S. Aukerman, "When Reading It Wrong Is Getting It Right: Shared Evaluation Pedagogy Among Struggling Fifth Grade Readers," *Research in the Teaching of English* 42, no. 1 (2007): 56–103; Mary Margaret Juzwik et al., *Inspiring Dialogue: Talking to Learn in the English Classroom* (New York: Teachers College Press, 2013).
13. Lisa Delpit, *Other People's Children: Cultural Conflict in the Classroom* (New York: The New Press, 2006).
14. Winn, *Justice on Both Sides*.
15. Howard Zehr, *Changing Lenses: Restorative Justice for Our Times* (Harrisonburg, VA: Herald Press, 2015), 240.
16. Danny C. Martinez and Elizabeth Montaño, "Toward Expanding What Counts as Language for Latina and Latino Youth in an Urban Middle School Classroom," *Literacy Research: Theory, Method, and Practice* 65, no. 1 (2016): 200–16; Cati V. de los Ríos et al., "Upending Colonial Practices: Toward Repairing Harm in English Education," *Theory into Practice* 58, no. 4 (2019): 359–67.
17. Kimberlé Crenshaw, "The Urgency of Intersectionality," Filmed October 2016 in San Francisco, CA, TEDWomen video, 18:41, www.ted.com/talks/kimberle_crenshaw_the_urgency_of_intersectionality?language=en.
18. Maisha T. Winn, "Toward a Restorative English Education," *Research in the Teaching of English* 48, no. 1 (2013): 126–35.

19. Rita Kohli and Daniel G. Solórzano, "Teachers, Please Learn Our Names! Racial Microaggressions and the K–12 Classroom," *Race Ethnicity and Education* 15, no. 4 (2012): 443.
20. Kohli and Solórzano, "Please Learn Our Names!," 445.
21. Fania E. Davis, *The Little Book of Race and Restorative Justice: Black Lives, Healing, and US Social Transformation* (New York: Simon and Schuster, 2019).

CHAPTER 11

1. Maisha T. Winn, *Justice on Both Sides: Transforming Education Through Restorative Justice* (Cambridge, MA: Harvard Education Press, 2018).
2. Winn, *Justice on Both Sides*, 39.
3. I was in college and had not yet read *The Dreamkeepers* by Gloria Ladson-Billings, a text that subsequently impacted my teaching.
4. Winn, *Justice on Both Sides*, 31.
5. Winn, *Justice on Both Sides*, 49.
6. Bert Bower, *History Alive! The United States Through Industrialism* (Palo Alto, CA: Teachers' Curriculum Institute, 2005).
7. I use the term *Latina/o/x* to include people who have roots in Latin America and a range of gender identities.
8. *History–Social Science for California Public Schools: Content Standards Kindergarten Through Grade Twelve* (Sacramento, CA: California Department of Education, 2000), https://www.cde.ca.gov/be/st/ss/documents/histsocscistnd.pdf.
9. Timothy Monreal, "The Middle Social Studies Curriculum as a Site of Struggle for Social Justice in Education," in *Handbook on Promoting Social Justice in Education*, ed. R. Papa (Switzerland: Springer, 2019), 1–29.
10. Ruchi Agarwal-Rangnath, *Planting the Seeds of Equity: Ethnic Studies and Social Justice in the K–2 Classroom* (New York: Teachers College Press, 2020).
11. LaGarrett J. King, "Interpreting Black History: Toward a Black History Framework for Teacher Education," *Urban Education* 54, no. 3 (2019): 368–96.
12. Timothy Monreal, "More Than Human Sacrifice: Teaching About the Aztecs in the New Latino South," *Middle Grades Review* 3, no. 3 (2017): Article 6.
13. Noreen Naseem Rodríguez, "From Margins to Center: Developing Cultural Citizenship Education Through the Teaching of Asian American History," *Theory and Research in Social Education* 46, no. 4 (2018): 528–73.
14. Maribel Santiago, "Historical Inquiry to Challenge the Narrative of Racial Progress," *Cognition and Instruction* 37, no. 1 (2019): 93–117.
15. Rita Kohli, Elizabeth Montaño, and Damany Fisher, "History Matters: Challenging an A-Historical Approach to Restorative Justice in Teacher Education," *Theory into Practice* (2019): 377–84.

CHAPTER 12

1. Maisha T. Winn, *Justice on Both Sides: Transforming Education Through Restorative Justice* (Cambridge, MA: Harvard Education Press, 2018), 36–37.
2. Winn, *Justice on Both Sides*, 38.
3. Carl A. Grant, "Cultivating Flourishing Lives: A Robust Social Justice Vision of Education," *American Educational Research Journal* 49, no. 5 (2012): 910–34.
4. Lilia Bartolomé, "Beyond the Methods Fetish: Toward a Humanizing Pedagogy," *Harvard Educational Review* 64, no. 2 (1994): 173–94.
5. Heidi Grasswick, "Epistemic Injustice in Science," in *The Routledge Handbook of Epistemic Injustice*, ed. Ian James Kidd, José Medina, and Gaile Pohlhaus, Jr.

(Oxford, England: Routledge, 2017), 313–23.
6. Bryan A. Brown, "Discursive Identity: Assimilation into the Culture of Science and Its Implications for Minority Students," *Journal of Research in Science Teaching* 41, no. 8 (2004): 810–34.
7. Miranda Fricker, *Epistemic Injustice: Power and the Ethics of Knowing* (Oxford, England: Oxford University Press, 2007).
8. Alison Bailey, "The Unlevel Knowing Field: An Engagement with Dotson's Third-Order Epistemic Oppression," *Social Epistemology Review and Reply Collective* 3, no. 10 (2014): 62–68.
9. Ben Kotzee, "Education and Epistemic Injustice," in *The Routledge Handbook of Epistemic Injustice*, ed. Ian James Kidd, José Medina, and Gaile Pohlhaus, Jr. (Oxford, England: Routledge, 2017), 324–35.
10. Kristie Dotson, "Tracking Epistemic Violence, Tracking Practices of Silencing," *Hypatia* 26, no. 2 (2011): 236–57.
11. Douglas B. Fisher and Nancy Frey, *Better Learning Through Structured Teaching: A Framework for the Gradual Release of Responsibility* (Alexandria, VA: ASCD, 2013).
12. Matthew Knoester and Wayne Au, "Standardized Testing and School Segregation: Like Tinder for Fire?," *Race Ethnicity and Education* 20, no. 1 (2017): 1–14.
13. Cynthia Townley, "Trust and the Curse of Cassandra (an Exploration of the Value of Trust)," *Philosophy in the Contemporary World* 10, no. 2 (2003): 105–11.
14. Fricker, *Epistemic Injustice*.
15. Bailey, "Unlevel Knowing Field."
16. Dotson, "Tracking Epistemic Violence."

CONCLUSION

1. Garrett Duncan, "Urban Pedagogies and the Celling of Adolescents of Color," *Social Justice*, 27, no. 3 (2000): 29–42.
2. Angela Y. Davis, *The Meaning of Freedom and Other Difficult Dialogues* (San Francisco: City Lights Publishers, 2012), 89.
3. Darnel Degand, "Stereotypes vs. Strategies for Digital Media Arts: The Case for Culturally Relevant Media Production," *Theory into Practice* 58, no. 4 (2019): 368–76.
4. Maisha T. Winn, "Futures Matter: Creating Just Futures in the Age of Hyper-Incarceration," *Peabody Journal of Education*, Forthcoming.
5. Stacey Lee, "Learning 'America': Hmong American High School Students," *Education and Urban Society* 34, no. 2 (2002): 233–46.
6. Ta-Nehisi Coates, *Between the World and Me* (New York: Spiegel and Grau, 2015), 25–26.
7. Ta-Nehisi Coates, *We Were Eight Years in Power: An American Tragedy* (New York: One World Publishing, 2017), 6.
8. Coates, *Eight Years in Power*, 7.
9. Marina Gorbis, "The Future as a Way of Life: Alvin Toffler's Unfinished Business," *Medium*, July 24, 2016, https://medium.com/@mgorbis/the-future-as-a-way-of-life-4bc314ec97de.
10. Gorbis, "The Future."
11. Bettina L. Love, "Anti-Black State Violence, Classroom Edition: The Spirit-Murdering of Black Children," *Journal of Curriculum and Pedagogy* 13, no. 1 (2016): 2.
12. Maisha T. Fisher, *Black Literate Lives: Historical and Contemporary Perspectives* (New York & London: Routledge, 2009); Russell Rickford, *We Are an African*

People: Independent Education, Black Power, and the Radical Imagination (Oxford: Oxford University Press, 2016).
13. Robin D. G. Kelley, *Freedom Dreams: The Black Radical Imagination* (Boston: Beacon Press, 2002); Robin D. G. Kelley, "Culture@Large" (paper presented at the American Anthropology Association, San Jose, California, November 17, 2018).
14. Fisher, *Black Literate Lives*, 67.
15. Haki R. Madhubuti, *From Plan to Planet: Life-Studies: The Need for Afrikan Minds and Institutions* (Chicago: Third World Press, 1973).

Acknowledgments

WE WOULD FIRST like to lift up the parents and families of too many Black children, women, and men who have lost their lives to state-sanctioned violence against Black bodies. We see you. Our hearts ache with yours and we see your children every time we look at our own.

We completed this edited volume at the intersection of COVID-19 and racial unrest with children in school at home, trying to determine how to engage in protest while also following protocols to prevent the spread of COVID-19 in hopes we could hug our extended family one day. Some of us wrote through the loss of and uncertainty of life and missed opportunities to celebrate and milestones of those close to us. The contributors in this volume continued to engage this work because they truly believe in the power of transformative justice and how it can and should show up in the teaching of the disciplines taught widely in schools. We are in awe of the careful and thorough work of these scholars: Subini Annamma, Karega Bailey, Deborah Loewenberg Ball, Melissa Braaten, Bryan A. Brown, Erika Bullock, Avanti Chajed, Roxana Dueñas, Abby Emerson, Hyeyoung Ghim, Maisie Gholson, Hannah Graham, Salina Gray, Tyrone Howard, Danfeng Koon, Eduardo López, Jorge López, Erica R. Meiners, Elizabeth Montaño, Adam Musser, Maureen Nicol, Alexis Patterson Williams, Darrius Robinson, Noreen Rodríguez, Carla Shalaby, Vanessa Siddle Walker, and our sister, Mariana Souto-Manning.

Our village at the Transformative Justice in Education (TJE) Center in the School of Education at the University of California, Davis offered inspiration and tangible support of our incredible graduate student researchers, Ambar Hernandez, Jeremy Prim, Vanessa Segundo, and Hodari Davis, who are compelling scholars who inspire us tremendously. We feel fortunate to be in community with these thinkers and doers.

There have been a host of scholars who have joined us at the TJE Center who shake us up and help us get on the right path when we are weary, including (but not exhaustive) Roger Viet Chung; Micia Mosely; Anthony Weeks; the aforementioned teaching trio Roxaña Dueñas, Eduardo López, and Jorge López (shout out to Roosevelt High School); H. Richard Milner; Carol D. Lee; Kris D. Gutierrez; Shaun Harper; Becky McCammon; Kara Beckman; Helen Bowen; and our forever teacher, Māttua Rawiri Pene.

Thank you to our teachers in Restorative Justice, sujatha baliga, Rita Renjitham Alfred, (Maisha) and the Community Justice for Youth Institute in Chicago (Torry) founded by Cheryl Graves and the late Ora Schub.

We are indebted to Tawnya Faye Switzer, who has become a trusted companion on this journey with keen thinking and fresh eyes.

In all things and in all ways our children, Obasi and Zafir, are our partners. They have spent many of their evenings at lectures we hosted and accompanied us to many conferences. They keep us honest in this work in embodying restorative and transformative justice at home.

And, finally, we cannot imagine a more attentive and encouraging editor than Jayne M. Fargnoli. Jayne asks all the right questions, holds up a mirror and a window, and always makes time to truly ask about your health and well-being in all of her communications.

We are grateful to the Spencer Foundation and their generous support of some of the foundational work of the Transformative Justice Teacher Education Framework. We assume the full responsibility of how this work is represented in this volume.

About the Editors

Maisha T. Winn is the associate dean and Chancellor's Leadership Professor in the School of Education at the University of California, Davis, where she cofounded and codirects the Transformative Justice in Education (TJE) Center. Much of Professor Winn's early scholarship examines how young people create literate identities through performing literacy and how teachers who are "practitioners of the craft" serve as "soul models" to emerging writers. Winn served as the Jeannette K. Watson Distinguished Visiting Professor in the Humanities at Syracuse University (2019–20). She is the author of several books including *Writing in Rhythm: Spoken Word Poetry in Urban Schools*, *Black Literate Lives: Historical and Contemporary Perspectives* (both published under maiden name, Fisher); *Girl Time: Literacy, Justice, and the School-to-Prison Pipeline*; coeditor of *Humanizing Research: Decolonizing Qualitative Research* (with Django Paris); *Justice on Both Sides: Transforming Education Through Restorative Justice* (Harvard Education Press), and *Restorative Justice in the English Language Arts Classroom* (with Hannah Graham and Rita Alfred). She is also the author of numerous articles in peer-reviewed journals, including *Review of Research in Education*; *Anthropology and Education Quarterly*; *International Journal of Qualitative Studies in Education*; *Race, Ethnicity and Education*; *Research in the Teaching of English*; and *Harvard Educational Review*.

Lawrence "T." Winn (PhD, Human Ecology, University of Wisconsin, Madison; MDiv, Princeton; JD, Vanderbilt University Law School; and BA, University of California, Berkeley) is an assistant professor of teaching in education in the School of Education at the University of California, Davis and the cofounder and executive director of the Transformative Justice in Education (TJE) Center. His program of research examines race, critical consciousness, and social capital in out-of-school learning spaces and transformative justice pedagogy and practice within schools. A trained ethnographer, Dr. Winn is interested in the relationship and dynamics between historically marginalized communities of color (BIPOC) and schools, nonprofits, and government entities such as police, elected officials, and so on. With over two decades of experience in the nonprofit sector, including projects with Casey Family Programs and the Annie E. Casey Foundation, Dr. Winn was a member of the Race to Equity Team (R2E), which published the *Race to Equity* report, a comprehensive study on racial disparities in education, criminal justice, workforce, and health care for Black and white families in Dane County, Wisconsin. He is the coauthor of articles that have appeared in *Theory into Practice, Race and Social Problems,* and *Adolescent Research Review.*

About the Contributors

Prior to her doctoral studies, **Subini Ancy Annamma** was a special education teacher in both public schools and youth prisons. Currently, she is an associate professor in the Graduate School of Education at Stanford University. Her research critically examines the mutually constitutive nature of racism and ableism, how they interlock with other marginalizing oppressions, and how these intersections impact youth education trajectories in urban schools and youth prisons. Further, she positions students as knowledge generators, exploring how their narratives can inform teacher and special education. Annamma's book, *The Pedagogy of Pathologization*, focuses on the education trajectories of incarcerated disabled girls of color. She was also a Ford Postdoctoral Fellow for the 2018–19 school year hosted at UCLA.

Deborah Loewenberg Ball is the William H. Payne Collegiate Professor of Education at the University of Michigan, an Arthur F. Thurnau Professor, and the director of TeachingWorks. Ball taught elementary school for more than fifteen years and continues to teach mathematics to elementary students every summer. Her research focuses on the work of teaching mathematics in ways that disrupt the reproduction of inequity and that make it possible for young people to enjoy and engage in mathematics in and out of school. She is an expert on teacher education, and her current work centers on how to improve the quality of beginning teaching. Ball has authored or coauthored more than 150 publications and has lectured and made numerous major presentations around the world. Ball has been elected to the American Academy of Arts and Sciences and the National Academy of Education, and is a fellow of the American Mathematical Society and the American Educational Research Association. She completed eleven years as dean of the University of Michigan School of Education in June 2016.

Karega Bailey is an educator, award-winning spoken-word poet, motivational speaker, and activist. He is a founding member of the Roses in Concrete school (Oakland, CA) where he currently serves as the dean of students. Bailey is a graduate of Hampton University and has a master of education (MEd) in special education at George Mason University. Bailey is a member of the soulful music group SOL Development.

Melissa Braaten is an assistant professor of STEM Education and Teacher Learning, Research, and Practice at the University of Colorado in Boulder. She is a former elementary, middle, and high school teacher whose research focuses on the complexities of teaching science in culturally sustaining ways that disrupt disparities and work toward greater justice. In research partnerships with teachers, she draws upon teachers' expertise to refine professional learning experiences across the career trajectory and to build strong explanations of how teachers learn. She is interested in how teaching is shaped by—and how teachers can shape—the political and institutional contexts of schools, educational reform initiatives, and policies. Along with Dr. Mark Windschitl and Dr. Jessica Thompson, Braaten is coauthor of the book *Ambitious Science Teaching*, which shares a framework for science teaching developed in long-term partnership with practicing teachers and youth who continue to offer inspiring examples of possible futures for science education in K–12 schools.

Bryan A. Brown is an associate professor of science education and former associate dean at the Stanford University. He holds a BS from Hampton University, a master's degree in educational psychology from the University of California, and a PhD in educational psychology from the University of California, Santa Barbara. His work focuses on the role of language in science teaching and learning. Brown studies how race, technology, language, and culture impact science teaching in urban schools.

Erika C. Bullock is assistant professor of mathematics education and curriculum studies at the University of Wisconsin–Madison. After teaching mathematics at the high school and two-year college levels in the Atlanta area, she earned the doctor of philosophy in teaching and learning with a concentration in mathematics education from Georgia State University in 2013. Bullock's research agenda consists of two key segments: conceptualizing urban mathematics education and historicizing issues in mathematics education. Bullock is a 2017 National Academy of Education/Spencer Foundation Postdoctoral Fellow. She won the 2017 Taylor & Francis Best Paper Award for her paper "Only STEM Can Save Us? Examining Race, Place, and STEM Education as Property" published in *Educational Studies*. She has also published work in *Educational Studies in Mathematics*, the *Mathematics Enthusiast*, the *Journal of Mathematics Education*, the *Journal of Education*, and *Teachers College Record*.

Avanti Chajed is currently a doctoral student at Teachers College, Columbia University. She is interested in ways that curriculum and pedagogy can be transformed to make education more equitable for students that the system dismisses and understanding the ways that these students and their families mediate identities and enact agency within these systems.

Roxana Dueñas is an ethnic studies teacher at the Math, Science and Technology Magnet at Roosevelt High School in Boyle Heights, California. Dueñas graduated from the University of California, Santa Barbara, with bachelor's degrees in women's studies and Chicana/o studies. This coursework inspired her to pursue a teaching career with a specific emphasis on social justice and transformative education. In 2009, she graduated from UCLA's Teacher Education Program with a master's in education and a teaching credential. In 2014, Dueñas helped cocreate the curriculum for an ethnic studies course titled "Boyle Heights and Me." The course places an emphasis on community history, student activism, and civic and artistic engagement, particularly with local organizations. The course focuses on developing a critical analysis of systems of oppression and methods of empowering transformative resistance and resilience. Every year, students in the course publish an anthology with the support of the nonprofit organization 826LA. The books, which often include testimonies and reflections on themes of resistance, resilience, and reimagination, have become part of the course curriculum. To date, students in the course have published several books: *This Is My Revolution*, *You Are My Roots*, and *We Are What They Envisioned*.

Abby C. Emerson is a doctoral student researching antiracist teacher education and parenting. In addition to studying these topics, she works as a teacher educator and facilitates workshops and action groups with white parents on antiracist parenting. Her current research explores whiteness, white supremacy, and their manifestations in formal and informal spaces where children are educated. She is particularly concerned with the personal work that white teachers and parents need to do when they are seeking to educate in antiracist, culturally responsive, and socially just ways. She is the mom to Melody and Felix. Previously, she was an elementary school teacher for ten years in NYC public schools. During that time she was named the 2018 National Association for Multicultural Education's Critical Teacher of the Year.

Hyeyoung Ghim received her EdD degree in Curriculum and Teaching from Teachers College, Columbia University. Her scholarship focuses on early childhood preservice teacher education, international preservice teachers, transmigrant/immigrant teachers, multilingual community, and multicultural social justice education. She is currently a research professor at Daegu University Center for Multiculturalism and Social Policy.

Maisie L. Gholson is an assistant professor in the School of Education at the University of Michigan. She is a former high school mathematics teacher and prior to that a patent writer in her hometown of Houston, Texas. Within a Black feminist framework, Gholson's research seeks to understand how our identities and relational ties to mathematics, peers, and teachers create different developmental trajectories and learning opportunities within mathematics contexts. She actively investigates that which is often dismissed as superfluous to mathematics—children's social relationships and networks. A driving force in her research is to foreground children's and adolescents' humanity—that is, to take seriously the constructed racialized and gendered backdrop of childhood and adolescence as a visceral context in the process of mathematics identity development. As such, Gholson deals explicitly with issues of race and gender, along with the theoretical and methodological challenges that these complex constructs entail. She is a recipient of the National Academy of Education/Spencer Dissertation Fellowship and the National Science Foundation Graduate Research Fellowship in STEM Education. She received her PhD in curriculum and instruction from the University of Illinois at Chicago (UIC) and her BS in electrical engineering from Duke University.

Hannah Graham is a teacher-educator focused on disrupting hierarchizing practices in schools and creating radically youth-centered classrooms. Her research examines how curricula and discursive practices reflect underlying classroom epistemologies, how such practices inform students' perceptions of themselves and others, and how teachers might spur or quash students' interest in—and reimagined social possibilities for—disciplinary tools. She is the coauthor of *Restorative Justice in the English Language Arts Classroom* and currently serves as assistant professor and program director of Middle Grades Education in the National College of Education at National Louis University.

Salina Gray has spent twenty-three years teaching in traditional public and charter schools as well as at the university level. In 2014, she received her doctorate from Stanford University in curriculum and instruction in science education with a focus on the intersection of racial and science identities After completing her two-hundred-hour registered yoga teacher training and wellness certificate through the Breathe for Change yoga training program, she went on to serve as a lead trainer for Social and Emotional Learning. Her commitment to mental health led her to pursue Resilience through Lumos Transforms. Gray is the resident science coach for the 2020–21 Institute for Teachers of Color at University of California, Riverside. She is currently as an adjunct faculty member at Mt. St. Mary's University in Los Angeles and teaches seventh-grade science in Moreno Valley, California. Her work has been disseminated at the National Association for Research in Science Teaching, the Teachers for Social Justice Conference, Free Minds Free People, and the American Educational Research Association.

Tyrone C. Howard is professor of education and the Pritzker Family Endowed Chair in the School of Education and Information Studies at UCLA. He is the director of the UCLA Pritzker Center for Strengthening Children and Families and the UCLA Center for the Transformation of Schools. Howard's research examines issues tied to race, culture, and educational equity. His work also examines the educational experiences of Black boys and men. A native and former classroom teacher of Compton, California, he was named an AERA Fellow in 2017.

Danfeng Soto-Vigil Koon is the faculty codirector of the Transformative School Leadership Program and assistant professor in the Department of Leadership Studies in the School of Education at the University of San Francisco. Her research focuses on educational law and policy as sites of political, economic, and socio-cultural contestation and explores the ways that these policies further or impede efforts to create a more just society. Her passion for, and commitment to, public education is informed by her roles as an educator, lawyer, organizer, and parent. She holds a PhD from University of California, Berkeley's Graduate School of Education, a JD from the University of Maryland School of Law, and an EdM from the Harvard Graduate School of Education. She is a recipient of the National Academy of Education/Spencer Dissertation Fellowship.

Eduardo López is a doctoral student in the Urban Schooling Division at UCLA's Graduate School of Education and Information Studies. His research focuses on the experiences of teachers and students of color at the individual and collective level as they learn and develop in critical K–12 ethnic studies curriculum, humanizing and healing centered pedagogies, youth participatory action research, and their intersection in the classroom and beyond on the path toward empowerment and liberation. Prior to the doctoral program, López taught for twelve years at Theodore Roosevelt Senior High School as a social studies activist/educator. At RHS, he cofounded and taught the ninth-grade Ethnic Studies program. In addition, he created and directed, for eight years, the Urban Scholar Compadres (Brotherhood) program, aimed at increasing the academic and personal success of young Latinx male-identified students. Presently, he serves as a social science teacher on special assignment for the Montebello Unified School District located in Los Angeles County, California. In this role López assists and collaborates on the development of social studies curriculum and the implementation of instructional strategies and professional learning opportunities. Currently, he supports the expansion of the Ethnic Studies curriculum across the district—at the elementary, middle, and high school levels.

Jorge López is a teacher of social studies at Roosevelt High School in the Los Angeles Unified School District. He has been teaching since 2002, after graduating from UCLA's Teacher Education Program. In 2009 he earned a second master's degree and administrative credential from UCLA's Principal Leadership Institute. He also currently serves his school as community outreach coordinator and arts lead. López is a member of LAUSD's Ethnic Studies Leadership Team and an instructional leader for the California Teachers Association, working toward the implementation of Ethnic Studies across the state. López is most passionate about teaching Ethnic Studies that address the culture and voices of youth of color, community history, social movements, and racial justice. He sponsors social justice student clubs and continues to collectively work with community organizations. López recently received his PhD in education from Claremont Graduate University. His research focuses on humanizing pedagogies and the impact of Ethnic Studies on high school Latinx youth. He examines Ethnic Studies curriculum and pedagogy that centers student narratives and testimonies of Boyle Heights youth. His published work is on Ethnic Studies and critical pedagogies. His interests also include community activism, social justice education, and critical race theory.

Mariana Souto-Manning is professor of early childhood education and teacher education at Teachers College, Columbia University. She serves as director of the Doctoral Program in Curriculum and Teaching and director of the Early Childhood Education and Early Childhood Special Education Programs. She holds additional academic appointments at the University of Iceland and King's College London. Souto-Manning is founding codirector of the Center for Innovation in Teacher Education and Development (CITED). Before becoming a university-based teacher educator, she was an early childhood teacher in public (pre)schools in Brazil and in the United States. From a critical perspective, her research examines inequities and injustices in early childhood teaching and teacher education, (re)centering methodologies and pedagogies on the lives, values, and experiences of intersectionally minoritized people of color. As she problematizes issues of colonization, assimilation, and oppression in schooling and society, she critically examines theoretical and methodological issues and dilemmas of doing research *with* communities of color. Souto-Manning regularly collaborates with teachers and engages in community-based research. She has published ten books, including the 2016 winner of the American Educational Studies Association Critics' Choice Award, *Reading, Writing, and Talk: Inclusive Teaching Strategies for Diverse Learners, K–2* (with Jessica Martell).

Writer, educator, and organizer, **Erica R. Meiners** counts among her current work the coedited anthology *The Long Term: Resisting Life Sentences, Working Towards Freedom*, the coauthored *The Feminist and the Sex Offender: Confronting Sexual Harm, Ending State Violence*, and *For the Children? Protecting Innocence in a Carceral State*. A Distinguished Visiting Scholar at a range of universities and centers, including Humbolt University, Trent University, CUNY Graduate Center, the Simone de Beauvoir Institute, and Chicago's Leather Archives and Museum, Meiners has been recognized by awards including the 2015 Henry Trueba Award from the American Education Research Association, a 2016 Soros Justice Fellowship, and other support from the Illinois Humanities Council, Woodrow Wilson Foundation, and US Department of Education. The Bernard J. Brommel Distinguished Research Professor at Northeastern Illinois University, Meiners is a member of her labor union, University Professionals of Illinois, and she teaches classes in justice studies, education, and gender and sexuality studies. Most importantly, Meiners is involved with a range of ongoing mobilizations for liberation, including movements that involve access to free public education for all, including people during and after incarceration, and other queer abolitionist struggles.

Elizabeth Montaño is associate professor of teaching and director of the Capital Area North Doctorate in Educational Leadership (CANDEL) program at the School of Education, University of California, Davis. Her previous research has explored the experiences of teachers and youth in culturally and linguistically diverse settings and the experiences of charter school teachers who are unionizing. She earned a BA in political science and Chicana/o studies from UCLA and an MA/credential in education, language, literacy, and culture from UC Berkeley. She taught middle school English, social studies, humanities, math, and science for eleven years in both Oakland and Los Angeles. She earned a doctorate degree in educational leadership for social justice from Loyola Marymount University and has published in *Linguistics in Education, Theory Into Practice, Equity and Excellence in Education*, along with various edited volumes. She was born and raised in Los Angeles.

Adam Musser is an abolitionist educator and restorative justice practitioner. He has learned with young people in high school classrooms, youth prisons, undergraduate seminars, and teacher education courses. Musser is currently a graduate student and Dissertation Year Fellow at the University of California, Davis.

Maureen Nicol is a doctoral student at Teachers College, Columbia University. Nicol's research interests include centering the joy and knowledge of Black girls and Black girlhoods through artistic experiences, specifically photovoice. With over ten years of experience in education, Nicol is a passionate educator and people connector who is determined to make institutions accessible and equitable for all, especially for marginalized groups.

Darrius D. Robinson is a doctoral candidate in educational studies with a concentration in mathematics education at the University of Michigan School of Education. Robinson studies mathematics instruction with a particular focus on instruction designed to enable Black learners to develop productive mathematics identities.

Noreen Naseem Rodríguez is an assistant professor of elementary social studies in the School of Education at Iowa State University. Her research uses critical race frameworks to understand Asian American education, the culturally sustaining pedagogies of educators of color, the teaching of difficult histories, and diverse children's literature. Rodríguez was a bilingual elementary teacher in Texas for nine years and was the recipient of the 2019 Early Career Award from the Children's Literature Assembly of the National Council of Teachers of English. Her work has been published in *Theory & Research in Social Education*, *Educational Studies*, the *Urban Review*, and the *International Journal of Multicultural Education*.

Carla Shalaby is a researcher on teaching and teacher education at the University of Michigan. Her professional and personal commitment is to education as the practice of freedom, and her research centers on cultivating and documenting daily classroom work that protects the dignity of every child and honors young people's rights to expression, to self-determination, and to full *human being*. She is the author of *Troublemakers: Lessons in Freedom from Young Children at School*.

Vanessa Siddle Walker is the Samuel Candler Dobbs Professor of African American Educational Studies. She has a BA from the University of North Carolina at Chapel Hill; MEd from Harvard University, and an EdD from Harvard University. For more than twenty-five years, she has explored the segregated schooling of African American children, considering sequentially the climate that permeated segregated schools, the network of professional collaborations that explains the similarity across schools, and the hidden systems of advocacy that demanded equality and justice for the children in the schools. Her research has garnered a number of awards, including the prestigious $200,000 Grawmeyer Award for Education and the American Educational Research Association (AERA) Early Career Award. In addition, she has received awards from the Conference of Southern Graduate Schools, the American Education Studies Association, and three awards from AERA Divisions, including the Best New Female Scholar Award, the Best New Book Award, and the Outstanding Book Award. Walker is a former National Academy of Education Fellow and in 2009 was named a Fellow of AERA. She also served as president of AERA (2019–20).

Alexis Patterson Williams is an assistant professor at the University of California, Davis. Patterson Williams's research lies at the intersection of equity studies, social psychology, and science education. Her work explores equity issues that arise from social hierarchies when students work together on group projects in science and teacher development of practices that support equitable and robust interactions between students that can deconstruct implicit and explicit language and literacy hierarchies. Her recent project has led to the development of an educational framework, (W)holistic Science Pedagogy, with her colleague and sister scholar, Dr. Salina Gray. Patterson Williams is a native Californian and received her undergraduate degree from UC Berkeley and her master's degree from Stanford University. She received her doctorate in curriculum studies and teacher education in science from Stanford's Graduate School of Education. Prior to graduate school, she worked in Oakland Unified School District as an assistant director of an afterschool program, as a middle school science teacher, and as an intervention instructor at an elementary school. Patterson Williams earned her multiple subject teaching credential from CSU East Bay.

Index

ableism, 29. *See also* Disability Critical Race Theory (DisCrit)
abolitionist approach to mathematics, 77–85
absenteeism, 132
accountability, 125, 129–130, 133–134
achievement-based commitments, 97
action research, 22–23
aesthetic care, 26
agency of students, 94–98
Andover Public Schools, 1–2
ankle monitors, 76
Anzaldúa, Gloria, 78
apologies, 163
attendance, 132
Aztecs, Spaniards and, 171–173

Bailey, Alison, 181, 191
Baker, Ella, 30–33, 39
Ball, Deborah Loewenberg, 154
Bartolomé, Lilia, 155
Between the World and Me (Coates), 195–196
Black, Indigenous, and People of Color (BIPOC), 138, 145–146. *See also* Black people; civic education; people of color
Black Lives Matter movement, 58, 196

Black people. *See also* people of color
 disproportionate discipline of, 2–3, 47–48, 49, 69, 122–123, 129
 erasure of, 8–9
 exclusion of Black teachers, 64, 199–200
 males seen as violent, 48, 69–72
 as never measuring up, 195–196
 recognition of, 89–90
 in STEM, 105–106
 surveillance and control of, 48, 51–52
 teachers not engaging with, 49–50
 violence against, 159–160
 as on watch list, 187
body cameras, 76
BOND, 43. *See also* the Spot
Brown v. Board of Education (1954), 61–62, 64, 145
Burroughs, Margaret, 199–200

Campbell, Fiona Kumari, 29
Campbell, Les, 198
cannibals versus missionaries, 97
carceral state. *See* school-prison nexus
Chicago police, 83–85
Cinco de Mayo, 175–176
circle practices, 16–17, 70–72, 119–122
"A City Budget in Pennies" activity, 84–85

civic education
  Slyvia and Aki story used for, 140–144
  transformative justice and, 138, 144–146
  white middle class norms in, 137–138
Civil Rights Data Collection, 49
civil rights generation, curriculum and, 10
civil rights movement, 139, 145
classroom discussion management, 94
climate, 14–15, 131–132, 181
Coates, Ta-Nehisi, 195–196
Coins, Cops, & Communities: A Toolkit, 84–85
colonization, 18–20, 170–171
colorblindness, 62, 97
Columbus, Christopher, 18–20
community building, 15, 161–162
community resources, 78–80
comparative language, 190–191. *See also* norms
Conkling, Winifred, 140–144
conquest, perspectives on, 169–173
Constitution, U.S., 173–174
"Continuous Learning Family and Caregiver Playbook," 1–2
creative writing, resilience and, 21–22
Crenshaw, Kimberlé, 159–160
critical consciousness, 107–109
critical mathematics education, 73
critical reflection, 107–109
curriculum
  civil rights generation and, 10
  dis/ability and, 37–38
  future student opportunities impacted by choices in, 81–83
  relevance of, 199–200
  review of, 81–83
  student-directed, 78–80, 94–96, 109–110, 127–128, 169, 188–190
  white supremacy and, 26

data days, 184–187
deficit model
  early childhood education and, 65, 67
  impacts of, 88–89
  mathematics and, 76–77, 87–88, 91–93, 97
  standardized testing and, 187–188
disability labels, 29–30
Disability Critical Race Theory (DisCrit)
  curriculum and, 37–38
  Ella Baker and, 30–33, 39
  intersectionality and, 28
  overview, 28–30
  relationships and, 38–39
  Rosa Parks and, 33–37, 39
discipline. *See also* restorative justice
  restorative justice approach to, 115–116
  suspensions and expulsions, 49, 69, 122–123
  zero tolerance policies, 123, 125, 127–129
Dozono, Tadishi, 26
Driver, Rosalind, 111–112
Du Bois, W. E. B., 44

early childhood education
  centering people of color in, 67–72
  literature review about, 63–65
  methodology used in study of, 67–68
  race and, 68–72
  racial segregation and, 62, 64–65
  transformative justice and, 66–67
  white privilege and, 61–62
EAST, 200
e-carceration tools, 76
Elk Grove Unified School District, 1–2
engagement, 32, 49–50, 81–83. *See also* relationships
English language learners, 165–167
epistemic justice
  defined, 180
  humanizing science teaching, 180–182
  importance of, 192
  language interpretation and, 190–191
  methodology used in study of, 183–184
  resistance and, 184–190, 192
  teaching for, 181–182

erasure
  of Ella Baker's health issues, 32
  of history of marginalized groups, 8–9, 145–146, 175–176, 197–198
  resistance to, 19
Evans, Lawton B., 8
Evans, Stephanie Y., 37
exclusion, whiteness as property and, 63–65
experienced-based commitments, 97–98
expulsions, 49, 69

5-Value Activity, 17
Freire, Paolo, 102
Fronius, Trevor, 129
Futures Matter stance, 193–200

Geography of Opportunity, Capital Region, Wisconsin, 47
Ginwright, Shawn, 114–115
Glacier City School District, 182. *See also* epistemic justice
Gone with the Wind, 8–9
good/bad dichotomy, 156–158
Gorbis, Marina, 196
The Great Teaching Initiative, 182. *See also* epistemic justice
Greene, Maxine, 118

hand art pieces, 17
Hickory Middle School (HMS), 179, 182. *See also* epistemic justice
Hispanic/Latinx students, 105–106. *See also* people of color
historical capital, 41–44. *See also* the Spot
Historiography for the Future project, 198–200
History Matters stance. *See also* Disability Critical Race Theory (DisCrit); Theodore Roosevelt High School Ethnic Studies course; the Spot
  full history, not selective, 8–9, 32–33, 35–36
  impacts of, 25–26
  importance of, 8–11
history narratives, effects of, 9–10
hooks, bell, 26–27
Hopkins, Belinda, 127
humanity, identification of, 124–125, 159, 180–182

inclusion versus tolerance, 112
Independent Black Institutions, 198–200
Indigenous people, circle practices and, 16–17. *See also* people of color
intersectionality, lack of consideration of, 28

Jackson, Kara, 88–89
Justice Matters stance, 90–98, 100–103, 190–191. *See also* civic education; restorative justice; (W)holistic Science Pedagogy

Keys, Sheila McCauley, 36
knowing field, 181, 191
Kohli, Rita, 162
Korematsu v. United States (1944), 145–146

lack of care, 55
Ladson-Billings, Gloria, 29
Language Matters stance. *See also* epistemic justice; social studies education
  changing meaning of language over time, 174
  community building with, 161–162
  comparative language, 190–191
  overview, 148–151
  purposes of, 168
  teacher education and, 153–164

Mackey, Janiece, 26
Madison, Wisconsin, 46–48. *See also* the Spot

Martin, Danny, 97
mass media, 110
mathematical identity
    justice-centered programs, impacts of, 90–98
    overview, 87–88
    race matters in, 88–90
mathematics
    deficit model and, 76–77, 87–88, 91–93, 97
    deification of, 73–75
    equity and, 75–77
    overview, 73–75
    punitive use of, 74
    reimagination of, 77–85
    relationships and, 89, 97–98
    student-centered approaches to instruction, 78–80, 94–96
Matias, Cheryl, 26
Mendez v. Westminster, 145
microaggressions, relationships and, 27
Millar, Robin, 111–112
Milner, H. Richard, 50
missionaries versus cannibals, 97
mobilizing versus organizing, 32–33
mock trial, 18–20
Morris, Ruth, 25

names, correct pronunciation of, 161–163
#NoCopAcademy, 83–85
norms
    administrators as source of discipline, 129
    as based on ableism, 29
    as based on whites, 26, 76, 145, 188, 190–191
    epistemic justice and, 181

oppression, 26–27, 31
organizing versus mobilizing, 32–33

pandemic, divide in response to, 1–2
Parks, Rosa, 33–37, 39
participatory action research, 22–23
Payne, Charles, 32–33
people of color. *See also* Black people
    centering in early childhood education, 67–72
    disproportionate discipline of, 2–3, 47–48, 49, 69, 122–123, 129
    erasure of, 8–9, 145–146, 175–176, 197–198
    positioning as less than, 29
    in STEM, 105–106
    surveillance and control of, 26–27, 48, 51–52, 76
Phillips, Robert, 113
police. *See also* surveillance and control
    body cameras, 76
    Chicago police budget, 83–85
    lack of care and, 55
    violence by, 159–160
politicized caring, 27–28
popular media, 110
Preamble of the Constitution, 173–174
Prilleltensky, Isaac, 113
prison-industrial complex, 76
property ownership, 18, 29
punishment. *See* discipline; restorative justice

race, 66, 68–72, 144
Race Matters stance, 58–60, 100–103. *See also* early childhood education; mathematical identity; mathematics
Race to Equity: A Baseline Report on the State of Racial Disparities in Dane County, 47
racial justice, need for, 58–60
racial segregation, early childhood education and, 62, 64–65
racism. *See also* Disability Critical Race Theory (DisCrit)
    good/bad dichotomy and, 156–158
    importance of discussing, 144
    mathematics and, 88
    in teacher education, 62–63, 65
    teacher's role in, 59

reading, white-hegemonic system of, 155–158
recognition, 89–90
redlining, 79–80
reimagination, 22–23, 77–85
relationships. *See also* restorative justice
  competitiveness in class as damaging, 89
  loving versus punitive, 38–39
  mathematics and, 89, 97–98
  oppression and, 26–27
  shaming and, 123, 124, 129
  youth building with adults, 52–55
representations in math, issues with, 92–93
resilience, 20–22
resistance
  acting out versus, 27–28
  epistemic justice and, 184–190, 192
  to erasure, 19
  mobilizing versus organizing, 32–33
  Theodore Roosevelt High School Ethnic Studies course, 16–20
  toll of, 34–36
  transformational resistance, 23
resource allocation, 29
restorative justice. *See also* early childhood education; Theodore Roosevelt High School Ethnic Studies course
  accountability and, 125, 129–130, 133–134
  apologies and, 163
  circle practices, 119–122
  context and, 178
  defined, 127–130
  disruption of injustice and inequality by, 23
  early childhood education and, 66
  example of, 119–122, 132–134
  importance of, 2
  language and, 154–155
  overview, 134–135
  research on, 130–132
  restorative practice compared, 3
  seeing causes of harm, 20

steps in process of, 120–122, 124–126
  what is being restored, 159
  (W)holistic Science Pedagogy and, 115–117
restorative practice, 3, 150
Robinson, Tony Terrell, Jr., 51
Rolle, Kaia, 2–3, 69
Roy, Arundhati, 2
Royston, Maxine McKinney de, 27
Rutherford, Mildred Lewis, 8

school climate, 14–15, 131–132, 181
School Climate Bill of Rights (SCBR), 14–15
school-prison nexus, 73–74, 76, 130–131
science, 105–106. *See also* epistemic justice; (W)holistic Science Pedagogy
Seigel, Micol, 74
self-awareness of teachers, 107–109, 118
Seven Pillars of Colonialism, 18–19
shaming, 123, 124, 129
social and emotional well-being of students, 112–115, 131
social and emotional well-being of teachers, 118
social justice, social and emotional well-being of students and, 114–115
social studies education. *See also* civic education; Theodore Roosevelt High School Ethnic Studies course
  English language learners, 165–167
  importance of language in, 167–168
  overview, 165
  transformation of, 176–178
  as transformative space, 168–176
Socratic seminars, 193–194
Solórzano, Daniel G., 162
Spaniards, Aztecs and, 171–173
special education labels, 29–30
standardized testing, 186–188
STEM, 105–106
story sharing, 22
structural racism, health conditions and, 30

student agency, 94–96
student-centered approaches
   to mathematics instruction, 78–80, 94–96
   restorative justice as, 127–128
   to science instruction, 109–110, 188–190
   to social studies, 169
surveillance and control, 26–27, 48, 51–52, 76
suspensions, 49, 69, 122–123
Sylvia and Aki (Conkling), 140–144
System of Empire, 18

Taíno, study of, 18–20
tardiness, 132
teacher education programs
   justice-centered programs, impacts of, 3–4, 72
   language importance and, 153–164
   racism in, 62–63, 65
   social studies preparation, 177–178
teachers
   administrators ignoring their knowledge of students, 185–186
   exclusion of Black teachers, 64, 199–200
   instructional decisions in math teaching, 93–94
   lack of engagement with Black students by, 49–50
   racism and, 59
   self-awareness and, 107–109, 118
   social and emotional well-being of, 118
teaching to the test, 188
Team Jazzy-Flashy-Cool, 179–180, 182–183. *See also* epistemic justice
TEDWomen Talk, 159–160
Theodore Roosevelt High School Ethnic Studies course
   beginnings of, 14–16
   reimagination, 22–23
   resilience, 20–22
   resistance, 16–20

transformative justice, 24
the Spot
   adult relationships with youth, 52–55
   description of, 44–45
   function of, 43–44
   history and, 56
   loss of pharmacy, 46
   role in youth's lives, 48–52
tolerance versus inclusion, 112
transformational resistance, 23
transformative justice
   civic education and, 144–146
   defined, 25
   early childhood education and, 66–67
   educational overhaul by, 24, 194
   futures and, 197
Transformative Justice Teacher Education, importance of, 3–4

urban pedagogies, 193–194
U.S. Constitution, 173–174

values, 108–109

Westbook neighborhood, 45–46. *See also* the Spot
Weusi, Jitu, 198–200
"What Shall I Tell My Children Who Are Black (Reflections of an African-American Mother)?" (Burroughs), 199–200
whiteness as property, 62, 63–65
white supremacy and privilege
   Brown v. Board of Education and, 64
   curriculum and, 26
   early childhood education and, 61–62, 65
   mathematics and, 76–77
   norms set based on whites, 26, 76, 145, 188, 190–191
   science and, 111
   teaching and, 59

(W)holistic Science Pedagogy
  commitment to science, 109–110
  overview, 106–107, 117–118
  restorative justice, 115–117
  science as transformative agent, 111–112
  self-awareness commitment, 107–109
  social and emotional well-being of students, 112–115

youth participatory action research (YPAR), 22–23

Zehr, Howard, 15, 159
zero tolerance policies, 123, 125, 127–129